AN INTRODUCTION TO ARIZONA HISTORY AND GOVERNMENT

Tenth Edition

Donald Gawronski

Mesa Community College
Mesa, Arizona

Learning Solutions

New York   Boston   San Francisco
London   Toronto   Sydney   Tokyo   Singapore   Madrid
Mexico City   Munich   Paris   Cape Town   Hong Kong   Montreal

Pearson Learning Solutions, 501 Boylston Street, Suite 900,
Boston, MA 02116
A Pearson Education Company
www.pearsoned.com

Printed in the United States of America

15 14 13 12 11 V3DZ 18 17 16 15 14

000200010270589006

LR

ISBN 10: 0-558-74514-8
ISBN 13: 978-0-558-74514-1

TABLE OF CONTENTS

Preface

The purpose of this text is to provide the student with basic information concerning the history and government of Arizona. The text emphasizes factual material rather than examples, the relevancy of which could quickly change. Political science is an "alive" discipline, in that its subject matter is always in an active and evolving state. It is, therefore, best left to the individual instructor to pick and choose whatever contemporary events best illustrate the point he or she is making.

This text makes no claims to be definitive. Most certainly in the introductory chapters on geography and history, the only purpose is to lay basic foundation for a discussion of political issues. Other more detailed works should be consulted for in-depth information.

Recommended are the following general works: Jay Wagoner, Early Arizona Prehistory to the Civil War, also Jay Wagoner, Arizona Territory, 1863-1912: A political History. John Golff, Arizona Civilization, Myles Hill and John Golff, Arizona Past and Present, Marshall Trimble, Arizona: A Panoramic History of a Frontier State. Also, Marshall Trimble, Arizona: A Cavalcade of History, Thomas Sheridan, Arizona: A History (the bibliographical essay at the end of this work is highly recommended), Robert Woznicki, History of Arizona, and Zachary Smith, Politics and Public Policy in Arizona.

This work is based on the efforts and research of many others. As is the case with most survey type courses, specific sources of information become lost in the maze of time. In the course of my teaching Arizona Constitution over the past fifteen years I have obviously consulted informally with many of my colleagues and incorporated their input into my lectures and mental database. Certainly, articles in the *Arizona Republic* and the *Arizona Capital Times,* or news items appearing on local television, had their influence. I am indebted to the current teachers of Arizona History and Arizona Constitution at Mesa Community College: Paul Heitter, Allen Meyer, and Juan Armijo, who, whether they realized it or not, from time to time made comments or presented ideas that I integrated into my own understanding. Special recognition is due to teachers of the Arizona Constitution now retired: Don Skousen, and especially, Fred Keyworth

The additions, innovations and corrections of earlier editions have been maintained. Newly discovered errors and omissions have been corrected. The new edition details the budget issues facing the state. Emphasis has been placed more on historical narrative and interpretation rather than on charts and budget detail. As a result much of chapter nine has been completely rewritten. A new section on immigration has been added to chapter thirteen. The historical development of immigration issues in Arizona is followed by a treatment of the various immigration laws the state has enacted in recent years.

All writing endeavors are group efforts. Special recognition is given to my friends and colleagues, Allen Meyer, for his suggestions and proofing of the previous edition, and Gretchen Anderson and Laura Ricci of Pearson Learning Solutions. The final typing, layout, and formatting require a degree of technical expertise, skill, and patience far beyond my capabilities.

And finally, to anyone else who has to put up with me as I go from one project to another, perhaps not knowing what are my self-imposed time constraints and pressures, you are all deserving of sainthood. Especially is this true for my wife Pat, who patiently endured all the evenings and weekends I spent in front of my computer screen, who consistently offers support and encouragement, and who has read and made suggestions for a number of my writing efforts. Thank you, Pat!

Scottsdale, Arizona   DVG

INTRODUCTION

Unique Features of Arizona's Past

A political system and its institutions comprise a physical manifestation of a political culture which, in turn, is a subset of culture in general. Culture, in this general sense, consists of an aggregate of the experiences, beliefs, perceptions, and the uniqueness of its participants, in whatever happens to be the resultant mix. Certain features of Arizona and its peoples need to be discussed as a prelude to understanding the political system currently in effect.

DURATION OF SPANISH/MEXICAN RULE

No part of the contiguous United States was ruled longer by outside forces than the American Southwest. Whereas indigenous populations and their cultures were largely displaced, destroyed, or assimilated in much of the United States, such was not the case in the Southwest, largely because no one group was powerful enough to totally dominate another.

Yet the Spaniard was here more than a half century before the founding of Jamestown, and laid claim to the Southwest long before northern and western Europeans were able to establish a firm foothold on the eastern seaboard. At about the time established statehood crossed the Mississippi with the admission of Missouri into the Union, Spanish rule shifted to Mexican rule, and Mexico would continue to lay claim to that area destined to become the American Southwest.

Spanish and Mexican populations were never extensive but what they lacked in density they perhaps made up for in duration. The Spanish-Mexican period lasted from 1539 to 1848, one and one half times the existence of the Constitution. When the Southwest did pass to the United States, the Treaty of Guadalupe Hidalgo and the Gadsden Purchase Treaty offered citizenship to the peoples of Hispanic origin residing in the affected areas.

Today, in the faces of many of its citizens, in place names whose origins might long be forgotten, in the presence of archeological and historical sites, in culture, and in language, the presence of the past lays heavily on the course of the future. Geographical proximity to Mexico, historic and economic ties, and ties by blood and language, aid in maintaining the existence of a part of our earliest culture.

INDIGENOUS POPULATIONS

Second only to Oklahoma, Arizona has the largest indigenous (Native American) population of any state. The tribes that currently reside in Arizona were here before the Spaniards came. They had not been relocated or driven from other homelands; this was home. And unlike their brethren before them who were displaced by the press of settlement to less desirable areas, there was no place else to go. Many of the names on reservation signs across Oklahoma reflect the presence of peoples long before associated with homes in the American East. The Apache, Navajo, Hopi, Pima, etc., were here first, and they stayed.

One of the first requests by territorial Arizona was for the federal government to use the military to place native populations on reservations. An initial allocation of 75,000 acres was followed by monetary appropriation of 1867 to accomplish this task. What followed were dark pages in Arizona history—the era of the "Apache wars"—replete with ample shedding of blood. The end result was native populations living on reservations comprising one fourth of the land mass of the State, meaning one fourth of the state ruled by tribal law, one fourth of the state not subject to state taxation, one fourth of the state subject to very limited jurisdiction by state government, one fourth of the state with a direct appeals process to federal rather than state courts, one fourth of the state semi-sovereign nations within a sovereign state.

A percentage of Arizona's native population has successfully maintained traditional lifestyles. This, coupled with a state dotted with the archeological remains of the past, has made Arizona truly a living museum. Cultural diversity is very real.

PRIVATE VS PUBLIC DOMAIN

In most western states a sizable chunk of the land is owned by the federal government, and Arizona is no exception—a whopping 44%. Another 17% is owned by state governmental entities. Add this to the reservation lands previously mentioned, and we come up with government ownership of roughly 85% of the entire state. Conversely, this leaves 15% for private ownership, and this means that only 15% of the state land is taxable.

In addition to the tax base issue, there exist several other problem areas, such as environmental issues with the federal government over the use of land under federal jurisdiction, interpretations of the Indian Gaming Act as applied on the reservations, the vast distances between islands of privately developed land that require the building of stretches of highway through non tax-bearing lands, and federal policy as it relates to logging, mining, and grazing, to name a few.

GEOGRAPHY

Begging the forbearance of geographers, the term used herein is to be interpreted in its broadest possible context.

Arizona is a large state. It is the sixth largest state in the Union. The state of Massachusetts would very easily fit within the boundaries of Maricopa County, and Connecticut could be enveloped within the Valley of the Sun. The smallest county in Arizona, Santa Cruz, is larger than the state of Rhode Island. All of Arizona's fifteen counties are larger than some eastern states.

Size, coupled with a widely dispersed population, yields some interesting political problems. To comply with the guidelines for congressional district apportioning contained within Baker v. Carr, all six federal congressional districts must include part of the Phoenix metropolitan area (Maricopa County lays claim to over half of the state population). Districts fan out over literally hundreds of miles, over changing climatic zones, differing peoples, different economies. For example, District 6 includes the reservations of the Four Corners area, among others, the settlements dotting the White Mountains and the Mogollon Rim (including Flagstaff), and the urban sprawl of Fountain Hills, East Scottsdale, and East Mesa. From the ponderosa pine to Sonoran Saguaro, mountain to desert, traditional indigenous peoples to sophisticated urbanites, there is one congressperson representing all. Not only is adequate representation rendered extremely difficult, if not impossible, but due to the distances involved, the time and expense of travel, the cost of political campaigns, and the cost of transportation and communications systems are greatly increased.

Arizona is a land of contrasts. The state symbol is the saguaro, yet more of Arizona is forested with the ponderosa pine than with the saguaro cactus. Snow skiing is a major winter attraction, and Arizona has more pleasure boats per capita than any other state except Florida. It is a land of contrasts, built on diversity.

DURATION OF TERRITORIAL STATUS

The Northwest Ordinance of 1787, one of the few notable successes of the Articles of Confederation government, provided a structure for the creation of new states that was loosely followed in the creation of all subsequent states except Texas and West Virginia. Basically, a three stage process was to be observed. In the first stage Congress would establish geographical boundaries and authorize the President to appoint a territorial governor and other territorial officials necessary to meet the needs of the territory in question. In the second stage an elected lower house and an appointed upper house of a territorial legislature was authorized. This legislative body was to enact measures that would meet the immediate needs of the territory and move it along the path toward statehood, subject to a line of vetoing authorities. With population growth the territory could petition Congress for permission to call a territorial constitution convention in preparation for statehood (stage three).

The length of the territorial status and the amount of hardship endured by people during their territorial experience varied tremendously. Whereas some states, California, went from territory to statehood in two years, Arizona's total territorial experience stretched from 1848 to 1912. This meant 64 years of rule from Washington, oftentimes by appointees with little or no interest in the concerns of the territory. Not that champions of Arizona's cause did not exist; they most certainly did! But problems of absentee government created distrust for government, most of it directed at the territorial governor. Current limitations on gubernatorial power and other structures within our constitution date from this drawn out and distasteful experience.

ISOLATION

One of the principle reasons for the unpleasant experience of territorial days was the mindset and perceptions of the eastern establishment about the region. Dating from the days when the myth of the "Great American Desert" was spread (circa 1820), Arizona and the rest of the Southwest was seen as being unfit for civilized people. It was perceived as a land inhabited by savage peoples, poisonous "critters," of hostile environment, devoid of culture, and lacking in economic opportunity. Ignored was the fact that all this was contrary to the successes of eastern entrepreneurs operating within the territory, and the lifestyles they were enjoying while here.

Yet except for the military telegraph and intermittent stagecoach forays, Arizona was isolated by distance and geography until the coming of the Southern Pacific Railroad to Tucson in 1880, and a spur to Phoenix in 1887. Even by rail it was a long way from the East, and the difficulties of access simply kept people and interest away. This mindset was slow to die even as Arizona moved into the twentieth century and it was a series of events around the World War II era that enabled Arizona to commence its phenomenal growth.

The isolation was double pronged. Not only did the rest of the country know or care little for Arizona, but Arizonans themselves were in large measure isolated from what was going on in the rest of the country. With a dominance in mining, cattle, and agriculture, and no appreciable business or industrial base, there was little need to pursue the infrastructure, the educational system, and the quality of life-type issues that were deemed essential "back East." So, after its "discovery" at mid-century Arizona would find itself somewhat out of synch with more developed parts of the country.

1
GEOGRAPHY

Arizona is located in the southwestern United States bordered by Mexico on the south, the states of California and Nevada on the west, Utah on the north, and New Mexico on the east. Arizona is usually considered a desert state, which is true of two-thirds of the land area, however, that description would be an oversimplification.

GENERAL TOPOGRAPHY

Arizona has three topographic zones that determine its climate (Figure 1-1). The Sonoran Desert zone is hot and dry, and it varies in elevation from sea level to approximately 3,000 feet in some of its mountains. The transition zone, or mountain area, crosses the state diagonally from northwest to southeast. The elevation of the region, from 4,000 to 12,670 feet, supports an alpine forest environment and accounts for the mild to frigid temperatures. The highest point in Arizona is Mount Humphrey in the San Francisco Peaks near Flagstaff. The high desert zone has an elevation from 4,000 to 5,000 feet on the average. In the winter the region does get snow, the temperature drops to below freezing, and the wind-chill factor can be well below freezing.

The mountains and rivers of Arizona are both travel routes and barriers. The Mogollon Rim is a formidable barrier to north-south travel. The White Mountains in eastern Arizona forced travelers to take a southern route in the early days. The Grand Canyon still forces people living in the strip country, that area north of the Colorado River, to travel hundreds of miles to reach the county seat on the other side of the Canyon.

RIVERS AND LAKES

Rivers have served as major transportation routes into Arizona (Figure 1-2). The Colorado River is the major river in Arizona both in size and importance. It enters Arizona at the north-central border with Utah and continues through the Grand Canyon, where it angles westward to form the border between Arizona and Nevada as well as California. South of Yuma the once mighty river, exhausted by the demands of urban centers and agriculture, turns into a marshland. No longer can steamboats find their way up from the Gulf of California. The Gila River is the only other river to traverse the state completely, entering from New Mexico and exiting by joining the Colorado River at Yuma. Several rivers have served as major routes into the state. The San Pedro and Santa Cruz rivers both flow north from Mexico into Arizona and combine with the Gila River. The Salt River, its lower reaches now dry except during periods of heavy consistent rainfall, along with its various tributaries are important primarily for their economic value to the Salt River Valley, in which the greater Phoenix metropolitan area lies.

There are a number of lakes in Arizona, for the most part owing their existence to the building of dams across natural waterways. The entirety of Arizona is either arid or semi arid, so the state cannot, therefore, afford to waste precious rainfall when it does occur. Runoff is preserved for future use behind the dams that create manmade lakes, or the countless reservoirs, large and small, that dot the entire state.

On the Colorado River, in addition to the most impressive Lake Powell and Lake Mead, there are two other artificial lakes, Mohave and Havasu, and two reservoirs near Yuma, Imperial and Laguna. The Salt River, first dammed to create massive Roosevelt Lake, is further contained by three other dams downstream, creating lakes Canyon, Saguaro, and Apache. The Aqua Fria River has been dammed to create Lake Pleasant in northwest Maricopa County, while the Verde River has been pooled in the northeastern part of Maricopa County to create Bartlett Lake. To the south, on the Gila River, is found San Carlos Lake.

Overwhelmingly, this water is used for irrigation, mostly for agriculture, but for domestic use as well. The bodies of water so contained provide the added benefit of recreation, as water starved Arizona boosts a very significant boating population. Most drinking water comes from deep wells, as ground water that accumulated from seepage and glacial runoff over thousands of years, is gradually being consumed.

LAND ROUTES

Arizona has fifteen counties widely divergent in size, population, and date of origin. Figure 1-3 shows the counties and the county seats and Table 1-1 shows the dates of incorporation and the approximate populations as of 1990.

Arizona's major land routes connect the communities of Arizona. (Figure 1-4). The southern route, Interstate Highways 8 and 10, passes through the cities of Willcox, Benson, Tucson, Casa Grande, Gila Bend, and Yuma. The northern route is Interstate 40 and it passes through the cities of Holbrook, Winslow, Flagstaff, Williams, and Kingman. Interstate 19, Interstate 17, and U.S. 89 span the state north and south and pass through Nogales, Tucson, Phoenix, Flagstaff, and Page. The interstate highway system was developed for transcontinental routes and not as a system for connecting cities within the state. In some instances, the cities owe their existence to the tourist trade using the highways. Yet, in other instances towns have dwindled as once traveled routes such as the historic Route 66 are replaced by modern interstate highways.

Railroads, too, were originally developed as transcontinental routes. Arizona was initially regarded as a place that had to be endured in order to reach desired California. First appeared the Southern Pacific Railroad across the southern portion of the state (it reached Tucson in 1881). In the late 1880's a series of railroad mergers resulted in a railroad route across northern Arizona, through Winslow, Flagstaff, and Kingman. Popularly known as the Frisco, in that it connected St. Louis with San Francisco, it was officially known as the Atchison, Topeka, and Santa Fe Railroad. It would later develop an additional route into Los Angeles.

In 1901 the Santa Fe Railroad created a subsidiary, the Grand Canyon Railroad, to carry tourist from the main line terminal at Williams, Arizona, to the South Rim of the Grand Canyon at Bright Angel Trail. The trip could be completed in reasonable comfort, a short period of time, and at reasonable cost. The railroad also built a quality hotel at the South Rim, named El Tovar, where visitors could stay and enjoy the scenery. Fred Harvey, who already operated restaurants and dining cars in conjunction with the Santa Fe, was commissioned to manage the hotel. For strictly commercial

reasons, the Santa Fe Railroad and the Fred Harvey Company transformed Arizona into the "Grand Canyon State."
Spurs branches out from the transcontinental lines. A spur of the Southern Pacific reached Phoenix in 1887, while the Santa Fe, Prescott and Phoenix Railroad connected from the northern route. The Southern Pacific crosses into California at Yuma, while the Atchison, Topeka and Santa Fe crosses at the northern end of Lake Havasu through Needles, California, and also further south through Parker, Arizona.

The state was subsequently crisscrossed with spur lines radiating from the major spurs and transcontinentals. These spurs were largely the work of the many mining companies operating in Arizona whose profitability depended on cheap transportation for their bulky ores. In the process, for being a sparsely populated region, Arizona became fairly well covered with railroads.

POINTS OF INTEREST

Several major points of interest in the state have become tourist attractions. The Grand Canyon National Park attracts almost 2.5 million visitors each year on the south rim. Not as famous as the Grand Canyon, the Salt River Canyon in eastern Arizona is also a most impressive site and serves the recreational desires of many from the Phoenix area. Floating the upper Salt River is a favored summer pastime. A more adventurous experience is the rafting of the Colorado River from Lee's Ferry through the Canyon to Lake Mead. Canyon de Chelly National Monument on the Navajo Reservation is not only scenic but is also a historic site for the Anasazi, Hopi, and Navajo Indians. The Painted Desert and Petrified Forest National Parks attract large numbers of visitors because of their proximity to Interstate 40. Historic sites also attract visitors, and many are unique for their excellent state of preservation. Montezuma Castle, Tuzigoot, Wupatki, Walnut Canyon, and Casa Grande National Monuments are all excellent examples of pre-Columbian Indian villages. Tumacacori, San Xavier del Bac, Tubac Presidio, and Coronado Monument are examples of the early Spanish mission and explorer period sites. Prescott's Sharlot Hall Museum, Jerome, Tombstone, Fort Bowie, and Pipe Springs attract visitors because of the folklore surrounding the cowboy and miner era in early territorial times.

The state is dotted with many ruins that have not been developed as tourist sites, the walls of Pueblo Canyon near Roosevelt Lake, for instance, contain numerous interesting and well-preserved ruins. Bone jarring travel over primitive roads and a somewhat more than leisurely climb are necessary to access such places. But the state is a living museum; evidences of past peoples and civilizations abound.

FIGURE 1-1. Topographical Zones

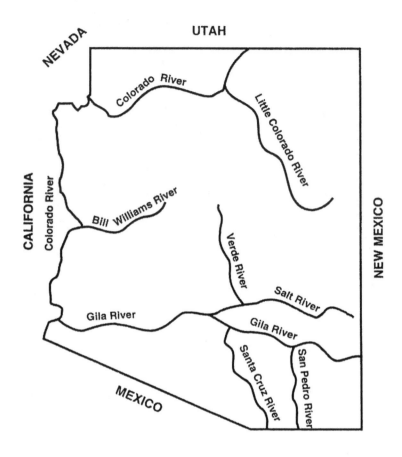

FIGURE 1-2. Rivers

TABLE 1-1. *Arizona Counties*

COUNTY	DATE OF INCORP	COUNTY SEAT	1990 COUNTY POPULATION	2000 COUNTY POPULATION
Yavapai	1864	Prescott	107,714	167,517
Mohave	1864	Kingman	93,491	155,032
Pima	1864	Tucson	666,880	843,746
Yuma	1864	Yuma	106,895	160,026
Maricopa	1871	Phoenix	2,122,101	3,072,149
Pinal	1875	Florence	116,379	179,727
Apache	1879	St. Johns	61,591	69,423
Cochise	1881	Bisbee	97,624	117,755
Graham	1881	Safford	26,554	33,489
Gila	1881	Globe	40,216	51,335
Coconino	1881	Flagstaff	96,591	116,320
Navaho	1895	Holbrook	77,658	97,470
Santa Cruz	1899	Nogales	29,676	38,381
Greenlee	1909	Clifton	8,008	8,547
LaPaz	1983	Parker	13,844	19,715

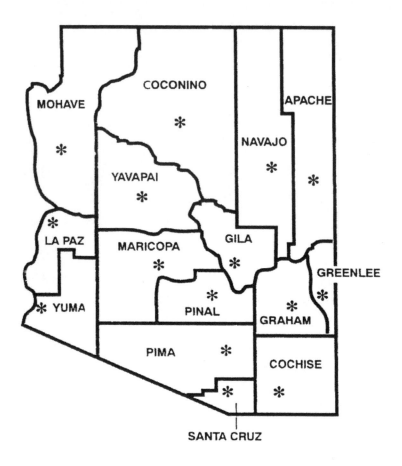

FIGURE 1-3. Map, Arizona Counties

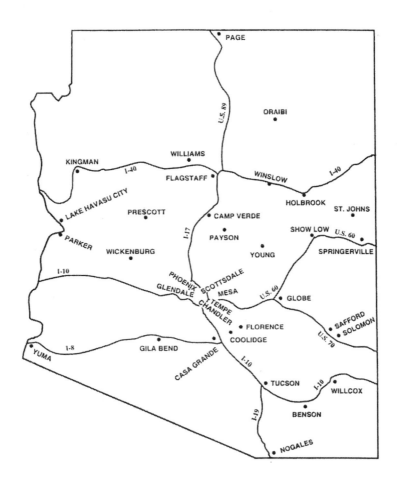

FIGURE 1-4. Highways, Cities, and Towns of Arizona

CHAPTER SUMMARY

✓ Arizona is a land of varied topography and climate.

✓ Rivers have been contained to conserve water for year-round use. Added effect is numerous water recreational areas in the state.

✓ Railroads played a major role in the early development of Arizona.

✓ Early land routes, both road and rail, were directed at reaching California, but provided benefits to Arizona territory as well.

✓ The state possesses abundant natural and native tourist attractions.

2
HISTORY

The American Indians were the only inhabitants of Arizona prior to the arrival of the Europeans. Indian history prior to the arrival of the Spanish is referred to as the pre-Columbian period that dates from approximately 15,000 B.C. to A.D. 1537. In the 1950s, documented physical evidence of early man in Arizona was found on the Lehner Ranch near Naco, Arizona. While no physical remains of the people were found, spear points in a mammoth (an elephant-like prehistoric animal) and the bones of other primitive animals were discovered and dated at about 9000 B.C. A report in the October 17, 1983, issue of The *Arizona Republic* credited Michael R. Walters, a University of Arizona graduate student, with discovering the burial site containing the remains of an adult Indian in Whitewater Draw near the present city of Douglas. Radioactive carbon test results of the remains indicated a rough date close to 10,000 years ago. The find is the oldest remains of a human found in Arizona to date.

ANCIENT INDIGENOUS CULTURES

This early period in Arizona is referred to as the Cochise Culture. The Cochise Culture is divided into three contemporary cultures from about 2000 B.C. to A.D. 1300. The Anasazi, Hohokam, and Mogollon cultures began at different places and at different times. Although they have unique beginnings, they seem to converge in the later stages.

The Anasazi developed in what is now northeastern Arizona, northwestern New Mexico, southeastern Utah, and southwestern Colorado. The latter period of their development is best recognized by extensive pueblo construction. Excellent ruins exist at Keet Seel and Betatakin in northeastern Arizona near Kayenta.

The Hohokam culture began in the lower desert and had extensive development in the Salt, Gila, and Verde River valleys. Hohokam are best known as irrigation farmers and are credited with building extensive canal systems. Some serve today as the canal routes of the Salt River Project. In the latter period, the Hohokam became pueblo dwellers, probably because of the extensive cross acculturation between the Anasazi and the Hohokam. Good examples of these ruins are to be seen at the Casa Grande National Monument near Coolidge and the Pueblo Grande ruins on East Washington Street in Phoenix.

The Mogollon culture began in southeastern Arizona and southwestern New Mexico. The Mogollons lived in caves and pit houses, and eventually built walled partitions in the caves, forming crude pueblos. In the latter stages of their development these pueblos became more elaborate. The Mogollon people were hunter gatherers who also practiced flood plain and dry land farming.

The Sinagua culture developed in the Verde Valley and the area around the San Francisco Peaks near the end of the pre-Columbian era. This group seems to have been heavily influenced by both the Anasazi and the Hohokam. The Sinagua were good farmers and pueblo builders. Because many of their remains have been protected from the elements, anthropologists have recreated a great deal of the life of these early Arizona residents. Excavations at Tuzigoot, Montezuma Castle National Monuments, and other sites have contributed significantly to the study of the Sinagua. Interesting displays of the artifacts of Sinagua Indians can be seen in the visitor centers at these national monuments.

The Patayan Indians resided along the Colorado River from the Grand Canyon to the Gulf of California. Less is known of these Indians since they built few structures, and most of the physical remains have been destroyed by wind and water erosion. What is known of the Patayan is primarily through their contact with contemporaries. Pottery and sea shells have been found at Anasazi and Hohokam sites, which indicates trade with the Patayan. The Patayan are believed to be the ancestors of the modern Yuma, Cocopah, Maricopa, Mojave, Walapai, Yavapai, and Havasupai tribes.

The reasons for the decline of these civilizations are not known, but several causes have been suggested. The twenty-three-year drought from A.D. 1276 to 1299 and the Sunset Crater eruption in A D. 1066 are given as climatic reasons for changes in living styles if not actual cultural decline. Another cause for change may have been the immigration of the Adhapascan Indians, the current Navajo and Apache tribes, into the area. The nomadic and raiding lifestyle of these tribes tended to put pressures on the centralized farming communities of the older cultures. Overpopulation, based on a centralized lifestyle, may have depleted the resources of the area faster than technology could respond. A simple decentralization of the people into smaller and more dispersed groups may have developed. Taken together, these events probably add up to a change in lifestyle. Some historians interpreted this change to be a decline from the large-scale dynamic period that existed in the area prior to A.D. 1300. The probable descendants of those early people are the Zuni, Hopi, Pima, Tohono O'odham and Yuman tribes.

MODERN NATIVE CULTURES

Modern Indian tribes were widely distributed throughout what is now Arizona. While there were some general areas where certain tribes were located, there was also a great deal of overlapping of territory. An area was not the exclusive preserve of one tribe until that concept was introduced by Europeans with the reservation system.

The Adhapascans are represented by the Navajo and Apache and their several subgroups. They are fairly recent arrivals in Arizona having migrated here at the beginning of the twelfth and thirteenth centuries A.D. While they were some of the most recent arrivals, the Adhapascans' nomadic lifestyle made them readily adaptable to the changes the Europeans were to bring. The group's dynamic growth, from 1540 until the arrival of the American army in 1848, made the Adhapascans among the most formidable Indians for the white man to control.

The Uto-Aztecan language group is represented by at least six tribes in Arizona: the Pima, Tohono O'odham, Hopi, Paiute, Chemehuevi, and Yaquis. The Pimas are known as river people who historically settled river and stream beds using the water to irrigate crops. Several of their villages, such as Sacaton on the Gila River Reservation south of Chandler, are well known and survive today as part of the reservation.

The Tohono O'odham, known as desert people, are dry land farmers, and in recent years have become cattlemen. Their major reservation on the southern border of Arizona surrounds Sells, a tribal village, and is the current tribal headquarters.

The Hopi are likely descendants of the Anasazi and share with the Pima and Tohono O'odham an ancient lineage with the Cochise culture. Their villages on the three mesas in northern Arizona are among the oldest villages in the United States. Oraibi, on Third Mesa, is the oldest continuously occupied village in the United States. Currently, there are twenty one reservations in Arizona (Figure 2-1).

EARLY SPANISH ACTIVITY

After Columbus' voyage to the new world in 1492, a host of Spanish explorers and conquistadors ventured into South America and Mexico. In 1536, Cabeza deVaca reached Culiacan, Mexico, after wandering eight years from Florida through the gulf states into Texas, New Mexico and, maybe, Arizona. Throughout the journey de Vaca and his companions heard stories of the seven cities of gold called Cibola, which existed some place to the north. When the Viceroy of Mexico heard the stories, he commissioned an expedition and selected Fray Marcos de Niza to lead it into what is now Arizona. Estevan, a Moorish slave and a member of the de Vaca party, was purchased as a guide for de Niza. Estevan led the party northward, following the San Pedro River entering Arizona near the present town of Hereford. It is unknown for sure how far de Niza traveled. However, the slave Estevan made it to the Zuni village of Hawikuh, where he was killed by natives who were not impressed by his claims of divine protection. Before his death, Estevan had sent a message to de Niza indicating that he had located the seven cities of

Figure 2-1. *Indian Reservations in Arizona*

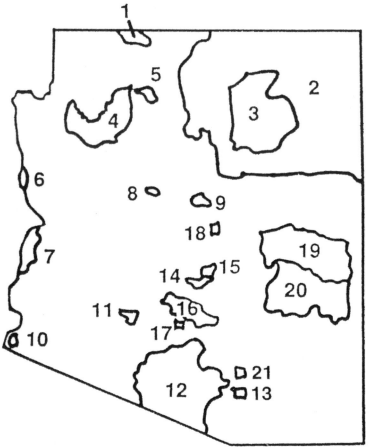

1. Kaibab	8. Yavapai	15. Fort McDowell
2. Navajo	9. Camp Verde	16. Gila River
3. Hopi	10. Cocopah	17. Ak-Chin
4. Hualapai	11. Gila Bend O'Odham	18. Payson
5. Havasupai	12. O'Odham	19. Fort Apache
6. Fort Mohave	13. San Xavier O'Odham	20. San Carlos
7. Colorado River	14. Salt River	21. Pascua Yacqui

Cibola. De Niza reported that he observed the cities, claimed them for the crown, and erected a wooden cross before returning to Mexico to report his discovery.

A giant expedition was then organized under Francisco Coronado in 1539. Coronado, with approximately 2500 officers, soldiers, Indian warriors, and slaves, departed from Compostela, Mexico, on February 22, 1540, in search of the seven cities of Cibola. With de Niza as a reluctant guide, Coronado followed the San Pedro River route past the Indian village of Quiburi to an area north of Benson. Leaving the river, he traveled north through rugged canyons and mountains to Chichilticale, or Red House, where the expedition rested before going on to the White Mountains east of Show Low. He continued to the plains of New Mexico, where he found the Zuni Pueblo of Hawikuh. To his disappointment, Coronado found no riches but only hostile Indians.

While conquering the Zunis, Coronado was injured and remained to rest and explore the surrounding area. One of Coronado's officers, Pedro de Tovar, led an expedition which discovered and conquered the Hopi villages in Arizona. Captain Cardenas also explored Northern Arizona beyond the Hopi mesas looking for the great river and was the first European to see the Grand Canyon and was not impressed. The canyon was seen merely as an impediment to travel, and the Colorado River, viewed from such a distance, was considered to be a tiny stream. Meanwhile, Captain Alarcon, who had sailed from Mexico to supply the expedition, explored the lower Colorado River in the process, and proved that the river could be navigated for a considerable distance. The association of the two discoveries, however, was not immediately evident.

Coronado, ever eager to believe the Indians' tales of riches, gold, and jewels, continued across New Mexico, stopping at pueblos near the Rio Grande. He then moved on to West Texas, Oklahoma, and the Arkansas River in Kansas. Finally, Coronado journeyed to Grand Quivira in central Kansas within 50 miles of the geographical center of the United States. On the windswept plains surrounded by friendly but poor Indians, Coronado surrendered to the reality that riches in silver and gold were not to be found in this area. He returned to Mexico City, a dejected and broken man, renounced for his failure to bring wealth and glory to the Spanish Empire.

Other explorers were to try for wealth and fame in Arizona before the advent of the mission period. In fact, Antonio de Espejo did discover some silver near the present site of Jerome in 1583. Espejo returned to Mexico with stories and rumors but little in the way of riches to show for his efforts.

Juan de Onate was a colonizer and explorer in the area between the Rio Grande River in New Mexico, and the Colorado River to the Gulf of California. In his travels, he contacted the Zuni, Hopi, and Mojave Indians and recorded some of their folklore and tales of riches. His men did find silver in the Prescott area, but like the earlier finding of Espejo, the ore was never mined in quantity. Onate was best known as the governor of the northern area of New Spain with permanent headquarters at Santa Fe.

SPANISH MISSIONARY ACTIVITY

While some mission activity continued in northern Arizona after the departure of Onate, Christianity was often rejected and the priests were killed. The Pueblo Indian revolt of 1680 was the largest expression of that rejection. However, in 1692, Governor Diego de Vargas recaptured the Zuni and Hopi villages and extracted from them a profession of the faith although little Christian practice was forthcoming.

In 1691, the most successful missionary of the Southwest was to enter Arizona. Father Kino, a Jesuit priest, had been sent to the Sonora region of Mexico to minister to the Pima Indians of the Pimeria Alta. This region extended northward to the Gila River and included the San Pedro and the Santa Cruz River valleys. In 1687, Father Kino established his headquarters at Dolores, Mexico, which is about seventy-five miles south of present day Nogales. Over the next fourteen years, Father Kino established several vistas and missions. The first of these was San Gabriel de Guevavi, which is north of the present site of Nogales on the Santa Cruz River. The Tumacacori Mission about twenty miles north of Nogales and San Xavier del Bac Mission near Tucson are better known Kino missions.

Father Kino was a mission builder who looked after the hearts, minds, and bodies of his people rather than the architecture of the mission buildings. The structures that are visible today were built later by Franciscan priests. The mission system, as established by Kino, had several characteristics that are important for understanding the Spanish-Indian culture as it was to develop in the new world. The San Xavier del Bac Mission was more of a ranch and farm community than a religious sanctuary. Kino was searching for some means of keeping the nomadic natives around so they could be religiously instructed. The method he hit upon was food. Kino introduced cattle, sheep, horses, and poultry to the Indians. He started raising grain crops and introduced several fruit trees: apple, citrus, and date palm. He replaced the metate with the grinding wheel and encouraged the Indians to use Spanish peasant housing, clothing, and tools. After Kino's death in 1711, mission work in Arizona declined, and the natives developed unique adaptations of Indian and Catholic religion over the next forty years. The German missionaries, who attended the missions from 1732 until 1767, were more doctrinaire than Kino and were sometimes considered cruel to the Indians.

The Pima rebellion of 1751 caused the Spanish to establish a presidio at Tubac to protect the mission at Tumacacori. This was the first civil settlement in Arizona and it grew to considerable size by 1775, when a new presidio was built at Tucson.

Of some importance to Arizona was the discovery in 1736 of a very pure form of silver about twenty miles west of Nogales. The Indians called this place Arizoniac or Arissona, an O'Odham word meaning "place of small springs." Although a mining rush soon exhausted the minerals, the name continued to be used in referring to an area west of Nogales. It is not known when the Spanish first started to refer to the whole region as Arizona, but by the time of Mexican independence in 1821, the name had become well established.

In 1767, the Jesuits were expelled from the New World and were replaced by the Franciscans. The Franciscan missionary explorer Fray Francisco Garces was one of the most dynamic personalities to traverse Arizona. He was a compassionate priest to the Indians and an untiring traveler, constantly seeking new places and new souls. Father Garces served as guide to Captain Juan Bautista de Anza in 1776 when de Anza led a group of settlers and opened the overland route to San Francisco. Father Garces was killed in the Yuma Massacre of 1781 in which fifty Spanish soldiers, settlers, and priests were killed and an equal number taken captive.

After 1781, the Spanish withdrew from the outreaches of the Arizona empire and concentrated on protecting the Santa Cruz Valley from the continuing attacks of the Apaches. The New Economic Policy of 1786 called for subsidies of whiskey, food, and outdated weapons to erode Indian skills and demoralize his character, thereby breaking resistance. Spain could well afford to underwrite this venture due to the wealth acquired from the new world, and did so even in the face of protest from the missionaries. "It works," was the response. As a result many settlers were able to move into the area. By 1790, a tentative peace was established with the Apaches. The Pima Indians were sufficiently colonized on to productive farms, and the new Spanish settlers had established commercial centers at the towns of Tucson and Tubac. The period from 1790 to 1821 is probably best known for the gold and silver mines the Spanish developed. Some mistakenly believed that this wealth had been hidden in the magnificent new buildings the Spanish were creating at the missions. The most outstanding example of the mission architecture of the period is the still active mission of San Xavier del Bac on the southwestern outskirts of Tucson.

THE MEXICAN PERIOD

The decline of Spain in the New World was related to events in Europe. The French Revolution in 1789 led to the Napoleonic wars, Napoleon's ultimate defeat, and the restitution of absolutistic rule in Europe. The United States government shared the liberal attitude of the French Revolution and, reacting to events in Europe, proclaimed the Monroe Doctrine as a deterrent to further European involvement in development of the western hemisphere. Thus began the chain of events that provided for liberation of several South and Central American countries, including Mexico.

As a result of Mexican independence in 1821, Spanish influence declined, loyal Spaniards fled the territory, and Mexico expelled the Franciscans as loyal supporters of the Spanish monarch. Mexico combined the old states of Sonora and Sinaloa into the new state of Occidente, which included what is now Arizona south of the Gila River and all of New Mexico. There was no centralized government in Arizona and the communities of Tucson and Tubac were governed by local patrons and businessmen. Arizona's fate was in the hands of the governor of New Mexico in Santa Fe.

To be noted also was the fact that independent Mexico lacked the wealth of Spain, and could not afford to continue the New Economic Policy. The end result was renewed hostilities with native populations and a general withdrawal of most settlers in the region south of Tucson.

In 1821, William Becknell, a trader, established relations with the newly independent country. The following year the Santa Fe Trail was established between Independence, Missouri, and Santa Fe, New Mexico. Later, the Spanish trail opened trade into California and the Anglo[1] entered the Southwest. Trappers, traders, and explorers worked the mountains of Arizona and New Mexico for the next several years. Men with colorful names and colorful histories added to the folklore of Arizona. These men included Kit Carson, Jedediah Smith, James Ohio Pattie and his father Sylvester Pattie, Bill Williams, Ewing Young, and

---

[1] Anglo in this context refers to English speaking North Americans

24

Pauline Weaver. Their contributions to the development of Arizona are many. They marked the mountain and desert trails which would later be used by travelers. They established relations with the Indians, some beneficial, others quite disastrous. James Kirker was one of the most successful Indian scalpers, paid bounty by the Mexican government. Many served as Army scouts in the Indian wars. Mountain men gave their names to rivers, peaks, creeks, and canyons. Most of all, they carried the story of a new land to the developing and ambitious eastern United States.

With westward expansion into Texas and America's desire to fulfill its manifest destiny, the West's settlement became a compelling desire. The precipitating incident leading to the war with Mexico was a boundary dispute involving the newly acquired state of Texas. But as events would reveal, the real cause was a desire by the United States to annex California and as much of the territory between the old Louisiana Purchase and the Pacific as possible. As was often the case, Arizona was not the prize but just a connecting part of the prized area. Colonel Stephen W. Kearney crossed Arizona along the Gila River in 1846 on his way to assist in the capture of California. Later that year, the Mormon Battalion, under the command of Captain Philip St. George Cooke, made a remarkable crossing from Council Bluffs, Iowa, to California with 340 men, five women, and several mules, horses, and wagons, proving that a wagon crossing through Arizona and northern Mexico was possible. Cooke raised the American flag over Tucson for the first time. The war had ended in 1848. In the ensuing settlement, the Treaty of Guadalupe Hildago, the southern boundary for Arizona was set at the Gila River. Tucson, the largest town, was excluded from United States control. The United States obtained all of Texas to the Rio Grande. The Mexican Cession included all or parts of the present states of California, Wyoming, Nevada, Utah, Colorado, New Mexico, and Arizona.

ACQUISITION BY THE UNITED STATES

In 1848, gold was discovered in California, and again Arizona became a pathway to the West. Although the best all weather route dipped into Mexico south of the Gila River, this was not a sufficient reason for the government of the United States to seek new land south of the border. Events in the East were responsible for Arizona's adding the land south of the Gila to its present boundaries. By 1850, the debate over the extension of slavery into the territories had reached a point where both North and South were competing for every advantage. Senator Douglas of Illinois argued for a northern route for a transcontinental railway, and Secretary of War Jefferson Davis supported a southern route. Both men realized that dependable transportation was the key to Western development. To support his claim, Davis ordered a survey for a southern rail route, thereby confirming the route Cooke used in crossing Arizona during the war with Mexico. James Gadsden was commissioned to begin negotiations to settle disputes and claims arising from the Treaty of Guadalupe Hidalgo.

The United States' payment to Mexico was $10 million in exchange for 45,535 square miles of land south of the Gila River. The railroad lobby in Congress was responsible for rotating the southern boundary slightly northward to prevent the possibility of an inland American port at the head of the Sea of Cortes. The current southern boundaries of the continental United States were established by the Gadsden Purchase, and as agreed in The Compromise of 1850, all of the land acquired from Mexico could be settled as slave territory with the exception of California and Utah. The stage was set for conflict with the United States government when Arizona petitioned for separate territorial status from New Mexico but was denied.

Santa Fe was neither inclined nor able to govern or defend Arizona. Therefore, Arizona remained essentially a military zone until 1863, when it was organized as a separate territory. From 1848 to 1863 only a few forts provided what passed for law and protection in Arizona. Because of Arizona's sparse population and its prosouthern sympathy, the United States government refused to admit Arizona as a territory. With the outbreak of the Civil War, the area of southern New Mexico and Arizona requested admission to the Confederacy as a territory. Acceptance was eagerly granted in that the Confederacy had great need for Arizona's mineral wealth. The Union was equally eager to prevent the acquisition. A small band of Union soldiers under the command of Lt. James Barrett encountered a Confederate scouting party from Tucson at Picacho Pass on April 15, 1862, and fought an indecisive skirmish. Later, a much larger party of the California Column occupied a deserted Tucson and reclaimed it for the Union, thus ending the Civil War in Arizona.

TERRITORIAL ARIZONA

Less than a year later, on February 24, 1863, President Lincoln signed into law the Organic Act of Arizona, making Arizona a territory of the United States. Lincoln, in selecting the first territorial officers for Arizona, established a pattern which was to gain widespread practice in the reconstruction of the South. Lincoln appointed two Northern politicians who had failed to win reelection to the House of Representatives in 1862, as well as other carpetbaggers who had served the war administration well, following a long established policy of appointing political chronies rather than territorial champions to guide the political development of the West. The only Arizonan to receive an appointment was Charles D. Poston, who was made superintendent of Indian affairs. Poston, known as the father of Arizona, had lobbied on behalf of the new territory. John Gurley was appointed governor, but he died before leaving for the new territory. Chief Justice John N. Goodwin took his place.

Much has been made of the desire of the Union to punish Tucson for its pro slavery sympathy by establishing the territorial capital at Fort Whipple near Prescott. An equally valid observation is that at the time of the creation of the Arizona territory the largest mining operations were in the Prescott area, and the new officials were notoriously attracted to prospecting and wealth.

Indian trouble in the territory had several effects, both on the new and the native inhabitants. The Apaches were raiders and nomadic hunters in pre-Columbian times. The Apaches grew rapidly in power with the introduction of horses, which had strayed or were otherwise acquired from the Spanish. Both Mexico and the United States tried to curtail the raiding of Apache leaders such as Cochise, Geronimo, and Victorio. Finally, in September 1886, after three hundred years of conflict, the United States Army prevailed and exiled the Apache leaders to Florida and later Oklahoma. The remaining peaceful Indians were placed on reservations.

The Easterner had the excitement of hearing and reading the dreadful tales of the atrocities of the wild Indians, and from them formed a romanticized view of Arizona and the West as a wild and lawless place. But what they rarely heard about were the atrocities committed by the settlers themselves. A notable exception was the Camp Grant Massacre of 1871. The good citizens of Tucson slaughtered a group of Apaches who had settled around the military installation known as Camp Grant. Most of the victims were women and children. Arizonians saw nothing wrong with this action; the nation on a whole was outraged. President Grant threatened martial law for the territory if the perpetrators were not brought to justice. A mock trial brought immediate and total exoneration. Having lived in the turmoil, fear, and distrust of the era, the Westerner became wary of the Indian and critical of the government for its policy. The Indian was probably the most affected of all and was forever changed in culture and outlook. Arizona and United States government Indian policies were greatly influenced by the conflicts of the nineteenth century. The policies emphasized exclusion and separation rather than inclusion of Indians in governmental affairs.

Settlements in the territory grew after the Civil War, and several groups added to the area's culture as it developed in preparation for statehood. Although some farmers, ranchers, and businessmen trickled into Arizona before the Civil War, the discovery of gold and silver at various sites during and after the war attracted the first large wave of settlers and miners. Places like the Vulture Mine near Wickenburg and the older mines of Mowry, La Paz, and Gila County attracted restless, aggressive, and frequently unstable persons; namely, the prospector and the individual miner. These men did not build towns or put down roots, for they rarely had family with them. They lived in a world of personal survival and independent action.

Later, in the 1880s, when silver and copper became important minerals, the mines and miners changed. Organized companies with machines and technology hired mine workers for wages to produce the metals. This in turn led to skilled labor being hired. Often these men came with their families and established permanent settlements. The most notorious of these towns, Tombstone, was founded in 1880 and continued for several years as a mining town. Its reputation was well established in the sensational press of the day, which reported and embellished such events as the infamous gunfight at the OK Corral.

Another group of settlers took advantage of the new Eastern beef market. This group included the cattleman, the rancher, and the cowboy. Prior to the Civil War, the country lacked the transportation and refrigeration technology to move and to store beef. Following the war, America's appetite for beef was satisfied by cattle drives to the railheads in Kansas and other midwestern points. With westward expansion of the rails, the cattle drives of the tough longhorn ended. Ranches raising the more desirable Hereford became big business wherever a railroad was available. The cattle business attracted capital from not only the East but from foreign countries as well. Hired hands came from the South, Midwest, and even the East. This cowboy lifestyle became legendary and, to this day, it is the hallmark of the state both for the pioneer and the newcomer, a highly romanticized view of an extremely harsh occupation.

The size of the ranches was enormous. One of the largest of these spreads was the Hashknife outfit, the ranching subsidiary of the Aztec Land and Cattle Company, which was owned by the same individuals who owned the Santa Fe Railroad. The spread covered most of the area from Holbrook to Flagstaff and ran as many as 65,000 head of cattle in the 1880s. Lust for land to graze cattle led to a variety of schemes, some legal, some illegal, and many violent. One of these illegal schemes concerns the famous Reavis claim, which may have been the largest land fraud case ever uncovered in Arizona. James Addison Reavis, known as the Baron of Arizona, based his claim to 11 million acres of land, stretching from Silver City, New Mexico to west of Phoenix, Arizona, on fraudulent documents, which he claimed granted his wife Dona Sofia Loreto Micaela de Maso-Reavis y Peralta de la Cordoba the entire region. The Baron of Arizona was exposed, tried for forgery, and imprisoned, but not before he had collected several hundred thousand dollars in rent from the occupants of the land.

Another event which demonstrates the violence that accompanied the greed and jealousy, which existed between the various ranchers, concerns the Pleasant Valley War. Some claim the feud started as a conflict between cattlemen and sheep-herders, while others claim that the feud started over rustling and thievery. For whatever reason, the Graham-Tewksbury feud lasted for ten years and accounted for the death of approximately fifty people.

The large spreads were gradually divided and ranching became a family operation. Resident owners frequently owned little land but leased large tracts from the government on grazing permits. While ranching is not associated with a dense population, the ranchers, with their families and hands, did provide a stable population around the communities that grew up to support their needs. Communities such as Payson, Young, Patagonia, Holbrook, and Kirkland developed in 1880s and 1890s.

The cowboy of this era was also immortalized in story and song that added to the nation's distorted view of the West. He was sometimes represented as a reckless villain and at other times as a victorious and gallant knight. Arizonans knew the truth to be somewhere in between.

Mormon pioneers that migrated from Utah established some of the first farm communities in Arizona. Successful farming in Arizona required more cooperation than it had in the East and Midwest. Irrigation was almost mandatory and necessitated the building of dams and canals. Furthermore, settlements frequently needed capital investment and skillful management in order to organize the labor, materials, and resources necessary to survive. The Mormon settlement patterns managed these problems in a skillful fashion to bring thriving communities to places where individuals working alone would have perished. The United Order provided for a well-balanced group which, sharing labor and using communal stores, could count on a variety of skills and mutual support in providing for its physical and spiritual needs. In a land often devoid of civil law, the Mormon theocracy ensured law and order with well-established roles and ample means of coercion and rewards. An orderly and energetic society resulted.

Jacob Hamblin, a Mormon, established Pipe Springs north of the Colorado River in The Strip Country. Later, he settled near Springerville in eastern Arizona. Pine, Strawberry, Heber, Snowflake, and St. Johns were all Mormon colonies in northern Arizona. Pima and Thatcher were in the eastern Arizona Gila River Valley, Lee's Crossing on the floor of the Grand Canyon. The White Mountain communities deemphasized the communalism of the United Order, favoring private ownership tempered by community cooperation instead.

Mormon pioneer David Jones was in the process of leading a group of saints to Mexico, and stopped to rest for a while in the Salt River Valley. This temporary settlement was known as Fort Utah, and later as Lehi. Other Mormon groups settled in the general area. By 1878 the Mexican destination was forgotten, and the Mormons were planting crops and laying out a town site known as Mesa. Settlement brought constant contact with non-Mormons and conflict was the result, most significantly, over the practice of polygamy. The issue was softened by the Proclamation of 1890, whereby polygamy was officially disavowed. Some Mormons refused to accept the change and were eventually excommunicated from the LDS organization. Over a century later polygamous communities, notably Colorado City, continue to exist. Controversy continues to surround the community. Its leader, Warren Jeffs, was recently convicted in a Utah court for forcing underage marriages, and faces similar charges in Arizona.

Statehood in Arizona was slow in coming for several reasons. To begin with, Arizona and New Mexico were both silver-producing territories and the gold standard supporters were fearful that their admission would swell the ranks of silver senators, possibly leading to a silver or bimetalist policy. A related issue concerned the general political liberalism of westerns disrupting the conservatism of the Eastern Establishment. Further, Arizona had been pictured as an undesirable place in Eastern literature. Indian wars, cattle rustling, and frontier lawlessness were played to the hilt in wild west shows and sensational publications. In addition, the territory was sparsely populated with only 204,354 inhabitants in the 1910 census.

Arizona's public relations improved considerably after the Spanish American War because of Theodore Roosevelt's popularity and his admiration for the West and the cowboys. Arizona's economic development was improved by the Reclamation Act of 1902, which funded the construction of Roosevelt Dam. Arizona's progressive politics, while still a drawback in some respects, found sympathy with the growth of populism and progressivism in other parts of the country.

EARLY STATEHOOD PERIOD

Arizona's constitution of 1912 was modeled after the federal constitution in form. It also reflected the ideals of the more recent admissions to the national union, Oregon and Oklahoma, for the progressive principles they included. The constitution contained a dominant legislature consisting of two houses, a plural executive with several quasi-independent elected officers, and an elected judiciary. The constitution also contained the direct democracy features of recall, referendum, and initiative, as well as the direct primary for candidate selection, the long ballot, and short terms for keeping officials responsive to the people. A list of thirty-three rights was included which, in most cases, assured that the state would abide by the same guarantees of rights as the United States government. While some features have been changed over the years by amendment, the intent has remained intact and the document represents one of the most progressive state constitutions in the country. (see Chapter 3)

Arizona's first elected officials reflected the prevailing political alignment of the state and were heavily Democratic. The first governor of Arizona, George W. P. Hunt, served six full terms and one half of a disputed term which he split with Thomas E. Campbell, Arizona's second governor. Governor Hunt was a labor advocate from the mining community of Globe. Although a wealthy man, he supported the cause of the common man in such issues as support for strikers, public education, the eight-hour day, workmen's compensation, and the abolition of child labor. Hunt was opposed by the state legislature on many of his social issues, and although popular with Democratic voters, he failed to control the democratic majority in the legislature.

By 1917, World War I was on the minds of Americans and Arizonans were proud to lend their support to the cause. Frank Luke Jr., a highly successful pilot, was recognized as Arizona's World War I hero. Arizona's Indians were particularly anxious to demonstrate their loyalty and were among the first to enlist. Civilian support was demonstrated by buying liberty bonds and conserving food. Patriotism led to some anti union activity as the IWW (International Workers of the World) was accused of obstructing the war effort and even sabotage. This sentiment was continued at the end of the war and a serious division erupted between the loyal Arizonans and the miners, who were often of eastern European or foreign descent. With the Russian Revolution of 1917, more distrust developed and anti unionism led to the Bisbee deportation of miners suspected of IWW or

Communist sympathy. Certain business interest saw no reason to discourage these feelings, using them instead to further stifle the union movement. Nativism also expressed itself in antiBlack, Chinese, Mexican, Indian, Mormon, and Catholic attitudes. There was some Ku Klux Klan activity in the state, but it certainly did not represent majority opinion.

On a more positive note World War I brought about a notable increase in agriculture and industry in Arizona. Led by Goodyear, tire manufacturing companies began moving into Arizona in 1916. Tires at the time were reinforced with cotton fiber, and long stand Pima cotton was ideally suited. Aircrafts of the era were covered with a cotton "skin." The result was a boom in cotton production; buyers were steady, and for a time cotton was king.

The period following World War I was one of rapid growth and development for Arizona. Agriculture became particularly important, with ever-expanding irrigation facilities and new ground being brought under cultivation. Mining grew into the largest industry in the state with the expansion of open pit mines and the crushing and smelting of huge quantities of low-grade ore. With the growth of Phoenix, real estate and construction industries began to grow, as did road and railroad construction.

Again, events outside of Arizona were to play an important part in its development. The Great Depression and the Dust Bowl caused a mass migration from the Midsouth: Arkansas, Oklahoma, and Texas. While some migrants settled in Arizona, most were on their way to California and only saw Arizona as an obstacle to be overcome. In response to the Depression, federal programs were created which were favorable to Arizona. The construction of schools, public buildings, dams, roads, and even the development of facilities in the national parks were especially important to the state as a foundation to the rapid growth that was to follow World War II.

MODERN ARIZONA

It is ironic that World War II would start for the United States with the attack on Pearl Harbor and the sinking of the battleship *Arizona*. In many ways, World War II set Arizona on the path that would direct it into the present. The invention and widespread use of the evaporative cooler and later refrigeration may have been the largest factor in allowing Phoenix and Tucson to become major year-round urban centers. Many service personnel were stationed in Arizona and returned after the war to settle. The migration patterns shifted and included more Midwestern farmers who were selling out as farms consolidated in that region. This growth especially caused the expansion of Phoenix and Tucson.

Other factors would include significantly improved transportation—air travel and interstate highways. The presence of military bases that continued to expand during the Cold War, with subsequent need for civilian support services and the increasing number of military retirees who chose to make Arizona their retirement home was another. Sanataria for the convalescing, dude ranches, a scenery popularized by the epic western movies, and the growth of high tech Sun Belt industry, all contributed to the population growth.

Phoenix area businessmen, in an effort to "clean up the town," in order to promote and attract business, had formed the Charter Government Committee. This organization provided the nucleus for Republican Party control, first in

Maricopa County, and eventually, statewide. The population change brought more Republicans into the state, and by 1950 Arizona had elected Howard Pyle, a Republican, governor. In 1952, Congressman John J. Rhodes, a United States House member, and Senator Barry Goldwater, both Republicans, were elected.

Arizona's growth pattern changed again following the 1972 energy crisis and the booming of the Sun Belt. While older winter visitors had discovered the sunny respite from cold weather that Arizona provided, they returned north each spring. A new migration began and was composed of younger workers from the midwestern and eastern industrial states who came to Arizona to work and live. The electronics industry had expanded tremendously from its infant beginnings in the 1950s. A highly skilled labor force was recruited to fill the jobs created by defense and industrial contracts.

As of April, 2005, the Voter Registration Report compiled by the Secretary of State, listed voter registration as 39.93% Republicans, 34.43% Democrats, 24.80% Independents, and .69% Libertarians. Arizona voters reflect conservative leanings when voting for the President, representatives in Congress, or state legislators. Individual Democrats can command support because of local constituencies or personal qualities but have taken a fairly cautious path in representing the Democratic party.

CHAPTER SUMMARY

✓ Arizona is home to many well documented indigenous cultures, many of which continue to exist.

✓ The existence of Arizona's early settlers is evidenced by the numerous reservations in the state.

✓ The early history of Arizona is associated with Spanish explorers who were searching for fabled treasures.

✓ Later Spanish presence was evidenced by its missionary activities.

✓ The Mexican government lacked the resources to combat the American push into the northern regions of the former Spanish Empire.

✓ The United States eventually acquired the Southwest by annexation, military conquest, and purchase. Arizona was acquired by the latter two methods.

✓ Early Anglos in Arizona were overwhelmingly pro-southern; Arizona was a Confederate territory before becoming a Union territory in 1863.

✓ Territorial Arizona was dominated by ranchers, miners, and loggers; permanent settlements were slow to develop.

✓ An exception was the many Mormon agricultural settlements that traversed the northern and eastern regions of the territory.

✓ Roosevelt Dam and the railroads made possible the development of the region.

✓ Substantial population growth was largely the result of effects associated with the Second World War.

3

THE CONSTITUTIONAL CONVENTION

Arizona's struggle for statehood was a lengthy ordeal. The first attempt to achieve statehood occurred in 1872. Led by a former territorial governor, Richard McCormick, who was then territorial delegate to Congress, the effort was premature. At the time, the population of the territory was approximately 12,000. The scant population, coupled with a general national lack of awareness or interest in the region resulted in little attention being given to the proposal.

The Indian wars of the 1870's focused national attention on the region, particularly due to the excesses being reported in the eastern press. Later, the request for statehood in 1886 by Arizona's sister territory, New Mexico, further brought the region into the national spotlight. Under normal circumstances the attention being given to the Southwest should have provided an impetus for statehood. But counterbalancing the positive issues involved in support of statehood was a more powerful national issue, the free silver issue.

STATEHOOD AND SILVER

At the time the national currency was backed by gold, and the dollar flourished in an appreciating market, sometimes exceeding its face value. Debtors oppose an appreciating currency; it requires them to pay back cheaper dollars with more expensive dollars. Eastern debtors, cash starved farmers, and westerners in general, favored an inflationary type currency, one that would be at least partially backed by silver (since it was a much cheaper commodity than gold). Western silver miners wholeheartedly agreed.

Political leaders in Arizona lined up on the pro-silver side of the monetary issue, while the Congress of the United States, reflecting eastern business interests, favored the maintenance of the gold standard. Statehood for Arizona would translate into an additional two pro-silver votes in the United States Senate. This anticipated increase in pro-silver political strength in the Senate was clearly not desired by eastern interests, and eastern interests controlled the Senate; statehood was simply not to be an option at the time.

An 1891 constitutional convention submitted a constitution that was immediately rejected by the United States Congress. This scenario was repeated each of the following three years, although in 1894 Congress split on the issue (the more liberal House approved it). Central to the repeated rejection was the perceived liberalism of the territory by eastern conservatives. The remainder of the century witnessed continual failed attempts to achieve statehood. In 1902, early in the presidency of Theodore Roosevelt, the House of Representatives introduced a bill calling for statehood for three territories: Arizona, New Mexico, and Oklahoma. The

Senate blocked the measure, again seeking to preserve its political composition.

CONTAINING LIBERALISM

The issue facing the Senate was clear: Oklahoma and Arizona were definitely of liberal persuasion, while New Mexico was not. A solution would be to combine Arizona with New Mexico, and let the much larger conservative vote of New Mexico absorb the smaller liberal Arizona vote. Thus, a conservative New Mexico would balance a liberal Oklahoma, and the political effect of the west would be neutralized. A powerful friend at court for this approach was found in the person of Senator Albert Beveridge, Chair of the Committee on Territories. In addition to the political issues involved, his views on the racial composition and literacy rate of the region convinced him that separate statehood for Arizona was not to be. A world wind tour through the territory, in which he successfully culled out the negatives, while ignoring the positives, further entrenched him in his position.

A 1904 bill proposed that Oklahoma become a state, and that New Mexico and Arizona be combined into a single state, with the capital to be located at Santa Fe and the name to be New Mexico. The measure passed the House of Representatives and was immediately met with a storm of protest from Arizona. Any political influence or identity for Arizona would be entirely lost under the new plan. The result was another committee being sent west to investigate the matter. This committee was headed by Congressman James Tawney, who did not share the views of his Republican colleague, Senator Beveridge, and who believed that any attempt to combine the two territories would be a mistake. The investigation delayed any further action on statehood until 1906.

In that year Senator Joseph Foraker proposed a solution. The voters in each territory would separately vote on whether or not they desired combined statehood. If the voters in either territory disapproved of combined statehood, then the combined statehood proposal would no longer be pursued by the Congress. During the late fall of 1906 the vote was taken. Over 16,000 people voted against combined statehood, compared to slightly more than 3,000 who favored it, in Arizona. The result was opposite in New Mexico. Slightly more than 26,000 voted in favor, while 15,000 opposed. (Note that the number of voters in New Mexico was twice that of Arizona.)
This should have been the end of the matter, according to the Foraker Amendment, but it was not to be.

Oklahoma had meanwhile acquired statehood (1907) while the combined statehood debate was raging in the Southwest. Oklahoma's liberal constitution met with no opposition from the current occupant of the White House, progressive minded Theodore Roosevelt. In the 1908 party platforms both major parties endorsed separate statehood for New Mexico and Arizona. But in 1908 the more conservative minded William Taft was elected president, and when he visited Arizona in 1909 he delivered an ominous warning. Announcing that he supported statehood for the territory, Taft warned against a constitution that contained the innovative features that the Oklahoma constitution contained. He further suggested that the territory take great care in choosing the right kind of delegates for its constitutional convention. The Enabling Act, that is, the authorization for

New Mexico and Arizona to proceed with the statehood process, finally passed Congress and was signed into law by President Taft on June 20, 1910. Due to the excesses found in Arizona's territorial history, the United States Congress placed a number of restrictions in Arizona in its Enabling Act, notably limitations on the use and disposal of federal lands deeded to the state, and various prohibitions on the ability to tax Indian land.

CONSTITUTIONAL DELEGATES

Delegates to the Arizona Constitutional Convention were elected on September 12, 1910. The 52 delegates were prorated among the counties on the basis of the number of qualified voters in each county. Total population was not a consideration; counties with high numbers of Hispanics and Native Americans were grossly underrepresented. A major ideological split among the delegates was immediately evident. Republican delegates wanted a short, conservative document, free of the recent innovative notions of the progressive era. Democrats, backed by the laborite element in the territory, wanted to incorporate all the latest innovations, including the recently adopted U'Ren system in Oregon (initiative, referendum, and recall elections).

The Democrats were destined to rule the convention. Of the 52 delegates chosen, 41 were Democrats and 11 were Republicans. Pima County sent 5 Republicans, Coconino sent 2, while Navajo, Santa Cruz, Gila, and Yvaipai counties sent one each. Republicans were in the majority only in Pima, Santa Cruz and Coconino counties. But despite the overwhelming 4-1 numeric advantage enjoyed by the Democrats, there was division within Democratic Party ranks. Counties that represented heavy mining interest were liberal, drawing their support from the laborite cause, whereas agricultural counties were of a more conservative persuasion.

Party caucuses chose convention officials and they were elected by a straight party vote, meaning, of course, that the Democrats chose convention officials by a vote of 41 to 11. George Hunt, a liberal, was chosen convention president (he would become the state's first governor), and Morris Goldwater was chosen vice president. Indicative of the split within Democratic Party ranks is evidenced by the fact that the caucus chose Hunt by a vote of 23 to 18, meaning that 23 Democrats were liberal and 18 were somewhat less so.

The composition of the convention was demographically heterogeneous. There were fourteen lawyers (but what percentage of them actually attended law school is another matter), and two physicians. There were also bankers, ranchers, miners, and skilled workers. It was a cross section of Arizona, with certain groups conspicuously not represented, but for the time, somewhat populist. The rich and the poor, the well educated and the poorly educated, rubbed shoulders. Delegates were appointed to working committees on the basis of their interests and expertise.

It became readily evident that, although the convention would pass liberal and progressive measures, it was not radical. The U'Ren system had been publicly endorsed by 39 delegates during the election process, and 30 of this number favored recall. The recall provision would be the most controversial in view of President Taft's stated conservative position. For although 60 percent of the delegates clearly favored the measure before the convention convened, their overriding focus was on achieving statehood. This was the main reason for the subduing of any radical tendencies. Yet, with some apprehension, the recall measure still passed by a 4 to 1 margin.

IDEOLOGICAL CONFLICTS

The liberalism that dominated the convention was not all encompassing. But neither, for that matter, was the much broader national progressive movement. Liberalism was spotty, interlaced with many deeply entrenched conservative pockets.

Female suffrage was considered, and then voted down, even though western states were noted for their early support of the suffrage movement. Allegedly, the primary reason for opposition in Arizona was due to the perception that women were strong backers of the prohibition initiative, and thirsty Arizona males were not about to strengthen the opposition. Prohibition was considered by the convention, but easily voted down. Ironically, within a year of achieving statehood, Arizona approved female suffrage by state constitutional amendment, seven years before ratification of the Nineteenth Amendment.

A proposal to mandate school segregation was also defeated, but not due to the tolerant views of the convention delegates. A somewhat related ban on interracial marriage was also defeated. In both instances the belief was that territorial statutes sufficiently addressed these matters, and a further delineation would not be necessary.

Populist influence was reflected by the inclusion of an elected regulatory agency, the Corporation Commission. Labor's influence was evidenced by the inclusion of an article mandating an eight-hour workday for government employees. Restrictions on child labor further witnessed prevalent progressive thought.

Other concerns, arising out of the territorial experience, were woven into the constitution. Since territorial governors were political appointees of the American presidency, not all had the best interests of the territory in their minds. Further, the territorial governor was viewed as the personification of an absentee federal government meddling in local affairs, more often than not ill advised, and as a result, dissatisfaction, complaint, and ire, was heaped more upon that office holder than any other, whether deserved or not. The result was a deliberately weakened governorship.

This weakening is witnessed primarily in two provisions. For one, the governor cannot perform the duties of governor if he/she is outside the boundaries of the state. This is true even if the governor is traveling on officials state business. The next in line for the governorship, usually the Secretary of State, assumes the duties. The other provision significantly limited the executive appointment power. Senior members of the executive branch are elected, not appointed. This seriously undermines the ability of the governor to develop an administration, in that key players may be elected officials of the opposing party, of divergent political views, or simply reflect conflicting personality. Most recently, the Republican governor, Fife Symington, had to contend with the Democrat, Secretary of State Richard Mahoney, as his second in command. Mahoney is reputed to have joked about his ability to cause mischief for the governor. And the current Democratic Governor, Janet Napolitano, has Republican Secretary of State Jan Brewer as her second in command. Several recent attempts to create continuity in succession by creating the office of Lt. Governor, have failed. Jerry Brown, when he was governor of California, and Mike Dukakis, governor of Massachusetts, after he had lost his presidential bid, both experienced problems due to this provision. These provisions in the state constitution have limited the ability of the governor to govern up to the present day. Territorial government experienced its share of abuses. Territorial legislatures had developed the practice of passing special laws for the benefit of particular individuals, businesses, or organizations. This even included legislative decreed divorces. Some public scandal was the result. The constitutional convention addressed this behavior when it specifically prohibited the state legislature from passing "special laws."

A WORDY DOCUMENT

Although the constitutional delegates comprised a very heterogeneous group (in terms of status, wealth, and education), they did share a common trait, this being a penchant for extreme detail which resulted in no lack of economy of words. The Arizona constitution is both detailed and quite lengthy. It is four times longer than the United States Constitution, a document noted for its brevity and conciseness. It is more than twice the length of what are considered standard guidelines for constitutions. Constitutions are meant to provide the broad guidelines of power and limitations on that power. Details are left to the legislative in making laws, and the judiciary in interpreting laws, constitution, and actions. When a constitution is overly detailed, thereby diminishing the role of legislative and judicial branches, the only manner in which change can occur is through the amendment process.

The generally held theory is that constitutions should be difficult but not impossible to change. It is not viewed as being in the interest of governmental stability to constantly change the basic structure of that government. Yet an overly detailed constitution can only result in an incessant need to amend—the only viable option available if unforeseen issues present themselves. The Arizona Constitution has been amended 141 times through the 2006 elections, 115 times by legislative referral to the voters and 26 times by voter initiative. There have been approximately 200 amendments proposed. By comparison the United States Constitution has been amended only 27 times in 215 years. But there is a factor other than too much detail that accounts for Arizona's rampant amending. The amendment process is exceedingly easy, and it may be initiated in a number of ways including voter initiative (see Chapter Five).

STATEHOOD DELAYED

The Enabling Act had granted $100,000 to the territory to defray the costs of the constitutional convention. Delegates were paid $4 per day for their services, but not to exceed 60 days total paid service (the constitution was written within 60 days—barely). Clerks and other employees of the convention were paid $5 per day. The convention organized itself into a series of committees, each responsible for specific issues. Then the entire convention debated and voted on each proposed article separately. The single most controversial article was the one dealing with the recall of judges.

According to the terms of the Enabling Act the completed constitution had to be approved by the voters of the territory before it could be forwarded to the federal government for its consideration. The vote was taken on February 9, 1911; it indicated acceptance by three-fourths of the voters. In mid August a Joint Resolution of Congress approved the admission of both New Mexico and Arizona into the Union, but this was before the Congress had heard from President Taft.

The Taft veto was aimed pointedly at the recall provision in the Arizona constitution, but there were a number of minor issues to be resolved with both territories. Congress passed another Joint Resolution the following week, admitting the two territories if they met certain conditions. Taft signed this resolution. Issues involving New Mexico were minor and statehood was not delayed. But Arizona was required to amend its proposed constitution to remove the provision allowing for the recall of judges. This entailed resubmitting to the voters, a time consuming process that resulted in a delay in achieving statehood. In an election held on December 12, 1911, Arizona voters removed the recall provision as it applied to judges. At the same time the first slate of state officials was elected in anticipation of formal admission to statehood.

STATEHOOD ACHIEVED

On February 14, 1912, President Taft signed a Proclamation recognizing Arizona as the 48th state. The federal constitution authorizes the admission of new states into the Union on free and equal footing with all other states. Subject to any restrictions contained within the United States Constitution, the state government is sovereign within its area of authority. The Tenth Amendment reserves all powers to the states that are not expressly granted to the federal government. A state is perfectly entitled to amend its own constitution, as long as it does not violate or conflict with the federal constitution.

It should not be surprising, then, that by constitutional amendment, Arizona immediately reinstated the recall of judges. Certainly Taft knew this would happen; he only succeeded in making his personal views known at the expense of earning the ire of the new state. Four other amendments were proposed during 1912. One providing for female suffrage and another defining the method of taxation passed, while one calling for prohibition and another for road bonds failed.

The first general election after achieving statehood was held November 5, 1912, a presidential election year. Voters clearly expressed their feelings concerning William Taft and his role in delaying Arizona statehood. The Progressive Republican, Theodore Roosevelt, the Democrat, Woodrow Wilson, and even the Socialist, Eugene Debs, finished ahead of Taft in the polling. Arizona's three electoral votes were not an issue, but its defiant expression of independence from federal control was characteristic of western attitudes, as the much later Sagebrush Rebellion indicates.

CHAPTER SUMMARY

✓ Arizona's struggle for statehood was a very lengthy process.

✓ The initial roadblock to statehood concerned the free silver issue.

✓ A later roadblock resulted from the predominant liberalism of the territory.

✓ The Constitutional Convention was dominated by Democrats, the majority of whom were liberal.

✓ The final document was liberal, but did reflect some conservative issues.

✓ Territorial experiences influenced a number of provisions in the Constitution.

✓ The Constitution is inordinately lengthy, a condition furthered by numerous amendments.

✓ The Arizona Constitution is very easy to amend.

✓ The most controversial feature in the proposed constitution was the recall of judges. Only by temporarily removing it could statehood be achieved.

✓ When Arizona became the 48th state in 1912 it had one of the most liberal state constitutions in the nation.

4
FEDERAL-STATE RELATIONSHIPS

The separation of powers doctrine is one of the mainstays of the American governmental system. Montesquieu, the French political theorist who delineated the doctrine in his *Spirit of the Law*, profoundly influenced the writers of the Constitution, who subsequently devised a government comprised of three distinct branches: legislative, executive, and judicial. This type of separation of powers, a horizontal separation, is fairly well understood, but less widely understood is a vertical separation of powers in our government: national, state, and local.

A FEDERAL SYSTEM

There are two types of multi-tiered governmental structures: federal and confederal. In a federal system the national government possesses ultimate sovereignty, whereas in a confederal system the regional governments are sovereign. The United States is a federal system, but the exact boundaries between national and state (regional) authority are sometimes vague and always shifting.

The United States Constitution states that the federal government is supreme within its area of authority. Exactly what that area of authority is has to be sought out. The Tenth Amendment provides that all powers not expressly granted to the federal government are reserved to the states. This has been generally held to mean the exercise of state police powers.

Essentially, the national government is supreme in those areas that are clearly national in scope: foreign affairs, the military, currency, interstate and foreign commerce, and certain basic guarantees of rights of citizenship, and restrictions and prohibitions are placed on the states in these areas. In general, the state regulates the day to day affairs of people and property: marriage and divorce, crimes against persons and property, determination of property law, health and safety issues, education, etc. The bulk of the visible contact with government by an overwhelming majority of citizens, is at the state level.

But why bring up this topic? When the original thirteen colonies formed the "Thirteen United States of North America," they ceded their western land claims to the new national (then confederal) government. At that time the so-called "backcountry" stretched to the eastern bank of the Mississippi River. The territories of the United States would eventually be held by the Congress for the free and equal benefit of the citizens of all the states. The Constitution that displaced the Articles of Confederation government after only six years placed numerous restrictions and obligations on the states with regard to the federal government and to other state's governments as well. It also spelled out some powers, duties, and responsibilities of the federal government toward the states.

States may levy no export taxes, there must be uniformity of national taxation, and states can only tax each other to the extent necessary to defray the cost of inspection programs for health and safety. States cannot enter treaties with other nations or with sister states, but they can enter into compacts (a form of agreement) with the approval of Congress. They cannot engage in war unless invaded, nor can they maintain troops and ships without the consent of Congress. States cannot coin their own money, violate contracts, issue titles of nobility, issue letters of marque or reprisal, emit credit, issue bills of attainder, or pass ex post facto laws.

Another part of the Constitution addresses the relation of states to each other. States must grant full faith and credit to the laws of all other states. This means that the laws of all states, as they apply to the bona fide citizens of those states, must be recognized by all other states. States must grant the privileges and immunities of their own citizens to the citizens of all other states who happen to be within their boundaries. A winter visitor to Arizona, for instance, is entitled to the same fire and police protection as is any Arizona citizen. On proper authority, states are required to return fugitives from other states who might be within their boundaries. And one that no longer holds, having been superseded by the Thirteenth Amendment, required states to return persons who had escaped from service, most commonly referred to as the fugitive slave clause.

For its part the federal government is required to guarantee a republican form of government, to protect the states from foreign invasion, and, on proper request, to aid states in the quelling of domestic violence (if federal issues are involved, no state request or authorization is needed for the federal government to intervene). The Congress may create new states, but not out of existing states, or parts of existing states, without approval of the state legislatures involved. In other words, state boundaries are guaranteed.

PROVISIONS FOR NEW STATES

A constitution provides a broad outline of governmental powers and responsibilities. The detail and subsequent implementation is the responsibility of the legislative body. The Congress, then, had to establish procedures whereby new states could be created and enter the Union. The blueprint was provided in 1787. The Northwest Ordinance of that year provided for a three staged process for the creation of new states. The original law dealt only with states to be carved out of the Old Northwest Territory, but its general guide lands were followed through Hawaii 50.

In stage one Congress would establish the geographical boundaries of a territory and authorize the President to appoint individuals to "govern" it. In as much as no laws would be in existence to govern the new territory, the appointees were to use whatever existing law they could find in the United States (federal or from any of the states) that fit the immediate situation.

In stage two the territory could elect a territorial legislature—originally, when the adult male population reached 5,000, but later, this would be ignored. The "citizens" of the territory would elect a territorial lower house, the territorial governor would appoint an upper house, and the territory could proceed to make its own laws. Acts of a territorial legislature were subject to a territory gubernatorial veto, a Congressional rejection, and a presidential veto. In effect, territories were wards of the federal government. During stage two the territory was to create the various structures and infrastructures requisite for statehood, and gain increasing experience in self government.

Stage three was initially based on population. When the total population of the territory reached 60,000, the territory could petition the Congress to begin the process for statehood. If Congress concurred, it would pass an "Enabling Act," authorizing the calling of a territorial constitutional convention to write a constitution for the proposed state. This would then be submitted to Congress for its approval, and eventually, to the President for signature. Either the Congress or the President could reject the proposed constitution, forcing changes in its writing. The new state would then enter the Union on free and equal footing with all other states.

Congress may impose specific requirements for admission of a state. This precedent was established with the passage of the Northwest Ordinance, which prohibited slavery from existing in any state carved out of the Old Northwest Territory. Other conditions were imposed at the time of the Missouri Compromise, the Kansas-Nebraska Act, the Compromise of 1850, on Alaska over environmental concerns, and also on Arizona over recall of judges.

The Arizona Constitution provided for removal of officials by the public before their terms expired, including judges. The President at the time, William Howard Taft, had a very strong bias for the absolute independence of the judiciary, and vetoed the Arizona proposal. The territory had no choice but to change the provision or remain a territory. But what happens after a territory becomes a state is another matter. Arizona, for instance, immediately amended its constitution to restore what Taft had insisted it remove as a condition for statehood.

TERRITORIAL ARIZONA

During their territorial phase, future states are far from independent, lacking many resources and services. New states in the eastern third of the nation experienced minimal difficulty. Abundant natural resources, fertile land for agriculture, substantial forests for building and fuel, adequate rainfall, geographical proximity to the established east, rapid introduction to new modes of communication and transportation, and the retreat of native populations were all factors. But with each new wave of territories and states the problems compounded. All of the advantages of eastern territories diminished, then practically disappeared.

Early Anglo settlers in Arizona were quite isolated from the East, and actively sought services from the federal government. Most specifically, they sought relief in the areas of communication and transportation, and demanded a military presence to "contain" native populations. With time they would seek measures that would encourage additional settlement.

The length of Arizona's territorial status, coupled with the vast distance from the established east, only compounded difficulties with the federal government. People in government in Washington literally could not comprehend the conditions and problems associated with a climate and terrain with which they were totally ignorant. Mindsets of a savage, inhospitable southwest were commonplace. The sparse territorial population lacked political clout, which came instead, from eastern mining, logging, and ranching interests, bent on achieving their own short term goals, then exiting the territory.

Still, the telegraph, a crude postal service, and the coming of the railroads, all financed by the federal government, brought some degree of outside contact to the region.

The federal Newlands Act would provide the funding mechanism to create the Salt River Project, and Roosevelt Dam would make possible the Valley of the Sun.

CONTINUED FEDERAL PRESENCE

Even after statehood in 1912, however, Arizona continued to languish, and it was the federal government that again gave the region an economic boost. Agricultural demands to support World War I brought federal monies to Arizona. One long lasting result was the growing of cotton, still a major agricultural product for the state. The various federal projects of the New Deal depression era left a legacy of irrigation, preservation, and economic development projects.

Federal programs during World War II provided the biggest boost. The fairly predictable climate, an abundant cheap labor supply, and the natural resources of the region, would locate the defense industry here to produce goods for war, train pilots for combat, and ultimately provide a civilian infrastructure to support it all. The presence of the military and defense are major in the development of modern Arizona.

During the last half of the twentieth century, the power of the federal government has grown tremendously at the expense of the states. Broadening interpretations of the interstate commerce power and the rights of federal citizenship were two key factors. For a time the judicial activism of the Supreme Court was a contributing factor. The national government also learned, during the Cold War, that adding the word "defense" to a new government proposal, was a fairly certain way of wrangling into formerly forbidden areas. The Federal Scholarship Defense Act enabled the federal government to move into the area of aid to education, a bastion of state initiative formerly. And the Federal Highway Defense Act went a long way toward standardizing a national system of limited access highways within state boundaries.

It was discovered that the federal government could pursue civil rights issues through such devices as grants or the withholding of grants, the issuance (or non issuance) of federal contracts, affirmative action programs, and a plethora of federal court decisions. Many state crimes do not exist at the federal level, but civil rights are a federal issue, and violations constitute a federal crime.

And finally, the grant-in-aid, or "dollar matching" programs of the federal government, enables the federal government to move into traditional state areas of authority. The process is quite simple: wave the federal checkbook, attach a number of requirements, and let the state decide for itself if it wants the money with conditions, or no money without. The result is fairly predictable. States have voluntarily given away some of their traditional areas of control.

Starting during the Nixon era, the "New Federalism" has been incrementally diminishing some of the vastly expanded federal power over the states. The problem here is that the federal government initiated programs, funded them (often with borrowed dollars), and over decades created a public expectation of their continuance. When the federal government began moving out of some areas, it did provide grants to the states, but not to the extent of former federal funding. And unlike the federal government, many states have constitutional limitations on borrowing. This has forced many states to either curtail programs or increase state taxation to fund them. Additionally, the federal government has mandated new programs that require the states to expend additional financial resources. An example is the Bush administration No Child Left Behind Initiative. But the federal government is still very much present within state boundaries.

A current highly charged issue concerns the role of the state government in immigration control, normally an uncontestable federal area of authority. Arizona is a major corridor for border crossings and various factious have polarized the issue. On one side of the issue there are "minute men" patrolling the border, a recently passed tough Employers Sanctions Law, and sweeps by the Immigration Interdiction Unit of the Maricopa Sheriffs Office. On the other side there are marches and demonstrations as well as a 2008 legislative action providing funds for English language instruction in view of threatened heavy fines by a federal District Court for failure to do so.

CHAPTER SUMMARY

✓ The federal government is supreme within its area of authority

✓ Powers not expressly granted to the federal government are reserved to the states.

✓ The federal constitution lists limitations on the states, obligations of states to each other, and obligations of the federal government to the states.

✓ Broad procedures by which new states are admitted into the Union are found in the Northwest Ordinance of 1787

✓ The purpose of territorial stages is to allow a region to gain experience in self-government and establish structures necessary for statehood.

✓ Territorial governments are dependent on the federal government for most of their immediate needs.

✓ The length of Arizona's territorial experience exerted a profound influence on the creation of its political structures.

✓ Federal presence in western states remained significant even after statehood was achieved.

✓ The federal government possesses many advantages with which to exert influence over all the states.

✓ The "New Federalism" would return to the states many functions that were assumed by the federal government in the decades following World War II.

5
SUFFRAGE, ELECTIONS AND REMOVAL

The Arizona Constitution was written during the Progressive Era, and thus embodied many of the liberal elements then being advanced. The recently enacted U'Ren System in Oregon had a pronounced effect on the Arizona political system. A number of articles promoting voter participation in government were written into the new document. In many respects, the constitution was quite revolutionary. It was only in the areas of racial and ethnic bias that the document fell short, the gender bias issue having been thwarted by constitutional amendment within a year of statehood approval.

Voter qualifications today follow the same philosophy and provide that any citizen eighteen years of age or older, who has lived in the county and state for at least twenty nine days preceding the election, and is able to write his or her name or mark, may register to vote. Exceptions preventing registering to vote include persons who have been convicted of a felony or treason and who have not had their civil rights restored, as well as persons who are under guardianship, or non compos mentis (mentally incompetent). The legal provisions for voting and elections are contained in Article VII of the Arizona Constitution and are paraphrased for brevity in this chapter. Since the Constitution was written almost a century ago, some of its language reflects a different culture than that of today. In 2000 the voters of Arizona approved Proposition 101, which provided for the modernizing of the archaic language found in the original document.

REGISTRATION AND VOTING PROVISIONS

A law passed in 1982 provides for continuous registration and allows a person to register to vote when applying for an Arizona driver's license. According to the National Registration Act of 1993 a person must take specific action to remove their name from the voter roll or an election official must provide positive confirmation that a person should be removed from the registration list. The act also requires that voter registration be available to a citizen at a variety of service sites. Otherwise, any county recorder, justice of the peace, or deputy registrar must register any voter upon request. Once registered, or if registration is changed, voters are eligible to vote after a 29-day residency period. The length of the residency requirement has been shortening over the years. Only a handful of states still have a residency requirement longer than a month; some states have abolished the residency requirement all together.

Historically, when voters registered for the first time, they were asked to declare a party affiliation. The reason for this was that Arizona was a closed primary state, meaning that only officially registered party members could vote in the primary election of their claimed party. The intent was to prevent crossover voting, that is, members of a party voting in the primary of the opposition party for the sole purpose of selecting the weakest possible candidate. How effective this practice may have been is arguable. The downside of the provision was that if a voter elected not to declare a party preference, then that person was effectively denied the right to participate in primary elections. A 2005 law requiring proof of citizenship as a condition for voting was vetoed by Governor Napolitano, who claimed the law would impose conditions on legitimate American citizens of Hispanic origin.

Proposition 103, approved by the voters in the 2000 election, allows registered independent voters and registered members of minor parties that do not conduct a primary election, to vote in the party primary of their choice. In 2000 approximately 14% of Arizona voters were registered independents. By 2007 the figure had risen to 27%. Registered voters of major parties continue to be limited to voting only in the primary of the party for which they announced allegiance. The proposition could have the long-term effect of transitioning the state to an open primary system.

The right to vote extends to non-English speaking persons and is facilitated by the requirement that the ballot be printed in Spanish and an Indian language understandable to the electorate. Voters also have some rights and protections while engaging in the election process. No person gains or loses residence in the state by reason of employment or service of the United States, while a student, while kept at any almshouse or asylum, or while confined in jail or prison. Electors shall be free from arrest except for treason, felony, or breach of the peace while going to or returning from voting. The Arizona Constitution, Article VII, Sec. 5, states, "No elector shall be obliged to perform military duty on the day of an election except in time of war or public danger." While voters have the right to cast a secret ballot, they may request assistance if they are unable to mark the ballot or if they wish to cast a ballot by mail. Voters may request in writing that a ballot be mailed to them to fill out and return. This recent change in the election process was motivated by a desire to increase voter participation and is known as the "Early Ballot Initiative." No reason must be given to vote by mail. This replaces the former absentee ballot system that required a notarized statement listing absence from the county on election day, physical disability, or religious conflict.

Arizona uses the direct or closed primary election to nominate candidates for the general election. As we saw above, the effective result of Proposition 103 was to make Arizona a modified closed primary state. A primary election is one in which voters choose candidates to run against candidates of other political parties in the general elections. A closed primary limits voting to registered party members only. An open primary allows any registered voter to vote in the party primary of their choice. This option is now available to registered independent voters in Arizona.

Primary elections for state, county, and national office candidates, and to choose political party precinct chairpersons are held on Tuesday, eight weeks prior to the general election. Candidates may also get their name on the ballot after the primary with a petition that contains the names of at least 10,000 registered voters who did not vote in the primary election. This is a very short window of opportunity given the proximity of the general election to the primary election. Ross Perot's minions were poised and ready and got his name on the Arizona ballot in 1992 utilizing this provision in the law.

ELECTION LAWS

State law regulates both primary and general elections. Candidates for primaries must file nomination papers, which declare their candidacy for an office, and show evidence that they meet the legal qualifications for the office. Candidates must also file petitions containing the required number of valid signatures for the office. Signers of petitions must be registered voters in the candidate's party, be residents of the jurisdiction of the office, and sign only one petition per office. All candidates are required to file a statement of contributions over $25 along with the names of the contributors. Proposition 200, passed by the voters in 1986, limited the amount any one person could contribute to a campaign. This provision was at the core of the recent AZscam scandal that resulted in the resignation and conviction of six legislators and charges against several lobbyists. The candidates are also limited by law in their expenditures.

The Clean Election Campaign Act, a 1998 voter initiative, provides public funding for candidates who meet certain minimum personal funding requirements and agree to prescribed campaign spending limits. Such candidates are known as participating candidates. Candidates are free to opt out of the system and spend as much as they want of their own raised funds. The intent of the law was to encourage more candidates to participate who otherwise could not afford to do so.

In the 2008 state elections the entire legislature and three corporation commissioners are to be elected. To qualify for public funding a certain number of $5 contributions set by the Clean Elections Commission must be obtained within a specified period. Corporation commission candidates must obtain 1650 qualifying contributions and state legislative candidates must obtain 220 in order to qualify for public funding.

Participating Candidate Expenditure & Contribution Limits for 2008 Elections

Office	Primary Election Spending Limits A.R.S.§16-961(G)	General Election Spending Limits A.R.S.§16-961(H)	Maximum Independent Expenditure Limit A.R.S.§16-941(D)	Maximum Early Contributions (Aggregate) A.R.S.§16-945(A)(2)	Maximum Early Contributions (Individual) A.R.S.§16-945(A)(1)	Maximum Personal Contributions A.R.S.§16-941(A)(2)
Governor	$638,222	$957,333	$610	$49,180	$130	$1,230
Secretary Of State	$165,378	$248,067	$610	$25,840	$130	$1,230
Attorney General	$165,378	$248,067	$610	$25,840	$130	$1,230
Treasurer	$82,680	$124,020	$610	$12,920	$130	$1,230
Superintendent Of Public Instruction	$82,680	$124,020	$610	$12,920	$130	$1,230
Corporation Commissioner	$82,680	$124,020	$610	$12,920	$130	$1,230
Mine Inspector	$41,349	$62,024	$610	$6,460	$130	$1,230
Legislature	$12,921	$19,382	$610	$3,230	$130	$610

The winner of the primary is the candidate who receives a plurality of the votes cast for that office and becomes the party's candidate in the general election. A plurality is the greatest number of votes cast for any candidate. A majority is more than one-half of all votes cast. An extraordinary majority (required for some bond elections) is a fixed percentage in excess of a simple majority. The general election is held on the first Tuesday after the first Monday in November of even numbered years. The secretary of state certifies the candidates and prepares the propositions that will appear on the general election ballot.

Winners of general elections must receive a plurality of all votes cast for the office. Proposition 100, passed in the 1992 general election, removed the requirement that executive department officials must be elected by a majority vote. The current requirement is the candidate receiving the highest number of votes will be elected.

The 1996 session of the Arizona legislature passed a bill consolidating Arizona elections to four preset dates. The legislature in amending section 16-204 stated the following: While the legislature recognizes that the method of conducting elections by political subdivisions including charter counties and cities may be a matter of local concern, the legislature finds and determines that for the purposes of increasing voter participation and for decreasing the costs to the taxpayers it is a matter of statewide concern that all elections in this state be conducted on a limited number of days.

Elections may only be held on the following dates:

1. The second Tuesday in March

2. The third Tuesday in May

3. The eighth Tuesday before the first Tuesday after the first Monday in November. A primary election that is held in an odd-numbered year may be held on this date.[1]

4. The first Tuesday after the first Monday in November. A general election that is held in an odd numbered year may be held on this date.

Proposition 101, approved by the voters in 2004, requires that any initiative that mandates revenue expenditures, to identify the revenue sources to cover the costs. Money cannot be taken from the General Fund or in any way reduce the General Fund.

INITIATIVE AND REFERENDUM

The initiative is a method of direct legislation which is conducted in conjunction with the general election and is included on the ballot as a proposition (question). The initiative power provides that registered voters equal to 10 or 15 percent of the total number of votes cast in the last general election for all gubernatorial candidates must sign petitions requesting that a measure be placed on the ballot. If the proposition is a constitutional amendment, 15 percent is required; if the measure is a proposed law, 10 percent is necessary. Political entities may conduct special elections

---

[1] This is the exact wording in the statute. At first glance it appears confusing but it is tied to the language that determines the November general election date. It is eight weeks before that time—the time of Arizona's primary election.

whenever they please, but if they do not schedule elections on the official election dates, they are required to pay the cost of their election. Initiative petitions must be filed with the secretary of state four months preceding the general election. Initiative measures must be approved by a majority of the vote cast in the general election. This is sometimes referred to as a "regular" referendum. It is much easier to initiate a proposition than it is to pass it. Of the 200 initiatives introduced, less than one half have been approved. Overwhelming, legislative enactment remains the domain of the State Legislature.

In addition to voter initiated petition, propositions can be referred to the voters by constitutional provision. A constitutional amendment proposed by the legislature is one example; it must be referred to the people for their approval. Another constitutional provision requires that any increase in legislative salaries be referred to the people.

A "protest" referendum is a proposition which allows the electorate to approve or reject any ordinary measure passed by the legislature. An ordinary measure is a law not containing the emergency clause. A referendum vote will be placed on the ballot if petitions bearing the signatures of registered voters equal to 5 percent of the number of votes cast for all gubernatorial candidates in the last general election are presented to the secretary of state. A simple majority vote of yes upholds the legislative action, a no rejects the law. Circulators of initiative and referendum petitions must declare whether they are paid or volunteer circulators and they must attest to the validity of all signatures on their petitions. Any political committee that makes an expenditure in connection with a ballot proposition must disclose its major funding sources. Ordinary Arizona laws do not go into effect until ninety days after the close of the legislative session in which they are passed. This ninety-day period is the time allowed for collecting enough signatures to "suspend" the law and refer it to the voters.

The legislature can protect its legislation from the protest referendum 90 blocking provision by declaring that the law is immediately necessary in order to preserve peace, health, or safety. Whether this is truly the case is not at issue. But it is a way of turning an ordinary law into an emergency law. Emergency laws require a two-thirds majority vote of both houses for passage and go into effect immediately upon the signature of the Governor.

Voters cannot set aside funding, general appropriation, or new tax laws, the reason being that such action could have an immediate detrimental effect on the state. However, voters do have the right to deal with these aforementioned issues through the process of future initiatives.

RECALL AND REMOVAL PROVISIONS

Every public official who holds elective office in the state is subject to recall. Recall is a process whereby the electorate may demand that an officeholder stand for reelection to the office if a sufficient number of qualified electors sign petitions stating the grounds for the official's removal. Recall petitions require signatures of 25 percent of the number of votes cast for all candidates for the office in the last general election. If the officer resigns, the office is filled as provided by law, usually by appointment. If not, the incumbent officer's name is placed on a special election ballot with all other qualified nominees, and the winner by plurality vote shall be declared elected and will hold the office for the remainder of the term. Recall petitions cannot be circulated against an elected official until six months of the term has expired. However, legislators may be recalled five days after the beginning of the first session of the term. The Arizona Constitution, Article VIII, Section 1, states that an official is required to stand for recall only once, and sets forth other provisions for removal from office.

Impeachment is another method for removing state executive and judicial officials except for justices of the peace. The Arizona House of Representatives must, by majority concurrence, charge the official with high crimes, misdemeanors, or malfeasance in office. The impeachment is tried by the Senate with the chief justice of the supreme court presiding, unless the chief justice is on trial or disqualified, in which case the Senate shall elect another judge of the Supreme Court to preside. The Arizona Constitution, Article VIII, Section 2, states that a vote of two-thirds of the Senate is required to remove the official from office, and carries a provision which prohibits him from holding future office in the state. The prohibition from holding office, however, requires a separate vote and may not be applied even though the officeholder is removed by impeachment.[2]

As a general rule, vacancies in offices are filled by appointment by a designated official at the appropriate jurisdictional level. In the case of a vacancy in the office of governor, the constitution provides that the secretary of state, if holding the office by election, shall succeed to the office of governor. The attorney general, state treasurer, and finally the superintendent of public instruction follow in that order.

---

[2] The various processes authorized for the removal of members of the judiciary are discussed in Chapter 8.

Vacancies in the United States Senate or the United States House of Representatives are filled by primary and general elections for the remainder of the term.

PARTY ORGANIZATION

Political party organization in Arizona is controlled by state law and provides for the following structure: Registered voters elect precinct committee persons for their parties at the primary election. The precinct is a voting district. Each precinct is entitled to one committee person from each party and one additional committee person for each additional 125 votes after the first 125 cast for the party's candidate for governor or presidential electors in the last general election. Precinct committee members make up the membership of the county committee. Chairpersons of each county committee plus an additional member for each 400 votes cast for governor or presidential electors in the last general election make up the membership of the state committee. The state committee, in turn, elects the executive committee and the state party officers.

Political party strength in Arizona is dependent upon location and office. Arizona is similar to other states in having a dominant party ghetto. East, north, and northwest Maricopa County make up the golden crescent of Republican support in the state. Tucson, Yuma, and southern Maricopa County are the strongholds of Democrats within the state. While this is a generalization, legislative districts in Arizona are thought to be safe constituencies in all but rare exceptions. The winner of the primary is virtually assured of election to a legislative seat.

Arizona's electoral votes for the presidency have been consistently Republican since 1948 with the exception being the vote for Bill Clinton in 1996. Until the election of 1994 Arizona had a Senator from each of the two major political parties for all but eight of the last forty-two years. The 1994 election resulted in a near sweep of the congressional delegation with both Senators and five of the six House seats being held by the Republicans. And it has remained unchanged through the 2000 elections.

Due to the increase in population as determined by the 1990 census, Arizona was entitled to a sixth Congressional district which was filled in the 1992 general election. The State Legislative redistricted the county supervisors districts, the State Legislative districts and the United States Congressional districts. An undercounting of some 500,000 citizens led Arizona to file suit against the federal government, claiming entitlement to a seventh congressional seat. The federal government acknowledged the error but stated that it was too late to do anything about it, in that reapportionment had been completed. Better luck in the year 2000 census.

If the elected corporation commissioners are counted, the Republicans have an edge of eight to one in the state executive offices. Republicans have a majority in both the Arizona State Senate and the House of Representatives. Democrats still hold more county offices but, again, this is dependent upon the area rather than any ideological identification. Probably the most important trend for understanding Arizona politics is the conservative orientation of both political parties at the state level. On ideological issues rural Democrats often ally with urban Republicans.

The 40 percent growth in population that occurred during the nineties translated into two additional representatives in the U. S. Congress, raising the total to eight representatives, which, counting the two senators, gives the state ten electoral votes next presidential election. At issue for the state is the redrawing of congressional districts. Up until 1966 County Boards of Supervisors drew state legislative district boundaries, while the State Legislature drew congressional boundaries. After 1966, with the establishment of guidelines by the U. S. Supreme Court, the state legislature took over both functions through the 1990 census redistricting.

Effective with 2000 reapportionment (the redistribution of seats based on population changes), Arizona is using a new process. Proposition 106, approved by the voters in 2000, provides for an independent commission to draw state and federal districts. The new approach is not without controversy. The major argument in favor of the new system involved the ending of the politicizing of the redistricting process. The argument against it centered around placing the process in the hands of non-elective officials.

A pool of 25 nominees selected by the Commission for Appellate Court Appointments or its designee, is forwarded to the State Legislature. The leadership of both major parties in both Arizona houses pick four commissioners. This, of course, means two Democrats and two Republicans. These four pick a fifth member from the same list who cannot be a member of a major party. No more than three commissioners can be chosen from any one county.

The commission is charged with redrawing state and congressional districts, pursuing the following guidelines as much as is reasonably practical. Districts should be equal in population. They should be compact and contiguous. They should be competitive. They should maintain communities of interest. And finally, they should follow established boundaries and natural features. These guidelines follow the standards set by the United States Supreme Court and the federal Voting Rights Act.

Nationally, the Republican Party is the smaller of the two major parties numerically. But more often than not Republicans tend to fit the profile of the most likely to vote. When Republicans hold a numerical superiority, coupled with their greater voter turnout, political domination is the result. As of March, 2008, there were approximately 2,695,000 registered voters in Arizona. Of that number 1,037,000 were registered Republicans; 916,000 were registered Democrats; the rest were Reform, Libertarian, Green, and Natural Law registrants, plus a growing number of Independents.

Maricopa County, wherein 60 percent of the state votes are cast, enjoys a comfortable Republican majority outnumbering Democrats 633,000 to 468,000. Much of the remainder of the state reflects a majority of Democrats. Of the fifteen counties in Arizona, eleven reflect a majority of Democrats. La Paz County enjoys a Republican majority, but barely. The three staunchly Republican counties are Maricopa, Mohave and Yavapai, where Republicans outnumber Democrats 725,000 to 522,000. In some counties controlled by the Democrats more Republicans turn out to vote than their majority Democratic opponents. With the exception of Pima and Coconino counties, the other Democrat controlled counties are the most sparsely populated in the state. There are now 725,279 registered Independents in Arizona and 16,933 Libertarians. The Independent category has grown substantially in recent years. Republicans controlled the Senate 17-13 and the House 33-27 during the 2008 legislative session.

The 2004 elections witnessed even greater gains for the conservative cause in Arizona. Traditional centers of Democratic power, notably counties with large percentages of Native Americans, voted for Bush. A majority of Hispanics, once overwhelming counted in the Democratic column, voted for Bush. Apparently values laden issues overshadowed economic concerns among traditionally based populations.

Arizona has exercised power in the national government out of proportion to its population size. Faithful support of exceptional officials has resulted in leadership roles based on both seniority and ability. Most notable was Carl Hayden, who served in Congress, first as a representative from 1912 to 1926 and then in the Senate from 1926 to 1968, for a total of 56 years. Senator Barry Goldwater served in the Senate for all but four years from 1952 to 1986. He is best known as the leader of the conservative wing of the Republican party during the 1950s and 1960s, and as the Republican presidential nominee in 1964. John Rhodes served from 1952 until his resignation in 1982, and at the time of his retirement was House Minority Leader. Ernest McFarland, senator from 1940 to 1952, became Senate Majority Leader and, along with Senator Hayden, was responsible for obtaining many of Arizona's military installations. Former governor Bruce Babbitt served as Secretary of Interior during the Clinton administration. Additionally, two recent members of the United States Supreme Court have been Arizonians: Chief Justice William Rehnquist (deceased), and Associate Justice Sandra Day O'Connor (retired). And at the time of this writing Arizonian John McCain is the presumptive Republican candidate for President in the 2008 election.

TABLE 5-1. *State of Arizona Official Canvass*

STATE OF ARIZONA REGISTRATION REPORT
2010 Special Election - May 18, 2010
Compiled and Issued by the Arizona Secretary of State

ACTIVE

	Precincts Date/Period	Green	Democratic	Libertarian	Republican	Other	TOTAL
Apache	45 JAN 2010	*	27,270	168	7,046	10,149	44,633
	45 MAR 2010	*	27,251	167	7,085	10,302	44,805
	45 S.E. 2010	33	26,215	160	6,844	10,063	43,315
Cochise	64 JAN 2010	*	23,836	307	28,048	22,353	74,544
	64 MAR 2010	*	23,748	317	28,187	22,780	75,032
	64 S.E. 2010	134	23,584	329	28,225	22,957	75,229
Coconino	85 JAN 2010	*	27,286	827	17,919	19,938	65,970
	85 MAR 2010	*	27,249	820	17,914	20,162	66,145
	85 S.E. 2010	252	27,140	818	17,807	20,175	66,192
Gila	39 JAN 2010	*	12,348	140	10,677	6,077	29,242
	39 MAR 2010	*	12,189	144	10,826	6,401	29,560
	39 S.E. 2010	23	11,965	146	10,723	6,393	29,250
Graham	18 JAN 2010	*	7,629	49	7,103	3,239	18,020
	18 MAR 2010	*	7,559	50	7,130	3,315	18,054
	18 S.E. 2010	6	7,441	49	7,120	3,348	17,964
Greenlee	8 JAN 2010	*	2,651	13	1,059	713	4,436
	8 MAR 2010	*	2,551	15	1,005	676	4,247
	8 S.E. 2010	2	2,448	14	932	626	4,022
La Paz	12 JAN 2010	*	2,969	31	3,273	2,705	8,978
	12 MAR 2010	*	2,912	32	3,232	2,696	8,872
	12 S.E. 2010	11	2,700	26	3,035	2,512	8,284
Maricopa	1,142 JAN 2010	*	567,111	16,066	707,631	563,058	1,853,866
	1,142 MAR. 2010	*	561,285	15,958	703,151	570,318	1,850,712
	1,142 S.E. 2010	2,130	539,477	15,232	688,733	554,084	1,799,656
Mohave	73 JAN 2010	*	28,391	497	44,471	37,091	110,450
	73 MAR 2010	*	28,278	507	44,637	37,663	111,085
	73 S.E. 2010	101	28,287	522	44,932	38,242	112,084

TABLE 5-1. Continued

	Precincts Date/Period	Green	Democratic	Libertarian	Republican	Other	TOTAL
Navajo	70 JAN 2010	*	26,539	420	19,369	14,432	60,760
	70 MAR 2010	*	26,314	432	19,093	14,488	60,327
	70 S.E. 2010	49	26,211	431	19,076	14,629	60,396
Pima	417 JAN 2010	*	186,166	4,052	148,315	132,073	470,606
	417 MAR 2010	*	182,987	3,933	146,283	130,939	464,142
	417 S.E. 2010	1,140	184,798	3,980	148,161	133,835	471,914
Pinal	88 JAN 2010	*	53,602	904	52,320	51,989	158,815
	88 MAR 2010	*	53,770	930	52,660	53,385	160,745
	88 S.E. 2010	152	52,709	926	52,162	53,239	159,188
Santa Cruz	24 JAN 2010	*	11,243	129	3,744	5,913	21,029
	24 MAR 2010	*	11,267	130	3,769	6,086	21,252
	24 S.E. 2010	24	11,317	134	3,775	6,304	21,554
Yavapai	112 JAN 2010	*	29,669	835	52,953	35,952	119,409
	112 MAR 2010	*	29,322	842	52,962	36,285	119,411
	112 S.E. 2010	238	29,300	847	53,287	36,786	120,458
Yuma	42 JAN 2010	*	27,685	388	23,721	23,537	75,331
	42 MAR 2010	*	28.076	395	23,819	24,046	76,336
	42 S.E. 2010	50	28,194	392	23,979	24,636	77,251
TOTALS:	2,239 JAN 2010	*	1,034,395	24,826	1,127,649	929,219	3,116,089
	2,239 MAR 2010	*	1,024,758	24,672	1,121,753	939,542	3,110,725
	2,239 S.E. 2010	4,345	1,001,786	24,006	1,108,791	927,829	3,066,757
PERCENTAGES:	JAN 2010	*	33.20	0.80	36.19	29.82	
	MAR 2010	*	32.94	0.79	36.06	30.20	
	S.E. 2008	0.14	32.67	0.78	36.16	30.25	

* - Party was not a recognized party during this cycle

Table 5-2 (on the following page) lists Arizona's national and state elected officials as of 2010.

TABLE 5-2. *Arizona's National and State Elected Officials (2008)*

OFFICE - NAME	PARTY AFFILIATION	TERM

United States Senate

John McCain	Republican	1986-2010
Jon Kyle	Republican	1994-2012

United States House of Representatives

District 1 Ann Kilpatrick	Democrat	2008-2010
District 2 Trent Franks	Republican	2002-2010
District 3 John Shadegg	Republican	1994-2010
District 4 Ed Pastor	Democrat	1991-2010
District 5 Harry Mitchell	Democrat	2006-2010
District 6 Jeff Flake	Republican	2000-2010
District 7 Raul Grijalva	Democrat	2002-2010
District 8 Gabrielle Giffords	Democrat	2006-2010

Governor

Jan Brewer	Republican	2009-2010*

Secretary of State

Ken Bennett	Republican	2009-2010**

*Former Secretary of State became Governor January 2009 when Governor Janet Napolitano resigned to become Secretary of Homeland Security in the Obama Administration.

**Appointed Secretary of State by Governor Jan Brewer January 2009 to fill her vacated Secretary of State position.

OFFICE - NAME	PARTY AFFILIATION	TERM

Attorney General

Terry Goddard	Democrat	2002-2010

Treasurer

Dean Martin	Republican	2006-2010

Superintendent of Public Instruction

Tom Horne	Republican	2002-2010

Mine Inspector

Joe Hart	Republican	2006-2010

Corporation Commission

Gary Pierce	Republican	2006-2010
Paul Newman	Democrat	2008-2010
Bob Stump	Republican	2008-2010
Sandra Kennedy	Democrat	2008-2010
Kristin Mayes	Republican	2003-2010*

*Appointed October, 2003, by Governor Napolitano to fill the vacancy left by the resignation of Commissioner James Irwin.

Both Houses of the Arizona Legislature are currently controlled by the Republican Party.

ARIZONA STATE GOVERNMENT ORGANIZATION

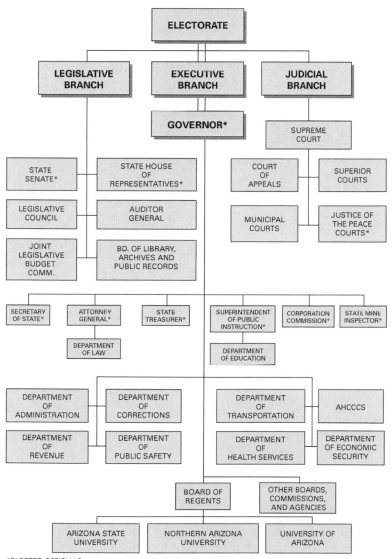

*ELECTED OFFICIALS

FIGURE 5-1. *Adopted Congressional Map*

The Independent Redistricting Committee completed its work in mid October, 2001. The completed plans for state legislative districts and federal congressional districts will be submitted to the United States Department of Justice during November. The review process could take up to sixty days and the final maps may not be known until early in 2002. The recommendations of the Committee are found in Charts........

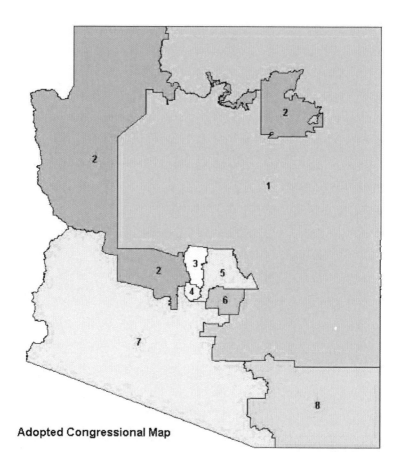

Adopted Congressional Map

FIGURE 5-2. *Adopted Legislative Map*

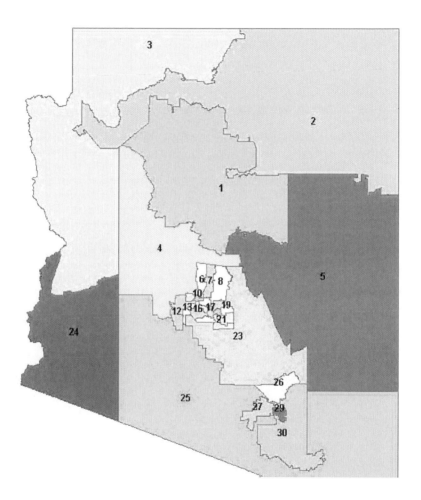

CHAPTER SUMMARY

✓ State voting regulations must be in accordance with the Federal Voting Rights Act and the National Registration Act.

✓ Initiative, referendum, and recall elections are clear examples of direct democracy.

✓ Arizona's closed primary system has been modified to allow participation of independent voters.

✓ The Arizona Constitution contains a number of provisions allowing for citizen participation in government.

✓ Executive and most judicial officials may be removed through the impeachment process. The legislative may expel or discipline members.

✓ Redistricting is a complicated and politically charged process.

✓ Ideologically, Arizona remains politically conservative, but demographic shifts could eventually brew change.

✓ Vacancies in state offices may be filled by appointment pending the next election; vacancies of federal office holders must be filled by election.

✓ The behavior of party organizations and the conducting of elections are regulated by numerous state and federal laws.

✓ The protest referendum may be avoided by invoking the emergency clause.

6
THE LEGISLATIVE BRANCH

Arizona has a bicameral legislature. The two houses are the Senate and House of Representatives. Since the 1966 Federal District Court decision in the reapportionment case (Klahr v. Goddard), the legislature has consisted of thirty senators and sixty representatives from the thirty legislative districts in the state. The 1991 redistricting was especially difficult because of several factors. First, the legislature was divided with the Senate controlled by the Democrats and the House controlled by the Republicans. Both houses must agree on the lines of the new districts, thus balancing the interests of both parties. Second, new Federal legislation requires that the new districts must not discriminate against minority voters. Third, population shifts have been significant in the past 10 years, thereby requiring significant changes in the old district boundaries. Fourth, incumbent office holders are interested in preserving their residences within their current constituencies. Some of these problem areas will be alleviated by the work of the new independent redistricting committee mentioned in the preceding chapter.

CONSTITUTIONAL PROVISIONS

Both senators and representatives are elected for a two-year term. The 1992 constitutional amendment on term limitations provides that neither state senators or representatives may serve more than four consecutive terms and they may not seek the same office again until they have been out of office one full term. This limitation began for all terms of office beginning on or after January 1, 1993.

Both senators and representatives serve for the same salary and allowances, and the qualifications are identical for holding either office. The only advantage in serving in the Senate is its smaller size, which gives each member greater power and, some believe, greater prestige. The qualifications for legislators include being a United States citizen, at least twenty-five years of age, a three-year resident of the state, and a one-year resident of the county prior to election. The statement prior to election means that before taking office, one must be of minimum qualifying age. A person is disqualified from holding legislative office if currently holding any other public office of profit or trust. Exceptions include state militia, notary public, justice of the peace, United States commissioner, and postmaster of the fourth class. No legislator will be eligible to be elected or appointed to any office or be otherwise employed by the state, county, or incorporated town, except for a school trustee or a teacher in the public school system. This information is found in the Arizona Constitution, Article IV, Part 2, Sections 1, 2, 4, and 5.

Members of the legislature shall be free from arrest in all cases except treason, felony, or breach of the peace. They shall not be subject to civil process during the session or fifteen days before a session. The recent AZscam case casts doubt on this provision because civil suits were filed against legislators before conviction or resignation, and, in one case against a legislator who was not even indicted. In the latter case the court dismissed the case and ordered reimbursement to the defendant for costs incurred during the defense. Legislators enjoy free speech in debate on the floor of the legislative chamber and are thus free from Civil suits for liable or slander. Legislators are subject to the rules of each house for punishment for disorderly conduct, or even expulsion upon concurrence of two-thirds of its members.

Legislative salaries were set by public vote at $24,000 per year in 1998 and despite several attempts to further raise them, remain at that figure. Prior to that date, despite repeated attempts, salaries held at $15,000 per year since 1980. Because Arizona has a single annual legislative session lasting approximately 120 days, some voters do not consider legislators as having a full time job, and therefore, not warranting higher pay. This is unfortunate, in that a number of legislative functions involve year-round activity and increasingly, there are multiple annual special sessions of the legislature. The legislature can set its own per diem and travel allowance without voter approval. Legislators are reimbursed at actual cost entailed.

LEGISLATIVE ORGANIZATION

The organization of the legislature is extremely important in determining the actions and operation of the lawmaking process. The division of power between the majority and minority parties is more important than seniority at the state level. Therefore, party support and loyalty become the determining factors in selecting committee chairpersons, speaker of the House, and president of the Senate, and making committee assignments. Majority party leadership is dependent upon support from a significant portion of the party in the caucus as well as the ability to raise campaign funds, to compromise extreme positions on issues, and to work with the minority, the governor, and the other house. The majority leader in each house must be a conciliator and pragmatic manager of the numerous interests which must be satisfied to reach legislative agreement. It has been said that the organization of the Arizona State Legislature is much better prepared to block legislation than to pass it.

The presiding officer in the House is the speaker of the House. The speaker is chosen by vote of the whole House. In reality, the majority party caucus in its organizational meeting agrees on who it will support for the speaker's position. A member of the House, seeking a leadership position, gains support from the majority party caucus by promising to appoint members to various committees, or chairmanships, or for helping with campaign or fund raising activities for the party's candidates. The majority leader is also chosen by the majority party as is the assistant floor leader. Committee chairmanships and committee assignments are made by the speaker.

The presiding officer in the Senate is the president of the Senate. The Senate also has a majority leader and an assistant floor leader. The Senate president appoints the committee chairpersons and assigns members to the committees.

The minority party also holds a caucus and by vote chooses a minority leader and assistant floor leader in both houses. The minority caucus makes committee assignments for its party.

The staffs of both houses are appointed by the majority party leadership, and the privilege of choosing certain staff members may be the price a leader must pay to obtain the support of a particular majority member. The Senate staff consists of a Senate secretary, assistant secretary, chaplain, sergeant at arms, pages, and secretaries. The House staff consists of a chief clerk, assistant chief clerk, chaplain, sergeant-at-arms, pages, and secretaries. Both the majority and minority parties have staff assistants to serve the party leaders in each house. The Arizona Legislative Council serves both houses, and its professional staff provides valuable services in research and bill drafting.

Regular and special sessions of the legislature are specified in Article IV, Part 2, Section 3 of the Arizona Constitution. Regular sessions shall be held annually at the capitol and commence on the second Monday in January of each year. Special sessions may be called by the governor when deemed advisable. The legislature may, by a petition signed by two-thirds of the members of both the houses, direct the governor to call a special session on a specified date. Special sessions called by the governor must specify the subjects to be considered, while those called by legislative petition are free to consider any subject.

Each house is charged with determining its own rules and procedures, and judging the election and qualifications of its own members. Each house has a set of rules and procedures which it adopts at the beginning of each session to guide the conduct of its action. The constitution defines a quorum as a majority of the members of each house. A quorum is the number of members necessary to do business. Neither house may adjourn for more than three days or meet in any other place without the consent of the other house.

LEGISLATIVE ACTIONS

Six types of action are possible in the legislature; the process differs slightly depending on the type of action being taken. A list of six kinds of action follows with a brief description of each (H. denotes House of Representatives, S. denotes Senate).

Bill: H.B. or S.B. Numbered in each house as introduced. Action or an appropriation.

A proposal for a new law, an amendment to an existing law requires governor's approval.

Joint Resolution: H.J.R. or S.J.R. Numbered in each house as introduced. Action requires governor's approval.

A high form of expression of legislative will and has the force of law.

Concurrent Resolution: H.C.R. or S.C.R. Actions of the legislature alone.

Used for ratifying amendments to the United States Constitution. Proposing amendments to the Arizona Constitution. Submitting legislative referendum to the voters. Authorizing joint legislative investigations.

Simple Resolution: H.R. or S.R. Action requiring agreement in only one house.

Expresses the opinion of one house. Used to influence actions by other bodies; not binding as law.

Joint Memorial: H.J.M. or S.J.M. An official statement of the state's position on a matter not in its jurisdiction. Requires governor's signature.

A request for action to some agency or official of the federal government.

Simple Memorial: H.M. or S.M. An expression of the position of one house, usually with the governor's concurrence.

A request from one house for an action over which it does not have exclusive control.

In addition to the types of legislative action mentioned, the constitution provides for emergency legislation. Ordinary bills require only simple majority approval by both houses and signature of the governor, or passage over the governor's veto by a two-thirds vote. An ordinary bill becomes effective ninety days after adjournment of the legislative session and is subject to referendum. A bill containing the emergency clause requires approval of two-thirds of the votes in both houses and the governor's signature for passage. If the governor vetoes an emergency measure, then a three-fourths vote is required to override the veto. An emergency measure takes effect with the governor's signature or veto override, and is not subject to referendum.

Proposition 108 passed in 1992, amended the Arizona Constitution to require a two-thirds vote in each house of the legislature to enact a net increase in state revenue. This provision requires that revenue increase bills be treated as emergency measures taking effect immediately without opportunity for referendum. The reason for this is that it would be extremely easy for a disgruntled 5 percent of the voters to block all revenue issues and effectively paralyze the state government.

The following is a description of the progress of a bill through the state legislature and includes both procedural and practical material. For the purpose of this description the bill will begin in the Arizona House of Representatives, but it must be understood that a bill may be introduced in either house, and that bills are often introduced in both houses in identical form but carry different numbers.

Step 1.   Any member of either house may introduce a bill. Bills may also be introduced by several members as sponsors or by a standing committee. Most bills are reviewed by the Legislative Council to ensure proper form and style.

Step 2.   The bill is given a number, receives a first read-
          ing, usually by title and number only, and is
          assigned by the Speaker to standing committees.
          Arizona uses the multiple reference system so that
          almost any chairperson may request the assignment
          of a bill to their committee regardless of the bill's
          content.

Step 3.   Usually one committee takes responsibility for con-
          ducting hearings and for marking up the bill to
          include or exclude features that important interests
          want. Usually less than one third of the bills intro-
          duced are passed by both houses. Even that is not
          a fair scoreboard because bills are often combined,
          and appropriation bills frequently appear in a pack-
          age. Differing Senate and House versions are com-
          bined in order to reach accord. The chairperson is
          responsible for making the committee agenda, and
          unless a majority of the committee members
          request a bill, the chairperson determines when,
          or if, a bill will be considered.

Step 4.   When a bill is reported from all committees to
          which it was assigned, it is sent to the Committee
          of the Whole. The Committee of the Whole con-
          sists of all the members of the House acting as
          one committee. Before it will be placed on the
          active calendar of that committee, it must receive
          Rules Committee approval. Again, an informal step
          usually includes the majority caucuses' recommen-
          dation for the consideration of any bill.

Step 5.   Committee of the Whole consideration is managed by the chairperson of the major committee that conducted the hearings and brought the bill to its current form. Members may offer amendments to the bill and even amendments to the amendments. Votes are taken by voice and the presiding officer determines the outcome. After the bill is amended, it is voted upon in its final form, referred to as the engrossed bill, and if it passes, it is ordered enrolled. It then receives its second reading and is ordered enrolled and engrossed. No record of this committee action is kept and the vote is not recorded.

Step 6.   The formal consideration of the bill takes place at this step. With the Speaker presiding, the bill is ordered to its third reading, where it must be read in its entirety. A roll call vote is taken and the vote is recorded in the House Journal. This is the official action on the bill. In reality, the bill will never get this far if it does not have sufficient support for passage.

Step 7.   The bill is then delivered to the Senate, where it may go through the same process. Frequently, a companion bill has been working its way through the Senate. Even where general agreement exists, the bills may pass in different forms.

Step 8.   If the bill passes both houses in identical form, it is sent to the governor to be signed. If the bill is not passed in identical form, and neither house is willing to accept the other's version, a conference committee is appointed by the Speaker of the House and the President of the Senate.

Step 9.   The conferees arrive at a compromise version and report it back to each house for final passage.

Step 10.   The governor has three options when the bill is received, sign the bill into law, allow it to become law without his signature, or veto all of the bill or an item of the bill (if appropriations).

Step 11.   If the governor vetoes the bill, it must be returned to House stating the reason(s) for veto. If the House and the Senate then pass the bill by a two-thirds vote for an ordinary bill, or three-fourths vote for an emergency measure, it becomes law. Ordinarily the threat of a veto with the conditions of its acceptance lets the governor influence the outcome without actually using the veto. Occasionally the majority will send the governor a bill that the governor has threatened to veto in order to establish a favorable image with the public.

Step 12.   Bills signed by the governor, as well as bills not signed or vetoed after five days, and bills not signed ten days after the end of a session, or bills passed over the governor's veto, are sent to the secretary of state who is responsible for publishing the Session Laws, and including the new laws in the Arizona Revised Statutes (A.R.S.).

INTEREST GROUP POLITICS

Pressure groups play an important part in government at all levels and in all branches, but state legislatures are particularly susceptible to the lobbying efforts of interest groups. Legislators represent various constituencies and they need to know how groups feel about pending legislation or the necessity of passing laws regulating some conduct. Pressure groups are formed in a democratic society when interested parties band together to speak as one voice on some subject. Pressure groups use the services of their members as volunteers to prepare and present information to the general public in order to create a favorable climate for their interests, or to influence legislators in making decisions. Some groups have significant economic or philosophical interests in the decisions. Usually success depends on the wise use of money, organization, information, and other pressures. Some groups hire professional representatives to present their case and to maintain an organization to mobilize the force available to influence decisions.

Special interest groups utilize individuals known as lobbyists. A lobbyist may be a paid professional or a volunteer who has the ability to gain access to political candidates and office holders. Lobbyists may be ex-office holders themselves, individuals who possess a degree of prominence, but always they are networked individuals. Lobbyists are the individuals who carry both the wishes of the organizations they represent and the offer of various forms of support to political candidates and office holders.

Anyone can be a lobbyist, but they must register with the Secretary of State office, maintain detailed records, and file periodic reports on money received, money disbursed, and from whom received and to whom given. An Arizona attorney may represent the interests of a group without being a registered lobbyist. Laws governing lobbyists and the forms lobbyists must use are available on the website of the Secretary of State.

All expenditures must be for legal purposes and any form of bribery would be counter productive to both the lobbyist and the public official. A 1996 bill which was passed by the legislature would have limited gift giving by lobbyists to state lawmakers. This bill with several others was vetoed by the governor. Political action committees have been formed by some of the groups as a method of directing campaign contributions to candidates who share their point of view. The most frequent abuse of lobbying efforts is the creation of a conflict of interest for the official, and the definition and ethics of this issue are unclear.

Both initiative and referendum have been explained in chapter 5, but it is important to note here that direct legislation has been very popular in Arizona. The secretary of state receives petitions, verifies signatures if they are contested, prepares the ballot propositions, and publicizes the issues by publishing pamphlets containing pro and con arguments. Some observers have charged that the frequent use of direct legislation is a reflection of the inability of the legislators to represent their constituents.

POWERS AND LIMITATIONS

The Arizona State Legislature has several duties besides passing law. The legislature has the following powers: to create and fund government offices and agencies, to approve appointments of the governor, and to remove an official by impeachment. These powers give the legislature a significant check on the other branches. When combined with its budget function of appropriation and taxation, it is clearly the most powerful branch of the state government.

The legislature sets the priorities for services by establishing and funding agencies to carry out the functions mandated by the law. The legislature sets the qualifications, duties, terms, and conditions of the employment for personnel in the state agencies. The budget appropriation determines the funding level for an agency and encourages vigorous service by full funding or minimal service by reduced funding. Since the state constitution prohibits deficit spending for operation in excess of $350,000 per year, it is equally necessary for the legislature to raise funds through taxation or other means to meet the cost of government service. The axiom that "each service has its cost" is clear to the lawmaker if not always to the citizen.

The governor is authorized to appoint numerous officials from the highest levels of the line agencies to the unpaid members of the state boards and agencies. In practice, virtually every appointment the governor makes has a limitation. The Senate must approve appointments and thus may convey to the governor a preference for the appointment or dismissal of a particular official. The governor must take into consideration the recommendation of various businesses, professions, and interests when appointing, regulating and licensing agencies. Finally, in the case of judges, the governor is limited to the consideration of only those persons recommended by the judicial nominating committees.

While the legislative power of impeachment has been considered in a previous chapter, recent events require a brief note on the impeachment of Evan Mecham. The impeachment power had lain dormant since 1964, when two corporation commissioners were impeached by the House, but not removed by the Senate. However, in 1988, the House voted impeachment articles, and after a lengthy and heated Senate trial, which featured several days of testimony by the accused, the Senate voted for removal of Governor Mecham. The Senate did not impose the so-called "Dracula clause", which prohibits an impeached official from holding future office. Mr. Mecham announced his candidacy for governor in 1990; he was not elected. The impeached governor was succeeded by Secretary of State Rose Mofford, and a called Recall election was canceled. Evan Mecham and his campaign chairman, Willard Mecham, were charged with crimes relating to the 1986 campaign. They were both found not guilty on all charges. The 1994 legislature voted to compensate Governor Mecham for the cost of defending himself against the impeachment and recall proceedings.

CHAPTER SUMMARY

✓ Party loyalty is far more important in the Arizona Legislature than is seniority.

✓ There is little difference, other than size, between the Arizona House and Senate.

✓ Even though Arizona voters possess the initiative, most legislation continues to be passed by the State Legislature.

✓ The interaction of special interest groups with the legislature is strictly controlled.

✓ Arizona limits its legislators to four consecutive terms; they may run again after a one-term hiatus.

✓ Lobbyists are required to register and to file periodic detailed reports on their expenditures.

✓ Special sessions of the legislature are occurring with increasing frequency.

✓ The Legislature is clearly the most powerful branch constitutionally in the Arizona government.

✓ Legislative salaries are low partly because the public has a perception of a part-time legislature, and partly because the public can express negative feelings by rejecting salary increases.

✓ The use of the "emergency clause" enables the legislature to avoid some popular control.

7
THE EXECUTIVE BRANCH

Unlike the federal government, which elects only one executive leader, Arizona has a plural executive branch, until the passage of Proposition 103 in 2000 (see below). The governor is designated as the chief executive and is responsible for the supervision of the state government, the execution of the state law, and the formulation and recommendation of policy, but all other executive officials are independently elected.

According to the Arizona State Constitution, Article V, the executive departments shall consist of governor, secretary of state, state treasurer, attorney general, and superintendent of public instruction. The office of state mine inspector was established in Article XIX of the Arizona State Constitution and is usually considered to be one of the executive offices. The office of state mine inspector is not in the line of succession, and the qualifications are different from those of the other state officers. The State Corporation Commission was also created by the constitution in Article XV, Section 1, and is included in the executive department as a separately elected body which has both policy and ministerial duties. Since each of the executive officers are elected independently, their powers and duties defined by the constitution, and their budget authorized by the state legislature, it is appropriate to consider each office separately in this chapter.

The term of office for the governor, secretary of state, state treasurer, attorney general, and superintendent of public instruction is four years. The 1992 constitutional amendment limiting terms for executive department officers states as follows "no member of the executive department shall hold that office for more than two consecutive terms." This limitation applies to terms beginning on or after January 1, 1993. They may not serve in the same office again until they have been out of office for no less than one full term. Two constitutional amendments passed in 1992 effect the term of office of the mine inspector. The first changed the term from two to four years and the second limited the office to four consecutive terms. The state corporation commissioners are elected for staggered four-year terms. Appointment to fill a vacancy of over half an unexpired term counts as a full term for reelection eligibility purposes. The terms of all executive officers end on the first Monday of January following the November general election. All elected officials of the executive branch serve four-year terms effective with the 2002 election.

GENERAL PROVISIONS

Executive officers have some standard qualifications, but there are additional requirements for the attorney general and the state mine inspector. All executive officers must be at least twenty-five years of age, citizens of the United States for ten years, and residents of Arizona for five years. The Constitution was changed by Proposition 103 in the 1988 general election to legalize women holding executive office in the state. This was a timely action in view of the fact women had been holding those offices for over 25 years, and the current governor at that time was a woman. The attorney general is required by law to be admitted to the practice of law in the state for at least five years preceding the election, and may not engage in private law practice while in office. The state mine inspector must have been a resident of the state for two years, be at least thirty years of age, and have at least seven years prior underground mining experience. State corporation commissioners may not have any financial interest in any corporation subject to their regulation.

Upon the request of the state legislature the five member Commission on salaries for elected state public officials makes Recommendations on salary rates to the governor. The recommendations are then submitted to the legislature for review. If the legislature does not disapprove or alter the recommendations, they become effective. Recommendations by the commission on legislative salaries must be approved by the voters at the next general election to go into effect the next legislative session.

THE GOVERNOR

The office of governor is assigned numerous powers by the constitution and statutes. Other powers of the governor have evolved through custom and the assertive action of some of the holders of the office. Political party alignment, ideological orientation, and personal political ambition are as responsible for a governor's use of power as are the legal prerequisites to power.

The governor is the chief executive and, as such, has the responsibility of overseeing the operation of the other executive offices. Also, the governor is the official representative of the state to the nation and to the other states. In addition, the constitution charges the governor with taking care that the laws are faithfully executed. The governor is also commander-in-chief of the military forces of the state if they are not in national service. Probably the most important executive function of the governor is the power to appoint public officials. The governor, through effective use of the appointive power, cannot only influence the agencies, boards, and commissions in the state, but can also build political power by rewarding supporters. Favors given must be returned, and in many cases this works to limit the governor's discretion in selecting appointees. In becoming governor, one accumulates many political debts to powerful interests and persons; and they, in turn, expect to have input into the selection process when their interests are affected. Furthermore, many appointments carry restrictive qualifications or are closely aligned to professions or businesses and almost require the blessing of the organizations which represent those interests. Finally, the Senate must confirm the governor's appointments, thereby wielding a powerful check on the governor's ability to appoint. Most appointees are independent of the governor's control since they are appointed for specific terms which often exceed that of the governor. The governor may only remove from office those appointees who do not have fixed terms of office. This effectively guarantees the independence of the membership of the various state boards, in that they rather consistently possess fixed terms of office.

The governor's legislative functions include methods to promote and to prevent legislation. The governor addresses the legislature at the beginning of each session in what has come to be known as the State of the State address. At this time, the governor outlines a program of legislative action. To the extent that he can bring public pressure on the legislature for his priorities, the governor can set the agenda that will dominate the legislative session. Another tool of the governor is to cast a veto under full view of the public; an aggressive governor may achieve significant effects. The veto is a double-edged sword because it can stop legislation that the governor opposes; or, by the threat of a veto, the governor may influence the final content of a particular law. The item veto by which the governor may reject a provision of a law is especially important in effecting the budget. While the governor has unlimited veto power, political considerations require a judicious restraint on its use.

The governor usually requires the support of a second party or another branch of government to fulfill judicial functions. However, in the case of extradition, the governor is the sole participant in deciding whether to comply with the request of another governor for the return of a fugitive from justice. Likewise, only the governor may initiate a request from Arizona to another state for the return of a fugitive. The governor is authorized to approve new divisions of the Superior Court and the Court of Appeals and to appoint judges to vacancies on the benches of these courts. The governor is limited to appointing persons recommended by the nominating committees for judges. The most traditional judicial functions of the governor include the power to grant reprieves and pardons, and to commute sentences. This power was limited early in the history of the state by the court's decision that a governor must follow the recommendation of the Board of Pardons and Paroles as provided by law. Inclusion of the following definitions is appropriate: A reprieve is a postponement of the sentence; a commutation is a reduction of a sentence; a pardon is the release of a criminal from confinement; and a parole is the conditional release of a prisoner to complete a sentence outside of prison. Arizona governors have been rather reluctant to commute sentences on the recommendation of the Board, even when the courts agree that an initial sentence was excessive. Apparently there is some concern over political fallout from such actions.

The line of succession to the governor's office established by the constitution provides that the governor may be replaced temporarily or permanently under certain conditions. In the event of the governor's death, resignation, removal from office, or permanent disability, the secretary of state, if holding office by election, shall succeed to the office. If any of the officers in the line of succession should fail to qualify, the office would evolve to the next in line. The order of succession after the secretary of state is the attorney general, state treasurer, and the superintendent of public instruction. In the event of absence from the state or a temporary disability, the line of succession is the same, but only until the absence or disability ceases.

Since executive officers are elected independently of each other, it can happen that those in the line of gubernatorial succession may be from different political parties and ideologies and might even be bitter political rivals.

THE SECRETARY OF STATE

The secretary of state is required to have only the minimum legal qualifications. The office is primarily administrative, and good management skills are required of the office holder. The duties of the office fall into two categories: 1) the collecting, compilation, and safe keeping of the nonfinancial records of the state, and 2) the administration of the election process.

In the first category, the secretary of state is responsible for the compilation of the official documents of the state, including the printing and distribution of the Journal of the House and Senate, the Session Laws, the Arizona Revised Statutes, and the Arizona Reports. All documents are public records and are open for public inspection. The secretary of state as the keeper of the seal is responsible for transmitting official communications to the national government and other state governments and for affixing the seal to official documents of the state.

The administration of the election process begins with the nomination petitions for the primary election. After the election, the secretary of state certifies the primary election winners and prepares the general election ballot. If propositions appear on the ballot, the secretary of state receives the petitions for initiative and referendum, prepares the ballot, and then prints and distributes the publicity pamphlet explaining the pros and cons of the issues. After the election, the secretary of state must receive the records on campaign finance as required by law and certify the results of the general election.

THE ATTORNEY GENERAL

The attorney general is head of the Department of Law for the state and as such is required to have the additional legal qualifications of being admitted to the practice of law before the Arizona Supreme Court, and is prohibited from engaging in private practice while in office.

The duties of the attorney general can be divided into three categories. The attorney general is the legal advisor to the public officials of the state, and provides legal advice to the legislature and advisory opinions to state officials upon request. Secondly, the attorney general has the responsibility of defending the state and its agents in the performance of their legal duties in civil actions brought against them in the state or federal courts. Additionally, the attorney general is responsible for the prosecution of crimes against the state of Arizona, and has the power to call for grand jury investigations. The grand jury tries to discover the commission of crimes and to indict those accused of committing those crimes. Most crimes are prosecuted by the county attorneys, but the attorney general has general supervisory responsibility over the county legal systems. The prosecution of cases involving consumer fraud, civil rights, and criminal antitrust are also within the jurisdiction of the attorney general. The office of attorney general is one of the most important in the state, and its holder can take an active part in promoting their party or their personal political ambitions.

THE STATE TREASURER

The office of state treasurer is primarily ministerial. The treasurer keeps the financial accounts of the state's revenues. The treasurer also reports to the officials the condition of the state's accounts, and pays warrants issued by the division of finance. The State Board of Investment, of which the Treasurer is chairperson, reviews the investment of State funds, serves as trustees of Land Trust Funds, and adopts and approves investment policy.

The constitution provides that the treasurer may not be absent from the state without permission of the legislature or the governor. While the state treasurer is in charge of huge amounts of money, the collection of taxes and other state revenue is the responsibility of the State Department of

Revenue. The likelihood of theft by the treasurer from the state treasury is no greater for the treasurer than for a host of other employees.

THE SUPERINTENDENT OF PUBLIC INSTRUCTION

As the state's chief educational officer, the state superintendent of public instruction serves as the administrator of the school funds of the state. The superintendent supervises a legislative funding formula which dictates the amount and method of distribution of these funds. Federal funds are also distributed through the state superintendent's office. The superintendent's office also administers the teacher certification laws and the textbook selection process. The state superintendent is also an ex officio member of the three state educational boards which set policy for the public schools in the state. They are as follows: The State Board of Education and the Board of Regents. Proposition 105 amended the Constitution in 2004 to add a community college chancellor or president to the State Board of Education. A free standing State Board for Community Colleges was abolished in 2003. The state superintendent also has general supervisory responsibility over the county school superintendents and is responsible to see that the state school laws are faithfully executed.

THE STATE MINING INSPECTOR

The office of state mine inspector was created in the constitution of 1912 under a separate article which indicates the importance the constitution's founders placed on the health and safety of the state's miners. The qualifications for state mine inspector required that the holder of the office be a two-year state resident, at least thirty years of age with seven years of prior underground mining experience, and not currently in the employ of any mining, milling, or smelting company. The duties of the mine inspector are to conduct mine inspections at least every three months for mines employing fifty persons or more, and once a year for mines employing six to fifty persons. The inspector is required to check safety ventilation, and emergency procedures, and to file a report with the mine owners listing any deficiencies. The mine inspector also is required to investigate mine accidents, establish cause and recommend corrective action.

There are 547 surface mines, underground mines, and sand and gravel pits operating in Arizona. Not all mines are inspected the number of times each year required by law, the reason most often given being lack of personnel. The Mining Inspector has the authority to temporarily close a mine if safety considerations warrant. Arizona's mines are also inspected by the United States Mine Safety and Health Administration. This agency performs its own independent inspections and is empowered to levy fines for safety infractions.

THE CORPORATION COMMISSION

The State Corporation Commission is the only remaining elected commission in the state that needs consideration. Its five members are elected for staggered four-year terms. The commissioners are considered full-time expert officials who are capable of wielding considerable power. Hence, unlike other elected members of the executive branch, their term of office is limited to one six year term.

Proposition 103, adopted by the voters in 2000, provides for a number of changes in the Corporation Commission. Effective with the 2002 election, the Commission was increased from three to five members, the two additional members to be elected initially to a two-year term. The reason most often cited for this change is to provide a broader base of interest on the Commission. At the same time the single six-year term was replaced by two four year terms, putting the Commission in line with other executive offices.

The general charge to the Corporation Commission is to regulate the public service corporations, sometimes called public utilities within the state. The prevailing attitude at the time of the writing of the Arizona Constitution was that since government license gave a public utility the exclusive right to provide a public service, there could be no competitive price or service standards. Therefore, it was the obligation of the state through elected representatives to set standards for rates, routes or territories, and conditions of service. The services mentioned in Article XV, Section 2 of the Arizona State Constitution define the scope of the commission's power:

> All corporations other than municipal engaged in furnishing gas, oil, or electricity for light, fuel, or power; or in furnishing water for irrigation, fire protection or other public purpose; or engaged in collecting, transporting, treating, purifying and disposing of sewage through a system for profit; or in transmitting messages or furnishing public telegraph or telephone service, and all corporations other than municipal, operating as common carriers, shall be deemed public service corporations.

In order to carry out this function, the Corporation Commission is authorized to issue certificates of incorporation to companies organized under the laws of this state, and to issue licenses to foreign corporations to do business within the state. Insurance companies are an exception and are under the jurisdiction of the Department of Insurance. The commission also has the power to establish rules regulating the sale and transfer of stock and other securities of corporations to the public. The commission has the power to adopt, investigate, and enforce rules and regulations pertaining to state licensed corporations.

Arizona has its share of appointive boards, commissions, and agencies. While it has been popular to criticize the use of volunteer public officials, they seem to serve two useful purposes. Democratic participation encourages those who have a stake in a government action to take a greater interest. Also, the activities the boards and commissions engage in are part time, and reflect policy determinations rather than time-consuming administrative services.

Table 7-1. Salaries of Elected Officials
(As of January 1, 2005)

Governor	$95,000
Secretary of State	$70,000
Attorney General	$90,000
State Treasurer	$70,000
Superintendent of Public Instruction	$85,000
State Mining Inspector	$50,000
Corporation Commissioner	$79,500

STATE BOARDS

Arizona government makes use of a number of boards and commissions. Currently, there are 266 active boards and commissions. By definition a board or commission is an independent body of citizens officially appointed by a public office holder to perform certain tasks. Appointed individuals may be paid, but most often they serve without pay and have their expenses paid.

Boards and commissions can be created in two ways. The State Legislature can create them by statute (state law) or the Governor can create them by issuing an executive order. In either manner the term of office, the functions, and the composition of membership must be outlined. Depending on the function board members may be required to possess certain expertise or professional credentials, or, a certain percentage of the membership may be so required.

There are two types of boards or commissions (the terms are practically identical): regulator and advisory. A regulatory board has the power of enforcement over violators and can invoke prescribed penalties, can investigate complaints, and can grant and revoke licenses. An example is the Arizona Medical Board. An advisory board recommends policies to public officials. The Governor's Advisory Council on Aging, for example, makes recommendations to the Governor's Office on matters dealing with Arizona's senior citizens.

Regulating education is the responsibility of two boards. The State Board of Education consists of eleven members, ten of whom are appointed by the governor, and the state superintendent of public instruction, who serves ex officio. Seven of the members are professional educators and four are lay members. The board's duties are to prescribe courses of study for the state's common schools and high schools, setting required courses, standards of achievement, and credits required for graduation. State board approval of texts and materials has been somewhat controversial in recent years. The board has adopted a textbook list from which districts may choose textbooks and, therefore, almost any point of view may be satisfied. The board also sets teacher certification standards which consist of required courses, special certificates, and more recently, tests demonstrating basic skills competency and knowledge of professional educational materials.

The Arizona Board of Regents consists of eight members appointed by the governor for eight-year staggered terms. The governor and the state superintendent of public instruction are ex officio members. A university student member is also appointed by the governor. The regents appoint the presidents and employees of the state's universities and establish conditions of work and salaries. They recommend the budgets of the universities to the legislature, approve curriculum, set standard fees and tuition, and grant degrees. They exercise general supervision over all aspects of university life including student and faculty conduct. Since the regents are lay members, they are the public representatives to the higher education establishment and their policies set the priorities of the institutions.

The regulation of businesses, professions, and occupations is handled by a multitude of licensing agencies, regulating boards, and commissions. Certain businesses by their nature need to be licensed and regulated by the state. In these cases, the regulations usually establish who can serve as officers, what the conditions of their operations shall be, and the regulation of their finances to ensure fair treatment of the public and stockholders. Such businesses as banking, insurance, racing, professional athletics, and liquor sales fall into this category. Certain activities are regulated in order to maintain standards to protect the public, such as nuclear energy, weights and measures, and the protection of worker safety by the Industrial Commission. The boards of examiners and the occupational and professional licensing boards are intended to ensure that persons who provide services are competent and skilled by virtue of training or experience. Licensed services are those such as provided by dentists, doctors, nurses, contractors, real estate salespersons, funeral directors, and barbers.

ADMINISTRATIVE DEPARTMENTS

In recent years, the administration of state government has been greatly improved by the creation of eight professionally managed line agencies. All directors of these agencies are appointed by the governor and confirmed by the Senate, and serve at the pleasure of the governor.

The first of the agencies, the Department of Public Safety, was created in 1969. The DPS consists of the Arizona Highway Patrol and the Division of Narcotics and Liquor Control.

The Department of Corrections operates the state prison system for adults and juveniles. It also administers the probation and parole system under the direction of the Board of Pardons and Paroles.

The Department of Administration is the key to the administrative reorganization. It serves to coordinate the housekeeping functions of the state bureaucracy by providing personnel services, purchasing, building and ground maintenance, finance and budget coordination, and data processing.

The Department of Economic Security is responsible for coordination of all human services programs in the state, especially those which administer federal funds. It administers programs for the unemployed, veterans, Indians, dependent mothers and children, poor, and disabled.

The Department of Emergency and Military Affairs was created to coordinate the activities of the Arizona National Guard. The department consists of a division of military affairs and a division of emergency services. The Arizona Division of Emergency Management develops programs to reduce or eliminate the impact of disasters. These include fire emergencies, energy distribution disruptions, hazardous products control, emergency response teams, flooding, storm damage issues, and is responsible for developing a plan to protect against terrorism. The Arizona Army National Guard serves the state in emergency conditions and the nation in time of need. Many members of the Guard have served in Iraq. The state also has a unit of the Air National Guard.

The Department of Health Services administers the federal, state, and local programs for health and safety. Although the department has some control over health care facilities, it is primarily responsible for the laws on the environment, communicable diseases, and sanitation.

The Department of Transportation was created to combine the Highway Department and the State Aeronautics Commission into a comprehensive planning agency to facilitate the movement of goods and people throughout the state. Legislative action taken in the 1985 session should greatly increase the activity of this department.

The Department of Revenue replaced the old tax commission and has the responsibility for collecting the state sales tax, income tax, luxury tax, and property tax. The department also has the duties of verifying property classifications, and supervising county assessors.

The executive function in Arizona reflects the attitude of the founding fathers. They were concerned with preventing a centralized authority and keeping the governor weak and subject to the people's control through the legislature. They believed that participation of many people in government is democratic and, therefore, the best protector of the people's rights. They also believed that anyone with average ability and with ordinary effort could perform the functions of most government offices.

Table 7-2. Executive Departments and Agencies

➲	Administration	➲	Highway Safety
➲	Agriculture	➲	Insurance
➲	Banks	➲	Juvenile Corrections
➲	Commerce	➲	Land
➲	Corrections	➲	Liquor Licenses and
➲	Economic Security		Control
➲	Emergency and Military	➲	Lottery
	Affairs	➲	Parks
➲	Environmental Quality	➲	Public Safety
➲	Game and Fish	➲	Real Estate
➲	Gaming	➲	Registrar of Contractors
➲	Government Information	➲	Revenue
	Technology Agency	➲	Tourism
	(GITA)	➲	Transportation
➲	Health Care Cost	➲	Water Resources
	Containment System	➲	Weights and Measures
➲	Health Services		

CHAPTER SUMMARY

✓ Arizona's plural executive can have a weakening effect on the Office of Governor.

✓ All elected members of the executive branch now have four-year terms and a two consecutive term limit.

✓ Of all elected executive officials only the Attorney General and the Mining Inspector have specific qualifications for holding office.

✓ In many instances state executive officials are limited to carrying out the orders of various appointed boards.

✓ Many appointees possess fixed terms of office and may therefore be beyond the ability of the Governor to control.

✓ A major function of the Secretary of State is to administer the state election process.

✓ The administrative structure of government was designed to prevent centralized control and to encourage citizen participation.

✓ A gubernatorial line of succession is well delineated in the Constitution.

✓ The office of the Attorney General is one of the most powerful positions in the state.

✓ A number of permanent professionally managed line agencies carry out the ongoing functions of government.

8
THE JUDICIAL BRANCH

Courts exist to keep the peace, to provide a non-violent way of resolving disputes, to maintain public order, and to protect society. They provide a more civilized version of the medieval trial by combat, the ordeal of fire, or the ordeal of water. They provide an ordeal of judges, lawyers, and juries.

ORIGINS AND NATURE OF THE JUDICIARY

The American legal system is based on the English common law tradition. In England, with the demise of feudalism, judges were royal appointees who were sent throughout the realm to administer justice in the monarch's name, thereby centralizing royal power. As outsiders coming into traditional communities, these judges were both ignorant of local issues and disputes, and were also viewed with considerable suspicion. To solve the former problem they would call together the leading citizens of the community to ascertain what cases or controversies existed. This is viewed as the origin of the grand jury system. To alleviate suspicion they had to somehow get the local people to "buy in" to the judicial process. The solution was a jury of one's peers. The locals themselves would be co-opted into the decision making process. To the present day juries are praised or blamed for the outcome of a process that is controlled by judge, prosecutor, and defense attorney.

Through evolution judges determine procedure, i.e., points of law. Juries decide on evidence received according to these judicial rulings. Juries determine innocence or guilt; judges determine punishment within the limits prescribed by the law.

Early in the development of this judicial system, a tremendous amount of time would be spent on each case. But gradually, the principals involved became progressively more aware that they had dealt with almost identical, or actually identical, cases in the past. Why reinvent the proverbial wheel! Hence, stare decisis, or precedent, came into being. And that entire body of judicial decisions and opinions becomes known as case law.

As government became more powerful, and with the parallel development of principles of democracy, rules dealing with how government could exercise its power gradually evolved. Today, we refer to this body of rules as due process, very much a part of American democracy.

TYPES OF PROCEDURES

The English system was the basis for the American colonial courts. These colonial courts eventually evolved into state courts, and later still, into the American judicial system. What follows is a discussion of how that system works in Arizona.[1]

---

[1] For what all the non lawyer needs to know about the Arizona judicial system, see the Arizona State Government web site, "Guide to Arizona Courts"

TRIALS

The Arizona justice system is based on the adjudication of conflicts. There are two types of cases: civil and criminal. Civil cases most often involve legal disputes between individuals, businesses, corporations, and partnerships. Most civil cases involve matters related to a breach of contract, the collection of a debt, or monetary compensation for personal injuries or property damage. The emphasis in civil actions is on compensation and restitution.

A special type of civil law is equity. Equity cases involve such matters as injunctions to compel a party to perform an obligation, or to prevent a person or business from continuing some type of alleged wrongdoing.

There are several specialized types of civil proceedings. One is probate, for the distribution of property of a person who has died and for payment of the deceased person's creditors. Another area of specialized civil proceedings is domestic relations. In these actions, the parties to the case seek to dissolve a marriage and, frequently, litigate issues related to the custody of children, division of property, and payment of debts.

Criminal cases are those which result from an alleged violation of the criminal code. Criminal actions are based on the premise that certain behaviors are detrimental to the interests of society. It is therefore assumed that the state must intervene to initiate action to protect society and punish wrongdoers. Criminal charges in general jurisdiction courts are initiated in two ways:

1. As the result of a grand jury indictment. A grand jury is a group of persons who

inquire into and investigate accusations in criminal cases, hear evidence, and issue indictments when they find probable cause.

2. By the filing of a document called an information, which charges the accused with the commission of a crime. The information can be filed by the county attorney or, in certain cases, by the attorney general.

FELONY PROCEEDINGS

In felony cases, before an information can be filed, a criminal complaint must be filed in the Justice of the Peace Court or before some other magistrate. Before the judge can issue an arrest warrant, there must be reasonable cause to believe that a crime has been committed and that the accused has committed it.

Arrest. In cases where the accused is not in custody and has not signed a promise to appear, the judge issues a summons or a warrant for arrest. A summons directs the accused to appear in court at a designated time, whereas a warrant authorizes the arrest of the accused.

Initial Appearance. A person who is arrested and taken into custody must be taken before a magistrate for an initial appearance within 24 hours of the arrest. At this appearance, the accused is informed of the charges and is advised of certain rights. Pretrial release conditions are also set at this time. If the offense charged is a felony, the defendant is informed of the right to a preliminary hearing and a date is set for the hearing.

Bail. When a defendant is released prior to trial, bail may be assessed in order to ensure the defendant's appearance at trial. The amount of bail is set by the judge. When bail is posted, the defendant is released. If the defendant fails to appear for trial after having posted bail, the security which was posted as bail is forfeited.

The Arizona Constitution (Article II, Section 22) was recently amended by the citizens of Arizona and states that: All persons charged with a crime shall be bailable by sufficient sureties, except for:

1. Capital offenses when the proof is evident or the presumption great.

2. Felony offenses committed when the person charged is already admitted to bail on a separate felony charge, and where the proof is evident or the presumption great as to the present charge.

3. Felony offenses if the person charged poses a substantial danger to any other person or the community, if no conditions of release which may be imposed will reasonably assure the safety of the other person or the community, and if the proof is evident or the presumption great as to the present charge.

In some instances, a defendant may be released without bail, that is, one's promise to appear. Release is granted if there is reason to believe that such a promise is sufficient to reasonably assure the defendant's appearance in court.

TRIALS

Preliminary Hearing.   When a complaint has been filed charging a felony, the defendant is entitled to a preliminary hearing. At the preliminary hearing the judge determines whether the evidence presented is sufficient to find probable cause to believe that the crime was committed and that it was committed by the defendant. If the judge finds probable cause, the case is bound over for trial in the Superior Court and a date for arraignment is set. If the judge does not find probable cause, the complaint is dismissed and the defendant is released.

Arraignment.   At the arraignment the defendant appears before the trial court and enters a plea of guilty, not guilty, or no contest to the charges contained in the information or indictment. If the plea is not guilty, a trial date is set. If the plea is guilty or no contest, a date for sentencing is set. Persons charged with felonies are arraigned in Superior Court.

Trial.   Trials in both civil and criminal cases are generally conducted in much the same manner. The judge is the central figure in the courtroom, and is there as an impartial tribunal to assure a fair trial by giving each side an opportunity to present its version of the disputed incident. All trials are conducted according to established rules of procedure and evidence.

Also present are a court reporter, court clerk, and bailiff. Each of these people assist the judge with some aspect of the trial. The court reporter records all proceedings. The court clerk records selected activities for official case file records and is responsible for all case exhibits. The bailiff is responsible for maintaining order in the court and overseeing the jury if there is one.

The other major figures in any trial are the litigants, or the parties to the action, and their attorneys. Attorneys are officers of the court. Their role is to protect individual rights and ensure just treatment of their clients. Attorneys present the evidence and legal arguments which they believe are necessary for the court to make a just determination.

Trials may be either to the court or to a jury. A trial jury is a group of persons called to decide the facts and render a verdict in the trial of a civil or criminal case. In most cases, either party may request a jury trial. In more serious criminal cases, the defendant has a right to trial by a jury. In a jury trial, the jury decides the facts of the case based on the evidence presented. In a trial to the court, the judge determines the facts in the case.

When the court is ready for the trial to begin, opening statements are made. The attorney for the plaintiff, the prosecuting attorney in a criminal case, speaks first and gives an overview of the facts which will be presented. The defense may present the same type of opening comment or may reserve the opening statement until later in the trial when the defense presents its case. Either party may choose to waive the opening statement.

The plaintiff in a civil case, or the prosecuting attorney in a criminal case, will begin to present their case by calling witnesses and asking them questions. Witnesses take an oath stating that what they say in court is the truth. All evidence presented in court, including testimony of witnesses and physical evidence, must comply with the Arizona Rules of Evidence, which specify what evidence is admissible in court. When the plaintiff or prosecution's side has completed its questioning of the witness, the defense is allowed to cross-examine the witness. When the plaintiff or prosecutor has called all of the witnesses for their side of the case and presented all of their evidence, they rest their case.

The defense now has the opportunity to present evidence establishing their side of the case. The attorney for the defense often waits until this portion of the trial to make an opening statement. The defense may choose not to present any evidence. The defense is not required to present evidence because the defendant in a criminal case is not required to prove innocence; rather, the prosecution is required to prove guilt. Likewise, in a civil case, it is the plaintiff who must prove negligence or liability. The burden of proof rests with the party filing the complaint. If the defense does choose to present a case and call witnesses, the same rules and procedures which govern presentation of evidence by the plaintiff/prosecution apply. The only difference is that the defense now calls the witnesses and questions them first.

When both sides have presented all of the evidence they wish to enter, they are each permitted to make closing arguments. Closing arguments are similar to opening statements. They provide an opportunity for the attorneys to address the judge or jury one last time regarding the merits of their case. The plaintiff/prosecutor speaks first, usually summarizing the evidence that has been presented and highlighting those items most beneficial to their clients. In a criminal case, the people of the state are the prosecutor's clients. The attorney for the defendant speaks next, usually summarizing the strongest points of the defendant's case and pointing out flaws in the case presented by the plaintiff/prosecutor. At this point the plaintiff/prosecutor is given one last opportunity to speak.

Finally, in a jury trial, the judge reads the legal instructions concerning the law applicable in the case. Jury members are to follow these instructions in reaching a verdict. The jury then goes to the jury deliberation room and elects a foreman. The jury proceeds to consider the evidence, determine the facts of the case, and reach a verdict.

When the jury has reached a verdict, court is reconvened and the judge or court clerk reads the verdict. The jury is then released. Failure of the jury to reach a unanimous verdict results in a hung jury and the judge may dismiss the jury and set a new trial date.

JUDGMENTS AND SENTENCING

The court enters judgment according to the jury's verdict, if there was a jury, or according to the judge's decision, if there was no jury. Under special circumstances in a civil case, a judge may enter a judgment notwithstanding the verdict; such a judgment is different from the jury's verdict. In a criminal trial, if the defendant has been found guilty, a date for sentencing will be set.

In Arizona, the legislature has established a range of sentences available for various crimes. The judge must impose a sentence within the range outlined by the legislature.

COURTS

The Arizona court system has three levels: 1) the limited jurisdiction courts, 2) the general jurisdiction court, and

3) the appellate courts. This is detailed in the Arizona Constitution, Article VI, Section I.

LIMITED JURISDICTION COURTS

Starting with the lower courts and working upward on Figure 8-1, there are two limited jurisdiction courts: Justice of the Peace Courts and Municipal Courts. They are called limited jurisdiction courts because there are various limits on the types of cases which can be tried in each of these courts. The county is divided into justice court precincts by the county board of supervisors.

The regular term of office for a justice of the peace is four years. Qualifications for election to this office include being at least eighteen years of age, a resident of the state, an elector of the precinct in which elected, and able to read and write English. Justices of the peace are not required to be attorneys. Justice court judges are paid according to a scale based on population of their districts.

Statutes provide that each justice court have a constable (A.R.S. pg. 22-102). The constable is an elected official whose primary duty is to execute, serve, and return various legal notices and documents as directed by the court.

The Arizona Constitution provides that the civil jurisdiction of Justice of the Peace Courts shall not exceed the sum of $10,000 exclusive of interest and costs, and that the criminal trial jurisdiction of Justice of the Peace Courts is limited to misdemeanors. In addition, justices of the peace are authorized to hold preliminary hearings for defendants charged with felonies.

Figure 8-1. Arizona's Judiciary Organizational Chart
January 1, 2008*
The Structure of Arizona's Judiciary
How the Courts are Organized
APPELLATE COURTS
Supreme Court: 5 Justices, 6 Year Terms
Chief Justice*
Vice Chief Justice*
3 Associate Justices
*Arizona Constitution, Article VI Section 3

Courts of Appeals
22 Judges, 6 Year Terms

Division One - Phoenix	Division Two - Tucson
Chief Judge* & 15 Associate Judges	Chief Judge* & 5 Associate Judges
5 Departments (A, B, C, D & E)	2 Departments (A & B)
Presiding Judge* & 2 Judges Each	Presiding Judge* & 2 Judges Each
Counties: Apache, Coconino, La Paz,	Counties: Cochise, Gila, Graham,
Maricopa, Mohave, Navajo, Yavapai, Yuma	Greenlee, Pima, Pinal, Santa Cruz

*A.R.S. Section 12.120.04

GENERAL JURISDICTION COURT
Superior Court: 159 Judges, 4 Year Terms
*Presiding Judge in each county

Apache	1	Greenlee	1	Pima	27
Cochise	4	La Paz	1	Pinal	6
Coconino	4	Maricopa	91	Santa Cruz	2
Gila	2	Mohave	5	Yavapai	6
Graham	1	Navajo	3	Yuma	5

*Arizona Constitution, Article VI Section 11

LIMITED JURISDICTION COURTS
Justice of the Peace Courts:
83 Judges, 79 Courts, 4 Year Terms

Apache	4	Mohave	5
Cochise	6	Navajo	6
Coconino	4	Pima	8
Gila	2	Pinal	8
Graham	2	Santa Cruz	2
Greenlee	2	Yavapai	5
La Paz	3	Yuma	3
Maricopa	23		

Arizona Constitution,
Article VI Section 32

---

* Numbers may vary due to retirements, resignations, or court expansion at any given time.

(continued)

Figure 8-1. Continued

Municipal Courts:
133 Full- & Part-Time Judgeships,
2 Year Terms, 84 Cities/Towns

	Judges	Courts		Judges	Courts
Apache	3	3	Mohave	4	4
Cochise	6	6	Navajo	4	5
Coconino	6	4	Pima	16	5
Gila	5	5	Pinal	8	8
Graham	3	3	Santa Cruz	2	2
Greenlee	2	2	Yavapai	8	8
La Paz	2	2	Yuma	4	4
Maricopa	60	23			

A.R.S. Sections 22-402 and -403

The Arizona Statutes provide that in civil cases the justice of the peace has exclusive jurisdiction in matters involving less than $500, and concurrent jurisdiction with the Superior Court in matters involving $500 or more, but less than $5,000. The justice of the peace also has jurisdiction in cases of forcible entry and detainer, provided that damages do not exceed $5,000. The voters approved a constitutional amendment in the 1990 election authorizing up to a $10,000 civil jurisdiction limit for Justice of the Peace courts. The legislature by statute increased the limits to $5,000. Justice courts may also hear small claims disputes not exceeding $2,500.

The Judicial Branch

ARIZONA SUPREME COURT

Andrew D. Hurwitz, Justice
Rebecca White Berch, Vice Chief Justice
Ruth V. McGregor, Chief Justice
Michael D. Ryan, Justice
W. Scott Bales, Justice

- Arizona State Bar
- Commission on Judicial Performance Review
- Nominating Commissions
- Commission on Judicial Conduct
- State Foster Care Review Board
- Arizona Judicial Council
- Staff Attorneys Office
- Clerk of the Court
- Administrative Office of the Courts Executive Office
  - Administrative Services
  - Adult Probation Services
  - Certification and Licensing
  - Court Services
  - Education Services
  - Dependent Children's Services
  - Information Technology
  - Juvenile Justice Services

Section 22-301 of the Arizona Revised Statutes provides criminal jurisdiction as follows:

1.　　　Petty theft.

2.　　　Assault or battery not charged to have been committed upon a public officer in the discharge of his/her duties, or to have been committed with such intent as to render the offense a felony.

3.　　　Breaches of peace, routs, affrays, and committing a willful injury to property.

4.　　　Misdemeanors and criminal offenses punishable by a fine not exceeding $1,000 or imprisonment in the county jail not to exceed six months, or by both such fine and imprisonment.

5.　　　Felonies, but only for the purpose of commencing action and conducting proceedings through preliminary examinations; and to hold the defendant to answer to the Superior Court; or to discharge the defendant if it appears that there is not probable cause to believe the defendant guilty of an offense.

Justices of the Peace have the least formal qualifications and one of the highest compensation plans of any elected officials in the state. Since compensation is tied to the case load of the Superior Court, Justices of the Peace in heavily populated counties can earn up to 70% of the salary paid to a Superior Court Judge, depending on the number of "judicial productivity credits" to which they are entitled. They can further augment their income by performing other services, such as marriages, on a personal fee basis.

Efforts to upgrade the judicial qualifications of Justices of the Peace (there currently are none) have gone on for decades. To date Justices of the Peace have been successful in resisting change. Reformers seek an integrated statewide court system, a college education, and a higher age requirement (30 instead of the current 18). These very basic reforms would disqualify most sitting Justices of the Peace from holding their offices, although a grandfathering provision would most certainly be a part of any reform package. Opponents to reform argue in favor of local autonomy and a populist approach to the judicial craft. There does not appear to be a quality of hard data to back up the efficacy of either position, although what is true is that the exercise of law at all levels has grown increasingly complex.

It has been suggested that one of the reasons the legislature has been reluctant to initiate reform is that some prominent retiring legislators retire to a Justice of the Peace position, with its much higher salary. Since the Elected Officials Retirement Plan is based on 4% times years of service times highest salary, this translates into substantial retirement income. The controversy remains volatile.

The second type of limited jurisdiction court in Arizona is the Municipal, or City, Court. Statutes require that each incorporated city or town have a court, and state laws refer to these as police courts. These courts have criminal jurisdiction in matters arising out of the ordinances of their city or town and have concurrent jurisdiction with the Justice of the Peace Courts over violations of state law committed within the city or town limits. The criminal trial jurisdiction of Municipal Courts is limited to misdemeanors.

Qualifications for judges in the Municipal Courts are set by the individual city's charter or ordinances. Some charter municipalities require that their judges be attorneys, while others do not. In most cases, Municipal Court judges are appointed by, and serve at the pleasure of, the city council.

GENERAL JURISDICTION COURTS

The Superior Court of Arizona is the state's only general jurisdiction court. It is a statewide trial court and is empowered to hear and decide a large variety of cases.

Article VI of the Arizona Constitution provides for one Superior Court judge in each county and permits one additional judge for every 30,000 inhabitants or majority fraction thereof beyond the county's first 30,000 inhabitants. These judges serve a regular term of office of four years.

According to the Arizona Constitution, judges of the Superior Court "shall be at least thirty years of age, of good moral character, and admitted to the practice of law in and a resident of the state for five years next preceding their taking of office" (Article VI, Section 22). In the ten counties having two or more Superior Court judges, the Supreme Court designates a presiding judge who exercises administrative supervision over the court.

Court commissioners may be appointed by and serve at the pleasure of the presiding judge of the Superior Court in counties with three or more judges. Commissioners usually determine masters where a default has been entered against a party and they may also preside at the initial appearance of a defendant charged with a crime.

As noted earlier, the Superior Court has general jurisdiction and it can hear almost any type of case except minor offenses and violations of city codes and ordinances. The Superior Court has original jurisdiction in the following matters:

> Cases and proceedings in which exclusive jurisdiction is not vested by law in another court.

> Cases of equity and at law which involve the title to or possession of real property, or the legality of any tax, impost, assessment, toll, or municipal ordinance.

> Other cases in which the demand or value of property in controversy amounts to $1,000 or more exclusive of interest and costs.

> Criminal cases amounting to felony and cases of misdemeanor not otherwise provided for by law.

> Actions of forcible entry and detainer.

> Proceedings in insolvency.

> Actions to prevent or abate nuisance.

> Matters of probate.

Divorce, now called dissolution of marriage, and for annulment of marriage.

Naturalization and the issuance of papers therefor.

Special cases and proceedings not otherwise provided for, and such other jurisdiction as may be provided by law.

The Superior Court also has concurrent jurisdiction with the Justice of the Peace Courts over civil claims involving $500 or more, but less than $5,000. The Superior Court is authorized to act as an appellate court hearing appeals from decisions made in the Justice of the Peace and Municipal Courts. Through its probation department, the Superior Court is responsible for supervising criminal defendants who have been placed on probation and juveniles who have been placed on probation after being adjudicated delinquent.

APPELLATE JURISDICTION COURTS

JUDICIAL SELECTION

The remaining two courts, the Supreme Court and the Court of Appeals, have appellate jurisdiction. These courts do not hear trials as the other courts do but hear appeals on cases that have gone to trial in other courts. When decisions of cases tried in the Superior Court are appealed, they usually go to the intermediate appellate court, the Court of Appeals. An exception to this is any case in which a sentence of death or life imprisonment has been imposed. These cases are appealed directly to the Supreme Court.

Arizona's intermediate appellate court, the Court of Appeals, was first established in 1965. This court consists of two divisions: Division One, with fifteen judges, is located in Phoenix, and Division Two, with six judges, is located in Tucson. To qualify for appointment to the Court of Appeals, a person must be at least thirty years of age, of good moral character, a resident of Arizona for five years immediately prior to taking office, and admitted to the practice of law in Arizona during that same period. The term of office for judges of the Court of Appeals is six years.

The Court of Appeals has appellate jurisdiction to determine all matters properly appealed from the Superior Court. In most instances, appeal to the Court of Appeals is not discretionary. This means that the court must hear and review all decisions properly appealed to it.

In addition to hearing Superior Court appeals, Division 1 has statewide responsibility for reviewing appeals and decisions arising from the Industrial Commission and unemployment compensation rulings of the Department of Economic Security. However, most of the caseload of the Court of Appeals involves appeals from Superior Court decisions. Judges for the Court of Appeals sit in three judge panels when hearing and deciding cases. As with the Supreme Court, there are three major decisions which can be rendered. The Court of Appeals may agree with the decision of the trial court and affirm that decision, it may disagree with the trial court and reverse the decision or it may remand the case to the trial court for further action or a new trial.

The Supreme Court is the state's highest court. The Arizona Constitution provides the Supreme Court with administrative supervision over all the courts of the state and gives the chief justice authority to exercise that supervision.

The Supreme Court consists of five justices whose regular term of office is six years. Justices of the Supreme Court must be of good moral character, admitted to the practice of law in Arizona, and a resident of the state for ten years immediately prior to their taking office.

The jurisdiction of the Supreme Court, as provided in Article VI, Section 5 of the Arizona Constitution, includes appellate jurisdiction, the issuance of extraordinary writs, and the power to make rules relative to any procedural matter in any court. At its discretion, the Supreme Court may review a decision of the intermediate appellate court when a litigant files a petition for review. The Supreme Court has original jurisdiction over all cases involving disputes between counties and disputes involving state officials in the performance of their duties.

Through its rule-making authority, the Supreme Court regulates the activities of the State Bar of Arizona and oversees the admission of new attorneys to the practice of law. The State Bar has responsibility for filing disciplinary and removal petitions related to the alleged misconduct of Arizona attorneys, but only the Supreme Court has authority to actually suspend an attorney from practice or disbar an attorney. The Supreme Court also serves as the final decision-making body when disciplinary recommendations against Arizona judges are filed by the Commission on Judicial Qualifications. The National Center for State Courts has consistently recognized the quality of Arizona's general and appellate courts.

TABLE 8-1. Judicial Salaries
(Effective January 1, 2008)

Chief Justice Supreme Court	$145,294
Associate Justices Supreme Court	$142,341
Appellate Judges	$139,388
Superior Court Judge	$135,844

There is a mandatory retirement age for Arizona judges; it is the age of 70.

JUDICIAL SELECTION

JUDICIAL EVALUATION

Superior Court judges are elected on a nonpartisan ballot in thirteen of the fifteen counties of Arizona. Superior Court judges in Maricopa and Pima are chosen by the merit selection system.

Commissions on judicial appointments are the core of the merit selection system. There are currently three such commissions on judicial appointments, one each for Maricopa and Pima Superior Court appointments, and one for appellate court appointments. Each commission has 16 members. Ten non-lawyer members are selected by the governor and five attorney members are chosen by the State Bar. Commission members are all nominated by the governor and must be confirmed by the state Senate. The chief justice of the Arizona Supreme Court presides over each commission and is thus a sixteenth member. However, the chief justice votes only in the case of a tie. Commission members serve staggered terms of four years. A constitutional amendment approved by the voters in 1992, provided for greater public participation in the process for appointing and evaluation judges in the courts of record in Maricopa and Pima Counties. The amendment requires that public hearings be held, testimony taken and public votes be made before any judicial selection commission could nominate to the governor a candidate for appointment to the court. It also increased the membership of the judicial appointment commission and expanded public process into recommending to the governor members for the judicial appointment commissions. It further provided that consideration be given to the diversity of the states' or county's' population in making court appointments but that the primary consideration shall be merit. An additional provision will take effect upon the establishment of a new evaluation process to be developed with full public participation.

When a vacancy occurs on a particular court, a call for nominations and applications is made. When the appropriate commission reviews potential nominees, its members are mindful of the constitutional requirements for the post. The constitution requires that the nominating commission submit at least three nominees, no more than two of whom, or in the case of more than three, not more than 60% shall be members of the same political party. Should the commission fail to submit names to the governor within sixty days after the vacancy occurs, the governor may appoint any qualified person to fill the vacancy. Should the governor fail to appoint one of the commission's nominees within sixty days after the names are submitted, the chief justice makes the appointment.

The judges appointed to office under the merit system initially hold office for a term which ends sixty days following the next regular general election after a two-year term of office. At the election, voters indicate yes or no on the issue of retaining the judge or justice. If retained, the judge serves a full regular term of either four or six years, depending on the court, and then the retention process repeats itself. When a judge is not retained, the office is vacated upon expiration of the term and the appropriate commission begins its nominating task once again.

In 1992 the voters established the Arizona Commission on Judicial Performance. The thirty member commission is appointed by the Governor and is comprised of a majority of public citizens and a minority of attorneys and judges not up for retention. The Commission is charged with establishing performance standards, evaluating judicial performance, and informing the public of its findings, for all judges and justices who are up for retention in any given election year.

For the 2004 elections, judges were evaluated in the following categories:

Administrative Performance
Communication Skills
Integrity
Judicial Temperament
Legal Ability
Settlement Activities

Information is gathered from attorneys, jurors, litigants and witnesses, and from the general public. The Commission sorts the data by percentages and votes on whether each judge meets the Arizona standard of judicial performance. Although most judges consistently earn high approval percentages in all categories, a few do drop into the 70th or 80th percentile ranges in some categories (usually judicial temperament is one of them). This is not considered to be sufficient for a negative recommendation from the Commission. However, it might be an issue of considerable importance to the voters. Data is published and mailed to all registered voters in advance of elections.

Article VI.I provides for a commission on judicial conduct. The Commission on Judicial Conduct consists of eleven members appointed to staggered six year terms, and represents a broad population base. It is the commission's duty to consider the disqualification, suspension, and removal, and the retirement of judges. The supreme court acts on the recommendation of the commission in accordance with the requirements of the Constitution.

CHAPTER SUMMARY

✓ In civil matters the purpose of the judicial system is to bring about peaceful resolution of disputes.

✓ In criminal matters the purpose of the judicial system is to protect the innocent and to punish those individuals whose actions are deemed detrimental to social order.

✓ A detailed body of law known as due process has evolved to govern judicial proceedings.

✓ Limited jurisdiction courts deal with minor infractions and issues, and require no formal training of judges, although municipal courts often do.

✓ General jurisdiction courts are the basic trial court of the state, handle all major issues, and require formal legal training of judges.

✓ Appellate courts hear only cases on appeal, except in the case of the Supreme Court where some limited original jurisdiction exists.

✓ The Arizona Supreme Court possesses supervisory authority over all courts in the state.

✓ Superior court judges are selected on a non-partisan ballot in thirteen counties, and by merit selection in Pima and Maricopa counties.

✓ Appellate judges are selected by a merit system and are periodically evaluated and approved by the voters

✓ Justices of the Peace are elected county officials, while municipal judges are selected according to procedures in the city charters.

9
BUDGET AND REVENUE

To understand government finance, one must understand that services cost money, that not all citizens receive services uniformly or equally, and that costs are not distributed equally. In the private sector one buys goods and services by direct purchase; in the public sector certain goods or services are deemed desirable for a portion of the population and publicly funded to provide those services. In education, the service receiver is not only the student who benefits, but also the society that enjoys the skills and abilities of the educated person. In law enforcement, the criminal frequently wishes to avoid the services of the police officer, but the public expects police protection. No one knows what their portion of the cost of service is, but most people have definite ideas about how they would like their money to be spent. The public has an absolute right to expect efficient, honest use of its funds for the services its elected representatives deem desirable.

THE BUDGET PROCESS

A major portion of the state's budget each year is committed to the ongoing programs and services the state provides. Any reduction in funding, except for increased efficiency, will usually be reflected in a reduction in services. Traditionally, the various departments and funded agencies have requested additional funds to expand services and meet inflation costs.

Arizona's budget-making process is as follows:

Step 1. The executive budget committee receives requests from agencies desiring funding under the state's budget. Each request must be accompanied by a justification both for the program and the funding amount. The justifications are most effective when they cite empirical evidence of the program's value and demonstrate the wise use of tax dollars.

Step 2. Budget requests are sent to the Joint Legislative Budget Committee (JLBC) for its review.

Step 3. The governor with the assistance of the executive budget committee staff prepares a budget.

Step 4. The governor presents a proposed budget to the legislature at the beginning of the legislative session in January. It is frequently the topic of the State of the State address.

Step 5. The legislature receives the recommendations of the JLBC based on staff analysis of needs and anticipated revenue.

Step 6. The legislature then begins the task of balancing the interests of diverse groups. The majority party in each house of the legislature has the responsibility of putting together a budget that will receive the necessary number of votes and not have any of it vetoed by the governor.

Frequently the appropriations committees of the two houses working independently arrive at different funding levels for the various agencies. Through compromise, they must reach agreement on an identical plan that will pass in the House, and then the Senate, and receive the governor's approval. Hopefully, the process can be concluded before the fiscal year ends the last day in June.

Arizona's budget for 2005 was $7.6 billion; the budget for 2008 rose to $10.6 billion. The money must come from current revenue sources. Since the state is constitutionally restrained from deficit spending, a reasonable reserve must be maintained to meet unexpected circumstances. Each year the state deposits or withdraws money from the Budget Stabilization Fund, a contingency fund designed to flatten out a fluctuating revenue stream.

The fund balance for 2006 was only $2 million; the following year it was $687 million. Over a two year period the state amassed a budget surplus approximating $1.5 billion. This was due to "boom" economic conditions. A hot real estate market meant more jobs and more consumer spending, with resultant huge increases in all state revenue sources.

The state deposited approximately $700 million of the surplus into the Budget Stabilization Fund and cut taxes by roughly $200 million, many of which go into effect in fiscal 2009. The state also increased spending massively during the "boom" years. As a result the 2008 budget, which is a 9.4% increase over the 2007 budget, only anticipates revenue growth of 6%. Various budget cuts, deferral of certain expenditures, and considerable depletion of the Budget Stabilization Fund will make up the deficit. It is important to bear in mind that economic cycles can swing suddenly in the modern world. A major downturn in the Arizona economy occurred due to the World Trade Center disaster. A sizeable portion of Arizona's economy rests on tourism, conventions and winter residents. All of these areas were reduced significantly after 9/11. The development translated into diminished sales, layoffs, and lowered purchasing power. Since almost one half of Arizona's revenues derive from sales tax, this amounted to a significant reduction in the revenue stream.

Another issue that negatively impacted the budget even prior to 9/11 had to do with huge unanticipated financial outlays necessitated by a loosely worded alternative fuel incentive program. The economic impact of the Employers Sanctions Law and the 2010 Immigration Act have not been determined. Certainly there is and will be some economic fallout from this legislation but hard data is almost impossible to obtain.

Through the Nineties and into the opening years of the new century Arizona's economy was fueled by growth. State political bodies consistently expressed optimism. But the Goldwater Institute, as well as a number of other monitoring organizations, cited problems with the budget. Their concerns were unheeded. Spending increases were outstripping population growth by almost twofold. And a state that provided itself with claims of low taxation (Arizona however ranks in the middle on overall taxation) continued to reduce taxes in some areas. User fees such as hikes in university tuition rates made ups for some of the loss. Lowering taxes was easy; it only took a simple majority vote of the legislature and would always be popular with the electorate. But to reverse the process, to raise taxes, was clearly a different matter. A two-third majority was necessitated and the electorate would not be pleased.

Ordinarily a reduction in spending results from a reduction in revenue and results in a reduction in public services. Each Governor and each legislature has its own priorities for state spending, and ultimately, these priorities will be reflected in the enacted General Fund budget.

It would appear from what has just been discussed that the budget process is relatively straight forward. This is simply not the case. Complicating the budget process are policy issues, ideology of government, partisan politics, special interest and so forth.

State legislators are elected from specific geographical districts. Thus, their individual constituencies may vary considerably. Local economic issues, long standing political culture, environmental issues, to cite a few examples, must be supported if the legislator is to be elected, and once elected, remains in office. Politics has been defined as a "study in perceptions, not realities." Successful politicians must treat these perceptions as realties. The governor, and other statewide elected officials, however, must not be so tied to localized issues. At the State level the generalized needs of the entire state must be taken into consideration. Current governor Janice Brewer, a lifelong fiscal conservative, proposed a sales tax increase, and for over a year failed to receive sufficient support from the legislative to achieve passage. (The tax was approved overwhelmingly by the voters on March 18, 2010.)

Bipartisanship is often talked but seldom walked. The major political parties to some extent exist to oppose each other. Election campaigns are based on emphasizing differences rather than similarities between opposing candidates. Often times slight differences give rise to grossly exaggerated rhetoric that goes far beyond the actual facts in an issue. Agreement and bipartisanship can be viewed as "me too" politics; it does not get one elected.

Ideological differences on the role of what government should or should not do have been around since the foundation of the republic. Should government be all encompassing or do as little as possible? Should there be free market, laissez fire, planned central economy, regulation, deregulation, social justice—What is the legitimate function of government? Words such as individualism, collectivism, capitalism, socialism are values laden words, often eliciting exaggerated responses. Well meaning people hold widely divergent views.

There are some fundamental differences between parties and candidates. The traditional constituent base of both major parties originated in the late nineteenth century—the stereotype of Republicans representing big business, the wealthy, the elites, and the Democrats representing the working class, minorities, the poor. Some of this stereotyping has diminished over the decade as ideologies have become somewhat blurred. Generally speaking Republicans do favor "free market," deregulation, privatization, low taxes and minimal government intervention. Democrats do favor market controls, progressive taxation, government intervention and involvement. However, individual Republicans and Democrats may vary considerably.

Obviously parties will approach problems differently. During a budget shortfall, for example, should government emphasize cutting services (decreasing expenditures) or raising taxes (increasing revenues). If taxes are raised, which ones? These are fundamental practical issues in politics. Complicating the above choices are the roles played by various special interest groups in politics. To whom does the politician give the most attention? Who has access to government and thereby effectively influence politics? In theory, in a representative government, politicians are supposed to represent the will of their constituents. In reality such is not often the case. For one, the generalized constituency is seldom unified, and therefore sends no clear message to elected officials. For another, some interests have far greater influence than others. Will the politician do what is in the best interest of the greatest number. A statesman has been defined as an individual who places the public interest above personal interest or ambitions. Then there is also the issue of how well individual elected officials fully grasp the issue at hand, especially as relates to fiscal matters.

There are no formal education requirements for Arizona legislators and most elected officials of the executive branch except for the ability to read and write English. So from what source comes the specialized knowledge needed to resolve complex issues, or even to address the prioritizing of issues. Does government suffer from restrictive "in the box" thinking, or do elected officials respond to their own prejudices and knowledge base? Clearly there is a wide range of responses to this. Organizations, those respectable and well financed, can present very concise and powerful views on what they want. The generalized constituency is scattered.

There also exists a structural difficulty in the political process itself. Politics has also been defined as the "art of compromise." Rarely does any elected official receive all he/she wants. To garner votes one must compromise their own initiatives and or provide political support for less than desirable initiative of other politicians. One need only review the various issues involved in the recent health care debate in the United States Congress.

Former Arizona House Speaker Mark Killian, in an editorial piece in the Arizona Republic on February 21, 2010, indicated that no extraneous issue should be allowed in budget bills considerations (earmarks). Budget building should be the top priority of every legislature and personal rancor solves nothing.

So how did the current budget crisis in Arizona come about? There exists both structural issues and policy issue independent of the national economics melt down. The 2010 Report on the Status of the Budget suggests that only one third of Arizona's economic woes are due to the national situation. Resolution of the current budget crisis can provide a blueprint for preventing or at least lessening any future fiscal crisis.

Government revenues derive from a number of general categories. One category can be termed "one-time receipts." This includes budget carryovers (money budgeted but not spent in a previous budget cycle.) It includes one time federal grants, such as the Federal Stimulus Program. It can also be a cyclical "boom" or highly expansive economic period, as what was recently experienced in Arizona. Cyclical "booms" mark high points in government revenues brought on by high employment, increased spending, speculation, various economic "bubbles," But there will also be low points, or corrections. Therefore, budgeting for long term initiatives should never be based on one time receipts.

There are also normal flow economic cycles, providing ebb and flow in revenues. The economy expands and contracts, and if not due to artificial issues, provides no disastrous effects. For normal cycle revenue, spending should be an average of high and low points, with saving during high points to provide level revenues for low points. The Budget Stabilization Fund was developed to meet this objective. It is, however much easier for government to want to spend rather than save.*

Finally, there are ongoing revenues—core income that goes on regardless of economic cycles. Even during the Great Depression the majority of workers kept their jobs and continued to pay taxes. Government did not cease to exist. Many of the wealthy continued to be wealthy. There are ongoing critical sectors of the economy. Prudent budgeting dictates that any monies used to implement new programs or expand existing ones should come form ongoing revenue sources only. Otherwise new programs may be initiated during good economic times only to be curtailed or abolished during bad economic times. Arizona's implementation and then retraction of full day kindergarten is a prime example.

Arizona State government possesses limited flexibility in fiscal matters. The Voter Protection Act of 1998 effectively curtailed the ability of the legislature to modify programs and revenues approved by the voters, specifically portions of AHCCCS (Arizona Health Care Cost Containment System), K-12 programs, and First Things First (preschool). Proposition 108 requires either a two-third vote of the legislature or a vote of the people to approve an increase in state revenues, while maintaining a simple majority legislative vote

*Established in 1990 the Budget Stabilization Fund initially called for maintaining 15% of the General Fund as a reserve for low revenue producing years. That percentage has been gradually reduced to 7% and as of 2010 there is no balance in the Fund.

to reduce taxes. Thus, it is very easy for the legislature to lower taxes and quite difficult to raise them. If the legislature cannot obtain the extra ordinary majority needed to raise taxes, the only other option is to refer the matter to the voters. This is how the temporary sales tax increase was approved on May 18, 2010.

The American Recovery and Reinvestment Act of 2009 made federal funds available to the states. These funds were not given without conditions. States are required to maintain funding at their 2006 levels from their own resources when the federal funding ends. In fiscal 2011 Arizona will be required to replace funding that the federal government provided for fiscal 2009, 2010 and some 2011. (See Chart 9-1 for that liability)

In the interim, however, this means that a substantial part of the budget in specific areas is protected from further legislative cuts. (See Charts 9-2, 9-3, and 9-4). The Technical

Chart 9-1. The ARRA FY 2011 Cliff

AHCCCS	201,806.9
DHS	90,343.5
DES	105,151.6
K-12 Education	379,314.0
Universities	64,000.0
Community Colleges	20,000.0
Corrections	50,000.0
TOTAL	910,616.0

January 08, 2010   Office of Governor Janice K. Brewer

Chart 9-2

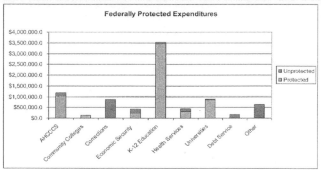

Approximately $2.4 billion unprotected

January 08, 2010   Office of Governor Janice K. Brewer

Chart 9-3

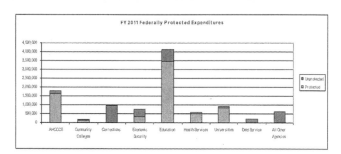

Approximately $3.2 billion unprotected

(note: Federal MOE for Medicaid currently ends on December 31, 2010)

January 08, 2010   Office of Governor Janice K. Brewer

Chart 9-4

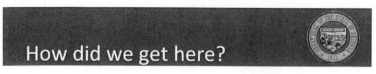

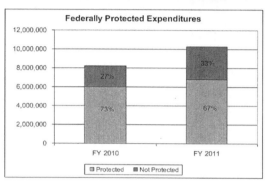

Federally Protected Expenditures

January 08, 2010   Office of Governor Janice K. Brewer

term for this requirement is MOE, standing for "Maintenance of Effort."

Yet in order to get through the 2010 fiscal year the legislature resorted to activities that created long term consequences in exchange for short term gains. State property was sold for $735 million in January, 2010, under a 20 year leaseback arrangement. The state is now committed to paying annual rents for what it formally owned—an additional expense for the next 20 years. Also, the state borrowed against future lottery proceeds, meaning of course, that the lottery revenue stream has been severely impacted.

Added problems derive from the fact that all major state general fund programs are equally protected. Nor has their growth been the same over the past decade. Federal funds for AHCCCS expire at the end of 2010. After that time the state will be able to alter eligibility requirements. The Education budget, however, is fairly safe from any further cuts. There are no MOE requirements for the Corrections budget, so it is entirely vulnerable. But can the correction budget, although unprotected, be severely cut? As of fiscal 2010 it costs approximately $880 million to incarcerate at current levels. This is roughly 10% of the General Fund Budget. Non-viable options include closing programs, furloughing guards, early release. But Arizona's mandatory sentencing laws retain most prisoners for most of their sentences. Further, the prison population of Arizona has grown dramatically, from 26,510 in 2000 to 39, 589 in 2008, a 49.3% increase. The State Corrections Department has considered transferring prisoners with less than a year remaining on their sentence to county jails (jails that are under the control of County Sheriffs). At the same time a number of municipalities are considering private jails in lieu of county jails.

Costs have increased from growth. According to the Governors office, over the past six years 121,500 students were added to K–12 at an additional cost of $1 billion annually. University enrollments increased by $18,100 at an annual cost of $395 million during the same period. AHCCCS in fiscal 2009 cost $1.5 billion more than in fiscal 2004. Some increasing state costs were hidden or ignored due to the boom conditions during the middle of the past decade. But these increases are staggering and even more astounding as the state was cutting taxes during the same period. Since 2000 the costs of many programs has more than doubled. So where is the money?

Chart 9-5. *General Fund State Budget*

**STATEMENT OF GENERAL FUND REVENUES
AND EXPENDITURES
SCENARIO 1: PROP 204 FUNDED**

	FY 2010 Revised	FY 2011 Revised
REVENUES		
Ongoing Revenues	$6,771,226,800	$7,020,888,400
Enacted Revenue Changes		10,607,600
Budget Legislation Changes	18,800,700	63,583,600
Sales Tax Increase - May Ballot		918,000,000
First Things First Redirect - Nov. Ballot		60,000,000
Urban Revenue Sharing	(628,649,100)	(473,986,800)
Net On-going Revenues	$6,161,378,400	$7,599,092,800
One-time Financing Sources		
Balance Forward	($480,713,000)	($150,185,000)
Other Revenue Changes	113,420,000	34,600,000
State Asset Leaseback/Other Financing	1,485,419,300	
Fund Transfers - November Ballot		448,538,600
Fund Transfers	386,505,800	180,292,300
Subtotal One-time Revenues	$1,504,632,100	$513,245,900
Total Revenues	$7,666,010,500	$8,112,338,700
EXPENDITURES		
Operating Budget Appropriations	$9,588,250,900	$9,508,835,500
FY 2010 Supplementals	132,583,200	0
First Things First/DES Redirect - Nov. Ballot		40,000,000
Administrative Adjustments	72,731,600	73,607,000
Revertments	(113,241,600)	(112,905,100)
Subtotal Ongoing Expenditures	$9,680,324,100	$9,509,537,400
One-time Expenditures		
Capital Outlay	$10,400,000	$4,000,000
Capital Outlay Prior Year Reversions	(450,000)	
Temporary Federal Assistance	(1,289,189,500)	(973,385,200)
SFB Debt Refinance		(60,000,000)
Payment Deferrals	(584,889,100)	
Subtotal One-time Expenditures	($1,864,128,600)	($1,029,385,200)
Total Expenditures	$7,816,195,500	$8,480,152,200
Ending Balance w/ Ballot Props [1]	($150,185,500)	($367,813,500)
Structural Balance (On-going Rev/Expend)	($3,518,945,700)	($1,910,444,600)
Impact of Ballot Proposition Failures		
Sales Tax Failure		(918,000,000)
Other Ballot Failures		(468,538,600)
Conditional Reductions		862,366,000
Revised Ending Balance w/out Ballot Props [2]	(150,185,000)	(891,986,100)

[1] Assume passage of budget-related ballot propositions

[2] Assumes failure of budget-related ballot propositions

FY 2012 Forecast	FY 2013 Forecast	FY 2014 Forecast
$8,024,988,500	$8,765,325,000	$9,412,533,500
(6,100,000)	(5,000,000)	(500,000)
(2,144,000)	(12,852,000)	
967,829,800	1,056,875,100	
120,000,000	120,000,000	120,000,000
(428,199,400)	(447,697,800)	(497,001,800)
$8,676,374,900	$9,476,650,300	$9,035,031,700
102,389,500	102,389,500	102,389,500
$102,389,500	$102,389,500	$102,389,500
$8,778,764,400	$9,579,039,800	$9,137,421,200
$9,642,043,900	$9,961,868,600	$10,122,764,700
40,000,000	40,000,000	40,000,000
73,388,300	74,853,500	77,086,600
(115,159,200)	(118,594,800)	(120,525,600)
$9,641,273,000	$9,958,127,300	$10,119,325,700
$0	$0	$0
$9,641,273,000	$9,958,127,300	$10,119,325,700
($862,508,600)	($379,087,500)	($981,904,500)
($964,898,100)	($481,477,000)	($1,084,294,000)
(967,829,800)	(1,056,875,100)	
(80,000,000)	(80,000,000)	(80,000,000)
862,366,000	862,366,000	862,366,000
(1,047,972,400)	(653,596,600)	(199,538,500)

163

REVENUE SOURCES

Arizona's political leaders are proud to claim that the state is a low tax state. The claim is a little simplistic. Considering only general state and local taxes Arizona ranked 41st as of fiscal 2008. But if all sources of taxation are included, and this includes escalating user fees, Arizona tends to rank around 25th, depending on which source is consulted. Some taxes are low-individual income tax for example.

There have been tax cuts enacted by the legislature in almost every one of the last twenty years. Some of the revenue loss is made up by higher user fees, such as increased tuition at the State University. Some loss is covered by curtailing service. But overall, while taxes have been cut, state spending has increased dramatically. It has been estimated that two-thirds of Arizona's fiscal problems is due to insufficient revenue not too much spending. In overall spending per capita Arizona ranks 45th. In spending for education it ranks 48th. Yet in tax burden per household it ranks 46th. The state literally needs more money.

The problem is compounded by the presence of wild budget swings. In 2003 the state experienced a $1 billion shortfall, whereas in 2006 there was a $1 billion surplus. Over 2008–2010 Arizona experienced a 28% drop in revenue. Such developments are not new to Arizona, so they should be anticipated. Resolutions of the current budget crisis could create a process for future fiscal responsibility.

Revenue to support the budget is as controversial as the spending patterns. Sales, income, and property taxes are all tied to fixed percentages. Inflation, growth, and the business cycle all cause fluctuations in the amount of revenue. Economists can predict with a high degree of accuracy-

anticipated revenue from these sources. Roughly speaking, the same level of taxation will maintain the same level of services. The addition of new or expanded services requires new sources of revenue. The Arizona Legislature has been limited by the constitution from deficit spending for operations to the $350,000 debt limit. Revenue from lottery games has been a windfall. Proposition 202, passed by the voters in 2002, created a twenty year compact with the tribes authorizing casino gambling; the tribes voluntarily agreed to pay taxes on their casino revenues. The estimated advantage to the state is $90-100 million annually. Also, recent voter approved legislation has appropriated $20 million from lottery revenue for the Heritage Fund. Property tax increases have resulted primarily from increased assessed evaluation rather than increases in the tax rate. Sales and income tax revenue has increased with business recovery and inflation. Escalating real estate values has enabled the state to sell school trust lands at favorable prices, netting $39 million in revenues in 2004. The down side is that once the land is sold and the proceeds are spent, the asset is permanently gone.

User taxes are popular where the users can be encouraged to pay the higher cost. Two examples are appropriate here: gasoline tax which is paid by highway users for the purpose of building and maintaining roads, and tuition payments to attend school, which are paid by those receiving the education. In 2000 the tuition rate at the state universities was $2272; for the 2009–2010 academic year it is over $5933. A tobacco tax of 40 cents per pack on cigarettes and a like amount on other tobacco products was passed by public initiative on the 1994 ballot. Subsequent increases have raised the tax to $2.00 per pack, one of the highest rates in the nation. The tax is to be deposited in separate accounts to be used for health care, health

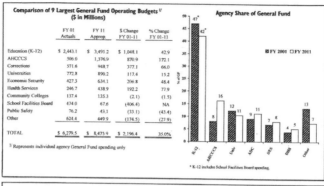

Comparison of 9 Largest General Fund Operating Budgets [1]
($ in Millions)

	FY 01 Actuals	FY 11 Approp.	$ Change FY 01-11	% Change FY 01-11
Education (K-12)	$ 2,443.1	$ 3,491.2	$ 1,048.1	42.9
AHCCCS	506.0	1,376.9	870.9	172.1
Corrections	571.6	948.7	377.1	66.0
Universities	772.8	890.2	117.4	15.2
Economic Security	427.3	634.1	206.8	48.4
Health Services	246.7	438.9	192.2	77.9
Community Colleges	137.4	135.3	(2.1)	(1.5)
School Facilities Board	474.0	67.6	(406.4)	NA
Public Safety	76.2	43.1	(33.1)	(43.4)
Other	624.4	449.9	(174.5)	(27.9)
TOTAL	$ 6,279.5	$ 8,475.9	$ 2,196.4	35.0%

[1] Represents individual agency General Fund spending only

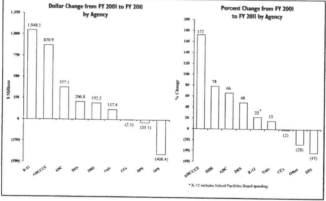

research and health education. User taxes can influence the use of a product or service when they are so high that they work a hardship on assessment of the population. The tax then becomes a social issue rather than a revenue matter.

There are several types of non-tax revenue which, taken together, are not large sources of income. The state raises money from the sale, rental, or lease of land or property. The state collects fees from users of state facilities such as parks and the coliseum. The state also sells licenses and permits to operate some regulated businesses, and to use a boat, car, or

General Fund Revenue, Expenditures and Ending Balances
($ in Millions)

Fiscal Year	Revenue	Expenditures	Ending Balance	Ending Balance as a % of Revenue
2000	6,215.7	6,012.3	203.4	3.3%
2001	6,381.0	6,367,7	13.3	0.2%
2002	6,339.6	6,338.6	1.0	0.0%
2003	6,232.8	6,040.6	192.2	3.1%
2004	6,876.2	6,515.8	360.4	5.2%
2005	8,184.1	7,545.1	639.0	7.8%
2006	9,814.9	8,768.4	1,046.5	10.7%
2007	10,672.2	10,200.5	471.7	4.4%
2008	10,038.2	10,037.2	1.0	0.0%
2009	8,273.7	8,754.4	(480.7)	-5.8%
2010	7,865.5	7,817.1	48.3	0.6%
2011	8,558.9	8,495.6	63.2	0.7%

trailer. The interest on state funds which are invested until used also goes into the general fund. From time to time the state receives gifts and bequests frequently earmarked for a specific purpose. Proposition 301, passed by the voters in 2000, authorizes additional revenues for public education by levying a 6/10 cent sales tax. It was originally believed the result would be $486 million for fiscal 2002, but that now appears have been a rather inflated figure. Federal funds help augment other state revenue sources. But these funds are not guaranteed. For example, the 2008 budget includes a $40 million reduction in disproportionate share payments from the federal government. Most federal funds are for special projects deemed desirable by the Federal government.

The largest single source of tax revenue to the state comes from the sales tax. The state general fund sales tax is 5.6 percent. Additional sales tax may be levied by charter cities for municipal services and by county government. The total sales tax rate from all sources cannot exceed 10.10 percent.

Sales tax applies to purchases made in Arizona; some items such as alcohol and tobacco are taxed at a higher rate as luxury privilege taxes. Food to be consumed off premises and prescription drugs are taxed at a lower rate or not taxed at all. General sales taxes go into the general fund. Special sales taxes such as motor vehicle fuel tax, rental car surtax, and the special education excise tax may go either to the general fund or to special accounts. At the time of this publication Arizona has no state inheritance tax.

Retailers are expected to collect the tax and remit it to the Arizona Department of Revenue based on their sales volume. This makes the tax easy to collect from the consumer at little cost to the state. However, the state's ability to collect from the retailers, construction companies, apartment owners, and others has sometimes been difficult. The Department of Revenue has asked for more agents to assist in this effort.

On May 18, 2010 the voters, by a 2-1 margin, approved a 1% increase in the state sales tax, thereby raising it to 6.6%. The tax increase has a 3 year lifespan and is intended to address the budget shortfall projected over that time period.

The tax increase will end automatically unless specific action by two-thirds of the legislature or a majority of the voters, act to the contrary. The additional revenues are specific to education, health services and public safety. The Joint Legislative Budget Committee anticipates $918 million from the increase for fiscal 2010–11 rising to over $1 billion for the third and final year of the increase. In addition various local taxing authorities are increasing or expanding the sales tax rate at their level in order to make up for budget shortfall.

While the income tax produces the second largest amount of revenue to the state a 1994 law changed the tax rates which is estimated to result in annual loss of 100 million dollars to the general fund. The effective income tax rate is the actual individual income tax liability as a percentage of the federal adjusted gross income. The rates for the 2007 tax year are as follows.

TABLE 9-1. Arizona's Income Tax Rate

2007
Arizona Tax Rate Tables X and Y
For Form 140
If your taxable income is less than $50,000, use the Optional Tax Rate Table. If your taxable income is $50,000 or more, use Tax Rate Table X or Y. Also, if your taxable income is $50,000 or more, you cannot use Form 140EZ or Form 140A to file for 2007. In this case, you must file using Form 140.

Table X–Use Table X if your filing status is Single or Married Filing Separate

(a) If taxable income from Form 140, page 1, line 19 is:		(b) Enter the amount from Form 140, page 1, line 19	(c) Multiply the amount entered in column (b) by	(d) Enter the result	(e) Subtract	(f) Your tax. Round the result and enter this amount on Form 140, page 1, line 20
Over	**But Not over**					
$0	$10,000	×	.0259 =	−	0.00 =	
$10,000	$25,000	×	.0288 =	− $	29.00 =	
$25,000	$50,000	×	.0336 =	− $	149.00 =	
$50,000	$150,000	×	.0424 =	− $	589.00 =	
$150,000	and over	×	.0454 =	− $	1,039.00 =	

169

Table Y - Use Table Y if your filing status is Married Filing Joint or Head of Household

(a)		(b)	(c)	(d)	(e)	(f)
If taxable income from Form 140, page 1, line 19 is:		Enter the amount from Form 140, page 1, line 19	Multiply the amount entered in column (b) by	Enter the result	Subtract	Your tax. Round the result and enter this amount on Form 140, page 1, line 20
Over	But Not over					
$0	$20,000	×	.0259	=	−	0.00 =
$20,000	$50,000	×	.0288	=	− $	58.00 =
$50,000	$100,000	×	.0336	=	− $	298.00 =
$100,000	$300,000	×	.0424	=	− $	1,178.00 =
$300,000	and over	×	.0454	=	− $	2,078.00 =

Effective July 1, 2010, Arizona's withholding rates are effectively decoupled from federal withholding. Instead state withholding amounts will be determined by the Department of Revenue, which the department is required to submit to JLBC by March 15, 2010. This provision has no fiscal impact.

A third tax is the state property tax. The property tax has been a traditional source of revenue for local governments in the United States since colonial times. Because it is hard to administer in a modern society, and because it is unfair to the extent that it bears little relation to either the ability to pay or the level of service usage, the laws regulating the property tax have become extremely complicated. Exemptions from taxation of property owned by certain persons or used for certain purposes exempt about 20 percent of the private property of the state. Government-owned property such as national, Indian, state, county, city, school districts, and nonprofit organizations' property is usually exempt. Inventory to be resold and agricultural livestock is exempt as is a portion of the property of widows, veterans, and the permanently disabled. The property tax rate is a product of the difference between the cost of government and what the other income sources will produce. Certain statutory limitations on the rate of property tax levy increases have forced both spending cuts and a search for alternative revenue sources.

Assessed evaluation of property depends on the use of the property. There are currently eight categories of property with a different percent of full cash value for each (Table 9-2).

TABLE 9-2. Arizona's Categories of Properties 1990

Class	Percent of Full Cash Value	Property Use
1	25	Mines, standing timber
2	25	Privately owned utility companies
3*	25	Industrial and commercial
4	16	Agriculture and vacant land
5	10	Owner occupied real and personal
6	14	Apartment and rental
7	24	Railroad and airline flight property
8	5	Certified significant historical
c	100	Producing oil and gas

---

* To be reduced to 20% over a 10 year period

171

The 1996 legislature passed a property tax reduction bill which would have reduced taxes on businesses and homes by $200 million per year. The governor vetoed the bill because it would have meant a tax increase for homeowners in 19 school districts which did not meet the qualifying tax rate. The legislature is expected to consider this and other school finance legislation in a special session later in the year.

Table 1

Budget Stabilization Fund
($ in Thousands)

General Fund Revenues	Actual FY 2002	Actual FY 2003	Estimate FY 2004	Estimate FY 2005
Adjusted Revenues	$6,239,325.1	$6,217,459.1	$6,551,569.9	$7,114,873.8
Statutory Limit of Revenues	7.000%	7.000%	7.000%	7.000%
Maximum Balance	436,752.8	435,222.1	458,609.9	498,041.2
Arizona Personal Income in Prior CY				
Real Adjusted Annual Income Growth	2.10%	1.67%	1.98%	6.82%
7-Year Average Income Growth	5.78%	5.26%	4.70%	4.63%
Annual Difference	-3.68%	-3.59%	-2.72%	2.19%
BSF Transactions				
Beginning BSF Balance	391,523.8	64,719.3	13,765.7	13,522.5
BSF Formula Recommendation	0.0	(224,085.4)	(169,505.0)	143,479.4
Actual Transfer In				
Conditional Appropriation - L'04, Ch. 275, Part 1 [1]	0.0	0.0	0.0	0.0
Conditional Appropriation - L'04, Ch. 275, Part 2 [2]	0.0	0.0	0.0	0.0
Actual Transfer Out				
ASH Construction Fund Payments [3]	(20,000.0)	(17,500.0)	0.0	0.0
Payment of Alternative Fuel Credits [4]	(61,942.9)	(5,528.7)	(643.2)	(4,500.0)
BSF Transfer to GF - L'01, 2SS, Ch. 4	(119,000.0)	0.0	0.0	0.0
BSF Transfer to GF - L'02, 3SS, Ch. 2, Part 1	(47,150.0)	0.0	0.0	0.0
BSF Transfer to GF - L'02, 3SS, Ch. 2, Part 2 [5]	(84,397.9)	0.0	0.0	0.0
BSF Transfer to GF - L'03, Ch. 262 [6]	0.0	(30,000.0)	0.0	0.0
BSF Transfer to GF - L'04, Ch. 275	0.0	0.0	0.0	(8,000.0)
Balance	59,033.0	11,690.6	13,122.5	1,022.5
Interest Earnings & Equity Gains/Losses	5,686.3	2,075.1	400.0	1,000.0
Ending BSF Balance	**$64,719.3**	**$13,765.7**	**$13,522.5**	**$2,022.5**
Percent of Revenues	**1.0%**	**0.2%**	**0.2%**	**0.0%**

Footnotes

[1] If revenues exceed the forecast by $102 million, $6.0 million would be appropriated to the BSF.

[2] If revenues exceed the forecast by $102 million, 50% of the additional revenue above $102 million would be deposited in the BSF.

[3] Pursuant to Laws 2003, 1st Special Session, Chapter 1, in FY 2003 the amount of $13.4 million was subsequently transferred from the Arizona State Arizona State Hospital Capital Construction Fund to the General Fund.

[4] The Alt. Fuels payout of BSF money was $(116.9) million between FY 2001 and FY 2003. Through the first 11 months of FY 2004, another $(0.6) million has been paid out. It is estimated that the ultimate total could be $(122) million. $4.5 million remains in reserve.

[5] Since revenues fell below the budgeted total in FY 2002, the BSF was used to make up the difference. A total of $84.4 million was withdrawn to balance the FY 2002 budget.

[6] The FY 2003 transfer to the General Fund was originally supposed to be in the amount of $(50) million. According to Laws 2002, Chapter 327. This amount was modified to $(30) million by Laws 2003, Chapter 262.

The county treasurer is responsible for collecting property taxes for the state, county, and special districts. Chart 9-6 shows the percentage of income derived from the various sources of revenue for the general fund.

The property tax rate for both the county and the state is determined by the following method. This general process is limited by laws regulating the amount of increase that can

Chart 9-6. FY 2000 vs. FY 2011 General Fund Revenue

General Fund Major Tax Sources as a Percent of Total Revenue[1]

Fiscal Year	Sales	Individual Income	Corporate Income	Other
2000	47.5%	38.4%	8.8%	5.3%
2001	48.3%	37.2%	8.8%	5.8%
2002	48.1%	33.4%	5.5%	12.9%
2003	48.8%	33.7%	6.3%	11.2%
2004	49.2%	34.5%	7.4%	8.9%
2005	46.1%	36.4%	8.8%	8.7%
2006	46.0%	39.7%	9.4%	4.8%
2007	46.9%	38.9%	10.2%	3.9%
2008	45.5%	35.6%	8.5%	10.4%
2009	45.5%	31.1%	7.2%	16.1%
2010	41.2%	28.8%	4.6%	25.4%
2011	53.1%	29.0%	5.2%	12.6%[2]

[1] Excludes balance forward from prior year.

[2] Includes $676.5 million in FY 2011 one-time revenue adjustments. See prior Appropriations Reports for earlier years.

be imposed in any year. Political reality also requires that tax rates remain fairly stable year to year.

1. All the eligible property in the state is assessed by the county assessors or the Arizona Department of Revenue.

2. A temporary budget is established.

3. A compilation of all other revenue sources is made.

4. The revenue is subtracted from the budget.

5. The deficit is then divided into the assessed evaluation of the property in the county and state, and the share of each property owner's portion of the deficits determined to be the tax rate.

The in lieu auto license plate, however, is a special case. Instead of assessing a personal property tax the state applies a number of fees. An auto plate cost consists of a $4 annual

Chart 9-7. FY 2001 vs. FY 2011 Total Operating Spending - All Sources

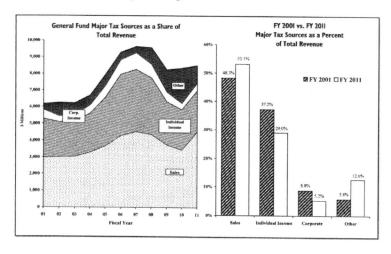

title fee, a $27.50 inspection fee whether conducted or not, and a license fee based on 60% of the manufacturer base retail price. This fee is reduced by 16.25% each year following initial new auto registration.

Chart 9-8. FY 1994 to FY 2009 Total Operating Spending by Fund Source

General Fund Spending as a Percent of Arizona Personal Income

Fiscal Year	Arizona Personal Income ($ in billions)	General Fund Expenditures ($ in millions)	Expenditures % of PI
1994	$ 77.4	$ 3,930.1	5.1%
1995	85.3	4,425.1	5.2%
1996	91.9	4,532.6	4.9%
1997	99.4	4,894.3	4.9%
1998	108.2	5,232.0	4.8%
1999	117.2	5,893.3	5.0%
2000	127.1	6,012.3	4.7%
2001	136.0	6,367.7	4.7%
2002	141.4	6,338.6	4.5%
2003	146.8	6,040.6	4.1%
2004	157.1	6,515.8	4.1%
2005	173.2	7,545.1	4.4%
2006	191.6	8,768.4	4.6%
2007	204.7	10,200.5	5.0%
2008	212.7	10,044.1	4.7%
2009	217.2 *	9,906.2	4.6%

*University of Arizona Economic and Business Research Center Forecast

CHAPTER SUMMARY

✓ Arizona lacks the flexibility in spending enjoyed by the federal government in that it has a constitutional limit on indebtedness.

✓ State legislators have great exposure to their constituencies and are therefore reluctant to raise taxes; the effect is limited services.

✓ The largest single source of state tax revenue is the sales tax.

✓ The Arizona budget has been increasing at a rate of ½ billion a year in recent years and will reach $7 billion in fiscal 2002.

✓ The largest single budget appropriation is for education; no other budget item is even a close second.

✓ If unemployment rises or consumer spending decreases, Arizona revenues are seriously impacted.

✓ The ill-fated alternative fuel incentives program had a major negative effect on the financial reserves of the state.

✓ Arizona ranks poorly among the states in its funding of social services.

✓ The new budget contains "triggers," that is, tax cuts or increased spending provisions, if revenues exceed certain defined levels.

10
COUNTY GOVERNMENT

Arizona had fourteen counties by the time of statehood; it now has fifteen. In 1983, La Paz County was created by dividing Yuma County. The Constitution, Article XII, has defined counties as a body politic and corporate of the state. This has been interpreted to mean that counties are political subdivisions of the state and are primarily responsible for the administration of state functions. Furthermore, the county does not have the separation of powers between the legislative and executive branches found in the national and state governments. The board of supervisors is the legislative branch and is a part of the plural executive branch of the county.

CLASSIFICATION AND JURISDICTION

Counties in Arizona are divided into two classes. Class one counties have 500,000 or more population and have certain prerogatives and limitations. Only Maricopa and Pima counties are currently class one counties. Because the class one and two designation implies greater or lesser importance, the terms larger and smaller will be used to designate the difference in classes of counties.

Sections 5 through 9 of Article XII of the Arizona Constitution were added by the voters in the 1992 election. These additions allow counties with a population of 500,000 or more (Maricopa and Pima counties) to establish a charter form of self government. For charter government to take effect in these counties two votes are required, one to approve the concept and to choose a charter committee to draft the charter, and a second vote would then be taken to allow the voters to approve the charter by majority vote. Maricopa County approved the creation of a 15 member committee to draft a home rule charter. The committee's work was completed in the summer of 1996. After hearings, throughout the county, the final draft was submitted to the voters for their approval at the November 5th 1996 general election. Charter county government would have permitted county voters broad powers over matters of local concern and allowed limited taxation authority if the powers were not in conflict with the Constitution or laws of the state. The proposition did not pass. Charter, or "home rule," county government is quite common in the United States.

To avoid conflict of jurisdiction, the county usually doesn't encroach upon cities in the pursuit of the same or similar services. In Arizona, a coordinating unit made up of representatives of the various cities, towns, and county governments called Councils of Governments (COG) was created in response to a federal government requirement that federal aid projects must be coordinated through a regional planning agency. The largest of these COGs is the Maricopa Association of Governments (MAG). Every county and city in the state is in one of the six regional COGs.

FUNCTIONS OF THE COUNTY

County government is one of the oldest forms of government, and before the urban growth of the past fifty years it was the most important agency for providing human services at the local level. The county poor farm, county old folks home, insane asylum, and orphanage were the mainstay of the welfare system. The county jail, road department, and school were the backbone of local government services. The list of statutory functions is still impressive, but much of the power is gone as the federal government and cities with greater tax resources have usurped the county in the performance of these functions.

Counties have the following functions:

Counties must perform certain election functions by dividing the county into election precincts, registering voters, conducting elections, counting ballots, and certifying the results.

Counties raise revenue by property tax. They must assess the value of private property within the county, register and license vehicles, set the tax rate, issue property tax statements, collect property tax, and provide a board for property tax equalization.

In order to maintain the records that underpin the institution of private property, they record property deeds, mortgages, liens, and other public documents.

They distribute school funds, provide services for schools, and issue warrants for school expenses.

They construct and maintain highways, bridges, and roads.

They provide health care for the indigent and maintain health standards.

They provide legal counsel to the county officials and school districts.

They provide law enforcement, maintain courts, prosecute offenders of state laws, defend indigents accused of crime, and maintain jails.

CONSTITUTIONAL COUNTY OFFICIALS

The constitution provides for the following county officers to be elected: sheriff, county attorney, recorder, treasurer, assessor, superintendent of schools, and at least three supervisors (five in larger counties). County officers shall have four-year terms without limitation to re-election. They take office the first day of January after the November presidential general election. County officers have minimum qualifications which include the following: they must be at least eighteen years old, a resident of the state and county, and be able to read and write English. Salaries for county officials are set by the state legislature by class of county and may be revised periodically. The following chart shows the approved salary schedule (Table 10-1).

TABLE 10-1. County Officials' Salaries
Effective January 1, 2005

OFFICE	500,000 OR MORE	LESS THAN 500,000
Attorney	109,450	109,450
Assessor	67,800	56,500
Recorder	67,800	56,500
Sheriff	89,225	89,225
Superintendent of Schools	67,800	56,500
Supervisor	67,800	56,500
Treasurer	67,800	56,500
Clerk of Superior Court	67,800	56,500

The County Board of Supervisors is composed of one member from each district in the county. There are five districts in Maricopa, Pima, Yuma, Coconino, and Navajo Counties. Three districts are used in the remaining counties. Supervisors need meet only the minimum qualifications. The supervisors choose one of their members to serve as chairperson. As in any multimember board, the authority of the board is limited to actions taken in public meetings as a group.

The supervisors are the legislative body of the county and have the power to pass county ordinances or laws, to approve the budget, and to set property tax rates. Serving as chief executive officers, they have the power to appoint replacements for vacancies in county offices and to exercise general supervisory powers over the other officers. Maricopa County and ten other counties have appointed managers to handle the administration of finance, planning, personnel, purchasing, buildings, and data processing services. The supervisors in all the counties appoint a county clerk to serve as secretary and administrator to the board.

The supervisors also have the power to build and maintain county roads. They are responsible for administering county health and welfare programs and for supervising the expenditure of all county funds. Supervisors also administer the election laws.

The county attorney is required to be a lawyer admitted to the practice of law in Arizona. As chief legal officer the county attorney gives advisory opinions upon request, defends public officials, and represents the county in civil suits. The major job of the county attorney is the prosecution of cases before the Superior Court. The legal department of the county attorney includes numerous assistants.

The county treasurer is required to have only the minimum legal qualifications. The treasurer is the tax collector for the county, school district, and any other special districts with a property tax assessment. The treasurer must prepare and distribute the tax statements, collect the receipts, and safeguard and distribute the funds as directed by law. The treasurer is also required to keep records of the accounts and report the status of accounts to the supervisors and other officials. The management of staff and equipment is a sizable undertaking requiring the services of an honest, energetic, and well-trained person.

The office of sheriff is one of the oldest offices in English history, and was originally known as the Reeve of the Shire, the king's representative in the local area. The basic duties of the sheriff are law enforcement, servant of the Superior Court, and custodian of the jail. To avoid jurisdictional conflict, the sheriff usually investigates crime and enforces the law outside of incorporated areas. The sheriffs office must assist the county attorney in the apprehension of criminals and the preservation and presentation of evidence against the accused. As a servant of the court, the sheriff must serve warrants, subpoenas, and legal papers, conduct sheriff sales to satisfy judgments, repossess property, and in short, carry out the orders of the court. As keeper of the jail, the sheriff is responsible for the safekeeping of prisoners awaiting trial and for administering sentences for those incarcerated in the county jail.

The county recorder has the historical obligation of maintaining the documents that underpin the institution of private property. Property deeds, mortgages, and liens against private property are a matter of public record and must be filed with the county recorder to be enforceable. The recorder is also in charge of the voter registration records and prepares the voter lists for the polls. And finally, the recorder is the officer who conducts elections for national, state, and county officials.

The county assessor is responsible for the classification and evaluation of all the real property within the county. The assessor must check building permits, check title changes, and use field surveys to ensure that property assessments are current. One of the largest jobs of the assessor is the registration of motor vehicles. This task alone requires a large staff and several facilities in larger counties. Personal inconvenience has been reduced considerably with the introduction of rotating expiration dates and mail-in registration.

The county school superintendent must be a certified teacher. The county superintendent administers the state school laws in the county, distributes the state and county funds, and administers the county accommodation schools. County superintendents have some discretion in the performance of their duties and can influence school districts in their operation by the approval or rejection of spending requests, and by influencing the policy-making school boards.

County judges are justices of the peace (see Chapter 8). They are aided in the performance of their duties by elected constables, who perform duties on behalf of justice courts somewhat similar to what sheriffs perform for Superior Courts at their level. The salary of constables, like that of their justices of the peace, is based on a sliding scale formula. Salaries for constables statewide range from a low of $23,500 to a high of $55,654 (effective January 1, 2001). There are no educational or experiential requirements to hold the office of constable.

STATUTORY COUNTY OFFICIALS

The clerk of the Superior Court is elected for a four-year term, and before entering into the duties of the office, shall take the oath of office and give a bond in the sum of five thousand dollars conditional upon faithful performance of the duties of the office and the payment of all moneys which may come into their hands as clerk to the person entitle to receive them. The clerk of the Superior Court and their deputies are also prohibited from practicing law or forming a partnership with an attorney. The clerk is the administrative arm of the court with responsibility for preparing the court docket, scheduling the cases into the court divisions, preparing the jury lists, and impaneling jurors. The clerk's office is also responsible for taking a verbatim account of the actions in a trial and preserving the record. The largest job is to administer the court ordered judgments, fines, fees, and costs, and distribute the proceeds appropriately. Additionally, the clerk issues marriage licenses and takes applications for United States passports.

Counties with community colleges also have elected boards of directors. They serve a five-year staggered term and are elected from districts within the county. Board members must be legally qualified voters residing in the district from which they are elected. Since they are lay representatives of the voters, they are not required to have any special qualifications. Because of their expressed interest in education, they frequently have unique personal educational qualifications and training that goes well beyond the minimum requirements. Board members receive no pay. The board is responsible for the operation of the colleges and serves to make policies and appoint administration, staff, and faculty. It also recommends the budget and sets tuition requirements. The board establishes graduation requirements and grants degrees.

THE COUNTY MANAGER

Arizona is very progressive in the use of the county manager. All but four counties now use this form of professional management to carry out the policy of the board of supervisors. The manager and staff are appointed by the supervisors and serve at their pleasure. The manager usually performs the general services functions of the county government. The manager has no authority to interfere in the operation of any of the elected officials' jurisdiction. Any power the manager may have comes from a close relationship with the supervisors and their power to adopt the budget.

Managers are public sector administrators who generally possess education and experience covering the general fields of government, law, or political science, combined with business administration or accounting, and possessed of good interpersonal skills. A degree in public administration is a close fit, but not necessarily the only fit for these positions. County managers are compensated at a much higher rate than are the elected officials who hire them.

Counties receive income from the property tax, sales tax residue, and federal grants. The largest source of income comes from the property tax. A law imposing a 10 percent limitation on increases in property tax poses a hardship on rapidly growing counties with a fairly small tax base. The second largest source of county income comes from sales tax returned to the county by the state. This formula requires that a percentage of the sales tax collected in a city or county be returned to support local services. Thus market centers receive extra income to support added road construction and maintenance, law enforcement, and other urban services resulting from increased commercial activities. Rural counties sometimes question the fairness of this distribution.

CHAPTER SUMMARY

✓ Arizona counties are administrative subdivisions of state government.

✓ Of Arizona's fifteen counties, the two large counties, Pima and Maricopa, are governed somewhat differently than the other thirteen.

✓ To date charter government does not exist in Arizona counties, although it is well established nationally.

✓ Most county officials and their functions are prescribed in the state constitution.

✓ The salary schedule for county officials is determined by the State Legislature.

✓ Many traditional county functions have been usurped by either strong municipal, or by state and federal governments.

✓ Councils on Government (COGs) coordinate functions among regional local governments.

✓ A substantial majority of Arizona counties employ a professional administrator, a county manager, to carry out the general duties of governance.

11
MUNICIPALITIES

Cities and towns in Arizona are created as a voluntary act on the part of the residents of an area. The act of incorporation determines whether an area can provide services and generate tax to support them. Cities and towns already in existence may annex an area, provide services, and receive revenue without the consent of the population. Although over three-fourths of the population of the state lives in incorporated cities, some of the largest population areas are not incorporated. Sun City, with a population of over 50,000, is not an incorporated city.

TYPES OF MUNICIPAL ORGANIZATIONS

The Arizona State Legislature is charged in Article XIII of the Arizona Constitution with the responsibility for providing for the incorporation of cities and towns by general law. General law towns must have a population of at least 1,500 but less than 3,000; any incorporated place over 3,000 is considered a city. A city of 3,500 or more may frame a charter for its own government, consistent with and subject to the constitution and the laws of the state. All communities may acquire incorporation in two ways. First, they may submit petitions containing signatures of two-thirds of qualified electors in an area requesting incorporation to the County Board of Supervisors. If the community meets all of the legal requirements, the supervisors will declare the community incorporated and appoint the first council immediately. Second, the community may submit a petition signed by 10 percent of the qualified voters to the supervisors requesting an incorporation election. If a majority of the electors in the defined area approves the incorporation, the board will appoint the first city council.

A general law town of less than 1,500 population must have a five-member council elected from the town at large for a two-year term. The council then selects one of its members to serve as mayor. All of these towns were created prior to the 1972 law raising the minimum population to 1,500. A town of between 1,500 and 3,000 has a seven member council elected from the town at large for a two-year term. The council selects one of its members to serve as mayor.

A general law city must have a population of at least 3,000 at the time of incorporation. General law cities elect a seven-member council which selects its mayor from the council itself. A city may choose to select its council from single member districts, and each district must represent an equal portion of the population.

All other officials of a city are appointed by the council. The city or town council serves as both the legislative and executive branch of the city government. As a legislative body, the council creates the departments, funds their operation, sets the qualifications of its officers, and defines their duties. As executives, the council selects the officers, supervises their performance, and promotes, terminates, or replaces officials at its pleasure. While this power may seem extreme and arbitrary, it is modified by national and state laws as well as public opinion. Elected municipal officials are subject to the recall provisions in the state constitution. Recalls are attempted more frequently at the local level than at the county or state level, and tend to be disruptive of government.

CHARTER CITIES

The constitution provides for the incorporation of charter cities in communities of 3,500 or more. Most cities in Arizona have adopted charters which provide them with much greater latitude to organize and perform their urban duties. Charter cities write their own "home rule" charter, which allows them to organize their government structure and exercise any powers not prohibited by a higher law. Most home rule charters have been initiated by city councils. Citizens may initiate a charter if 25 percent of the number of voters voting in the previous municipal election sign petitions requesting that the mayor hold an election. In either case, an election must be held to determine if a majority of the voters wish a charter, and to select fourteen electors from the city who will compose the board of freeholders to write the new charter. At least a majority of the freeholders must agree on the wording of the charter and submit it to the voters for approval. If the charter is ratified by a majority of the voters, it is then submitted to the governor, who shall approve it unless it is in conflict with the state constitution or the laws of the state. Upon approval, it becomes the organic law of the city superseding any charter then existing. Charter cities may have any number of council members elected for any term from the city at large or from districts. Charter cities may pay council members any amount the charter provides. Charter cities also may have a popularly elected mayor who is paid and has powers beyond the council in executive matters. However, in legislative matters the mayor is still just one member of the council with one vote.

Probably the most important difference between general law and charter cities exists in the taxing structure. A charter city may levy any tax not prohibited by state law. Thus charter cities usually have at least a 1 percent city sales tax and may even levy special sales taxes with the permission of the voters.

The city council usually establishes the services and appoints department heads to administer the organization. The chief administrator of a city is the city manager, who is appointed by the council and serves at its pleasure. The departments are under the direct control of the manager. City managers generally adopt a low profile, allowing the elected officials, particularly the mayor, to bask in the public arena. Some of the line agencies, such as personnel and finance, may answer not only to the manager but, also, to the mayor and council. The city clerk serves as a secretary to the council and is often the most important employee of the council when there is no manager. The city attorney and the city magistrate are somewhat independent of the manager and serve the council more directly. Most cities also have advisory boards and commissions which hold hearings, make studies, and make recommendations on topics such as planning and zoning, health, housing, tourism and recreation, transportation, and citizen police review boards. The role of the manager's office is to provide staff assistance to these boards.

City services are provided by the police department, fire department, planning and zoning department, parks and recreation department, sewage and sanitation department, streets and utilities, and a budget or finance department. Each of these departments is headed by a chief or director. Good management policy requires that the manager be responsible for the actions of the departments, and may remove department heads when their performance is unsatisfactory. In reality, the mayor and council will become involved if voter interests are affected.

SCHOOL DISTRICTS AND SPECIAL TAXING DISTRICTS

All cities and towns are entitled to state and federal revenue sharing and the local property tax. Charter cities may have special taxes. The cities may also raise revenue from the sale of utilities, water, and in some cases gas and electricity. City budgets are growing rapidly as they must provide more and more services in a highly complex urban environment. Much has been made of the dependent status of cities and towns since they rely on state law for authority and much of their funding. As Arizona changed from rural to urban dominance, the legislature, in response to urban demands, passed laws that cities wanted. The dependence of cities on legislative action is an inconvenience but not an insurmountable obstacle.

Arizona has two kinds of school districts, the common school and the union high school. In some districts, the boundaries and jurisdiction of the two have been joined into a unified district. The common school district governs the elementary schools, kindergarten through eighth grade; the union high school district governs the ninth through twelfth grades. Each district has a five-member board of trustees which serves a staggered four-year term. The board is responsible for making policy and for supervising the staff, administration, and faculty. The board sets the budget, the dates of the school year, and the educational requirements for the district as long as they are not contrary to state requirements. In a unified district, the same board governs both the common and the union high school districts, using one administrative staff to run both levels of schools. The superintendent of a school district is appointed by, and serves at the pleasure of the board. The administrators and principals of a district are usually responsible to the superintendent. The faculty and staff of a school, although legally employed by the board, are under the supervision of the principal of the school.

Schools receive about 50 percent of their funding from the state by a formula based on average daily membership. The remainder of funds comes from federal revenue grants and local property taxes. The mix of these moneys depends on the nature of the community, its assessed evaluation, and the effectiveness of its staff in attracting funding.

Another form of local governing district is the special taxing district. It can be created for any purpose: flood control, fire protection, water conservation, etc. Such districts can often accomplish what established government cannot accomplish due to such factors as solidarity of purpose, less governmental restriction, and greater flexibility in funding strategies. Quite often special taxing districts are created in unincorporated areas where perceived needed services simply are not being provided by any existing governmental entity. Special taxing districts also have been created to finance quasi commercial ventures such as the building of the multi-purpose sports complex, more popularly known as the Arizona Cardinals Football Stadium.

The special taxing district possesses certain advantages. Specificity of purpose avoids the traditional divisiveness of local government. Control is proximate to its source, and oftentimes, considerable volunteerism reduces overall costs, for example, a fire district with a volunteer fire department. On the negative side, whether the knowledge and the skill level of volunteer organizations is adequate, is an arguable issue.

NEIGHBORHOOD ASSOCIATIONS

Oftentimes overlooked in any discussion of local government is the neighborhood "association." Arizona law (33-1901 through 1907) defines "association" as a nonprofit corporation or an unincorporated association of owners created by a "declaration" (popularly referred to as covenants) to own and operate portions of a planned community, and which has the power to assess association members for expenses entailed in carrying out the declaration.

Planned community refers to real estate owned and operated by a nonprofit corporation or unincorporated association of owners. The stated purpose is to manage, maintain, or improve the property. All owners of individual parcels within the development are required to pay assessments to the association to carry out its purposes.

Association powers include setting architectural standards, establishing landscape schemes, controlling parking and storage, enforcing color themes, and can even mandate the size and position of properties and the use thereof. The intent is to preserve the value of the community, and usually the intent is addressed. But since occasional association officers have run amuck, the Arizona legislature has seen fit to limit the extent to which association powers can be exercised.

Law limits assessment increases to no more than 20 percent of the previous year, limits late payment penalties to the greater of $15 or ten percent of the amount owed, requires open meetings and mandates at least one general meeting annually, establishes stated exceptions to open meetings, and provides for disclosure and exceptions to disclosure of association records. The law further requires the association to provide any new purchaser with all pertinent materials relating to the association, and if failure to do so results in damage to seller or purchaser, remedy against the association is provided.

The 2003 and 2004 legislative sessions placed significant limitations on the powers and practices of homeowner's associations, particularly in the area of foreclosure to enforce liens. Whereas at one time homeowner's associations could actually foreclose on homeowner's to collect both fines and assessments, their ability to foreclose is now limited to non payment of assessments. All other actions are by civil suit. Also, recent legislation forbids homeowner associations from restricting the installation of any external energy conservation device, such as solar panels.

Once a planned community is sufficiently established, association officers are generally elected by the membership at an annual meeting. They possess the legal authority to enforce the declarations of the association, and to assess (a form of taxation) that membership. All enforcement issues of an association are according to civil law. In many respects, associations are a form of local government.

CHAPTER SUMMARY

✓ The creation of a town or city is a voluntary act of the residents of the area in question.

✓ Charter cities allow the citizens to select a government of their choice, subject only to the laws and constitution of the state.

✓ Arizona's charter cities employ a council-mayor structure, with the ordinary affairs of government managed by a professional administrator.

✓ School districts are oftentimes a contentious form of local government.

✓ Special taxing districts may be created to meet the specific needs of a community or region.

✓ Elected municipal officials are subject to the recall provisions contained in the Arizona constitution.

✓ Professional city managers tend to be low profile administrators.

✓ Often overlooked as a form of local government is the neighborhood improvement association.

✓ Perceived abuses by the management of neighborhood improvement associations has led to an increasing of state regulation.

12
TRIBAL GOVERNMENT

Native Americans who are official members of a tribe and who live on a reservation are not only tribal members subject to tribal law, but they are also citizens of the state of Arizona and the United States as well. Native Americans possess the right to vote for state and federal officials, are subject to varying degrees of state law on the reservation, and entirely so off the reservation. In a sense, tribal government is a form of local government, the major characteristic of which is the high degree of autonomy in which it is encased.

Almost one-fourth of Arizona is under tribal law, an area considerably larger than most eastern states. Many stretches of state and federal highways, and some urban streets as well, are on tribal lands. Many of the popular recreational and tourist sites in the state are on tribal lands, and the businesses thereon are owned and/or controlled by the tribe. In urban areas, such as the greater Phoenix area, urban sprawl has provided economic opportunities for nearby tribes as traditional agricultural pursuits give way to shopping centers, casinos, and a variety of other business interests.

Thus, tribal affluence varies greatly. Tribes located in the proximity of urban areas become increasingly entrepreneurial, and are able to provide considerably more service to tribal members than those tribes remote from population centers, and who are lacking in economic opportunities and tend to be much more traditional in their lifestyles. As a consequence, differences between "progressive" and "traditional" mindsets renders it quite difficult to make standardized observations concerning the structure of Arizona's many Indian communities.

ORIGINS OF THE RESERVATION SYSTEM

It is estimated that there were approximately three million indigenous people residing in what was to become the United States when Columbus made Europe aware of the New World. The cultures of European settlers were in almost immediate conflict with those of native peoples.

As the numbers of settlers swelled, this cultural conflict eventually led to the American policy of relocation, that is, the forced removal of native populations from areas desired by the newcomers, and placement in areas deemed undesirable. Fueled by the geographical ignorance generated by the myth of the Great American Desert, coupled with the settlers never ending lust for even more land, native groups were consistently pushed to the trans-Mississippi West, a movement characterized by such ignominious events as the Cherokee "Trail of Tears."

By the time Anglo culture was preparing for an assault on Arizona, settlement had already developed around the region. The continuing push from the east, the Mormon drive across Utah and Nevada, and Mexican settlement in Sonora and Sinaloa, left no unoccupied area to push native populations. The vastness and harshness of the terrain, and the mobility of many of its native inhabitants, also promised a most challenging task for the United States Cavalry. Unlike Oklahoma, whose huge native population consists primarily of transplanted eastern tribes, Arizona's native population is native Arizonian. They were here first; they had neither the place nor the will to go elsewhere, and so they stayed.

One of the actions of the Arizona territorial legislature of 1864 was to request federal aid (this meant the military) in placing all Arizona Indians on reservations. Congress responded with an initial allocation of 75,000 acres for eventual reservations, and began providing funds for this purpose in 1867. Yet, it was the massacre of the Aravaipa Apache by white settlers on April 30, 1871, and their subsequent exoneration by a sham judicial proceeding, that provoked national interest and federal action on the "Indian Issue".

President U.S. Grant appointed agent John Clum to negotiate with the tribes, the purpose of which was to separate them from whites by implementing the reservation system. It was a combination of negotiation and military action that eventually resulted in most Arizona Indians residing on reservations by the late 1870s.

The creation of Arizona's reservations spans more than a century, dating from the Gila River Community (1859) to the most recent Pasqua Yaqui Reservation (1978). Reservation lands account for roughly 27% of the state's land mass, and the lands held by the tribes continue to expand as more affluent tribes purchase adjacent territories for planned economic growth or engage in favorable land swaps with government.

In 1887 Congress passed the Dawes Severalty Act, the purpose of which was to break down tribal identity by introducing private land ownership and establishing assimilation requirements. The failure of this act, coupled with continued growing criticism of it, eventually led to its being replaced with the Indian Reorganization Act of 1934. This latter measure restored aspects of tribal communalism, and also created an array of tribal governmental structures closely modeled after the U.S. Constitution.

In a sense the Indian Reorganization Act was a more covert attempt to break down tribal identity. By creating tribal governments that were microcosms of the U.S. government, the federal government was imposing an alien structure on cultures that were based on kinship and long standing custom. Artificial authorities were created to replace traditional ones. Yet many traditional authorities defied extinction, resulting in a medley of overlapping and confusing lines of governance.

Ten years earlier, the United States Congress, in 1924, passed the Indian Citizenship Act, yet in Arizona, Indian participation in state government was effectively blocked through the enactment of a "literacy test" that remained in existence until 1948.

A few years later, when the Eisenhower administration was involved in some serious discussions over the dismantling of the reservation system, native American "progressives" protested. They had already figured out how to work the system. Power had been placed in the hands of tribal chairpersons and councils, those individuals who had sought to participate, and they increasingly used their power to engage in entrepreneurial activities. Not unchallenged, however, the result was schism in Indian communities as "progressives" and "traditionalists" squared off over the issue of the true course of the Indian future.

TRIBAL GOVERNMENT

There exists no one reservation governmental template. Tribal government exists under national government supervision on lands held in trust by the federal government, but within state boundaries. The key issue is tribal autonomy, or, the right of the tribe to govern itself, but how complete that autonomy is depends on who one asks. Yet certain generalizations can be made concerning tribal government.

There is an elected tribal chairperson and vice chairperson—the executive. The legislative function is handled by an elected tribal council. Council members are elected from prescribed districts on large reservations and at-large on smaller ones. Tribal judges are generally appointed by the tribal chair.

More like a prime minister than a president the tribal chairperson appoints all committees and committee chairpersons. This selection enables the tribal chair to strongly influence the outcome of committee recommendations. A similar observation could be made concerning the appointment of tribal judges. The vice chair generally has the duty of being available should the position of the chair become vacant.

Council members hold regular district meetings on large reservations. On all reservations, large and small, the tribal council tends to meet quarterly to deliberate on issues of concern to the tribe. It is resolutions of the tribal council that govern the tribe. Additionally, council approval is required to validate any tribal contract.

Appointed tribal trial courts handle violations of tribal criminal law and civil suites involving tribal members. A tribal appeals court is generally appointed by the tribal chairperson on a per case basis. The authority of tribal courts dealing with tribal law for tribal members is undisputed. All appeals from tribal courts are through the federal court system. What is an area of potential controversy is the twilight zone between tribal and state government jurisdiction.

State law applies on tribal lands only if Congress agrees and it does not conflict with tribal law. Yet there are some who maintain absolute sovereignty for native Americans and allow that whatever state or federal law operates on a reservation is with the agreement of the tribe, and that agreement may be withdrawn at any time.

The Indian Gaming Act, passed by the Congress, authorized gaming (casinos) on reservations as an economic development measure, but only to the extent allowable by state law. This suggests that the Congress gave the states the authority to regulate gaming on reservations residing within their boundaries, and this is exactly what the state of Arizona attempted to do during the recent Symington administration. Proposition 202 granted the tribes twenty year compacts authorizing casino gambling in exchange for a "voluntary" payment of taxes on their profits. The Proposition further allowed tribes that operated casinos to use the allocation of gambling machines authorized to tribes who chose not to engage in casino gambling, and to share the subsequent profits. The Proposition was generally regarded as a win-win for all parties concerned. Similarly, the United States Supreme Court in 1990, in *Oregon v. Smith*, recognized the power of a state to disallow the use of a hallucinogenic substance (in this case sacramental peyote) in traditional native American religious ceremonies, if the state so chooses. The State of Oregon did so choose, but Arizona has not invoked this decision and native Americans, on the reservation, can use such substances in their traditional ceremonies. Yet the case law suggests that Arizona could disallow the practice, yet how it could be enforced is another matter. So there exists a very broad gray area of jurisdictional never-never land.

THE SOVEREIGNTY ISSUE

In most instances the tribe is sovereign. Non-tribal law enforcement agencies only have jurisdiction on the reservation if the officers involved possess dual certification by agreement between the tribe and the outside jurisdiction. Usually this is limited to pursuit situations involving non-felony offenses (in 1885 the Congress had passed the Indian Major Crimes Act, placing all Indian felony offenses under federal jurisdiction).

Native Americans cannot be extradited from the reservation for trial in state courts. State courts only have jurisdiction on the reservation over issues involving non-Indians committing alleged offenses against other non-Indians. In *Montana v. United States* (1981) the Supreme Court stated that tribes possess inherent power over their internal affairs and civil authority over non-tribal members on their reservations to the extent necessary to protect the integrity of the tribe. This suggests the possibility of considerable litigation. Yet in *Duro v. Reina* (1990) the same court stated that tribes did not have jurisdiction over non-tribal members but could eject "undesirable persons" or detain them and turn them over to non-tribal authorities. Issues of jurisdiction are obviously not well defined.

Any number of agreements or arrangements may exist between a tribe and neighboring political entities or state government. These may involve service or enforcement issues on and off the reservation. They tend to exist more in urban areas. In many instances contractual agreements require the approval of Congress. Further, a tribe cannot be sued without its permission and the permission of Congress as well.

Tribal members pay no state taxes for activities performed on the reservation. Employment off the reservation is subject to state taxation. There is no exemption from federal taxation. A recent issue concerned the enforcement of the state tobacco tax on tobacco products sold on the reservation. The solution was to tax the wholesaler before the products got to the reservation where a jurisdictional dispute most certainly would have occurred.

In *Worcester v. Georgia* (1832), in which the United States Supreme Court claimed exclusive jurisdiction over the territory of the Cherokee Nation, Chief Justice John Marshall referred to Indian tribes as being "dependent nations." Hence, the ongoing controversy over the scope and meaning of such terms as "sovereignty," or "autonomy."

Arizona's Indian Communities

Ak Chin Indian Community
Cocopah Tribe
Colorado River Indian Tribes
Fort McDowell Mojave-Apache Indian Community
Fort Mohave Indian Tribe
Fort Yuma-Quechan Tribe
Gila River Indian Community
Havasupai Tribe
Hopi Tribe
Hualapai Tribe
Kaibab-Paiute Tribe
Navajo Nation
Pasqua Yaqui Tribe
Salt River Pima-Maricopa Indian Community
San Carlos Apache Tribe
San Juan Southern Paiute Tribe
Tohono O'odham Nation

Tonto-Apache Tribe
White Mountain Apache Tribe
Yavapai-Apache Tribe
Yavapai-Prescott Indian Tribe

CHAPTER SUMMARY

✓ The Native American presence in Arizona is quite formidable.

✓ Tribal lands account for approximately 27% of the state land mass.

✓ Arizona's Indians are indigenous to the region; they were not relocated here from some other part of the country.

✓ The federal government engaged in a number of futile attempts to destroy tribal identity.

✓ In general tribal government is a loosely structured version of other governmental levels in the United States.

✓ The line of appeal on reservation issues is through the federal court system rather than the Arizona court system.

✓ A significant issue from the tribal perspective is one of sovereignty—the right of self-government.

✓ The national government tacitly recognized sovereignty when it negotiated treaties with indigenous peoples, thereby acknowledging nation status.

✓ The current issue is not one debating the existence of sovereignty, but rather its extent (absolute or relative).

13
ARIZONA TODAY

The relatively new discipline of futurism purports to identify current trends in order to project possible futures and the consequences of these futures. This process is partially speculative, in that the very act of identifying and projecting trends can bring about intervention that will alter them. Many of the trends in Arizona are easily discernible. Some are controlled by external forces. Others are based simply on how decision makers choose to view the world. Still others are moored in stark statistical data. This chapter will identify these trends and attempt to project the course of a rapidly growing state.

A STATE DIVIDED

There are two Arizonas, or, better still, there are two perceptions of what Arizona is, or should be. During the candidate debates of the 1998 state legislative elections, Republican candidates rather universally cited a $523 million budget surplus and their record of cutting income taxes by some 28% during the Nineties, as their outstanding achievements. Democratic candidates countered with charges that the surplus should never have been; the funds should have been allocated for many Arizona social programs that rank in the lower half nationally when compared with other states.

They further questioned the wisdom of cutting taxes while many unresolved issues face the state.

Republicans see a prospering Arizona, and believe that lower taxes will further stimulate the economy and attract more business and workers to the state. Democrats see an Arizona that one poll cited as one of the worse places to raise one's children. What kind of Arizona is it? While many live in poverty, while the state has the dubious honor of one of the highest high school drop out rates in the nation, the state boasts of a higher than average standard of living, more pleasure boats per capita than any other state except Florida, and with an ample supply of golf courses and prestigious resorts.

Until recently Arizona boasted one of the lowest unemployment rates in the nation coupling it with a booming economy. The bulk of all new jobs were either in information age industries or the hospitality industry, both of which are included in the general category of "service industry." Prior to the economic meltdown the construction industry was a prime mover in the economy.

There exists no consensus for the future. Long standing Arizonians tend to adhere to the romanticized frontier notions of rugged American individualism—fairly common among the western states. Newcomers to the state, on the other hand, have been mellowed by past experiences of living in states that have had long standing social agenda programs. There exists a general western reluctance to devote energy and resources to social issues. Opportunity abounds; take advantage of it! Yet, many of the newcomers come from areas where the prevalent attitude favors a proactive government in these areas.

Long time Arizonians had disproportionate political power, not by deceit, but rather by default, so their views continue to prevail. Newcomers are slow to socialize into the political scene, and there is also a reluctance to fully accept them until they have "paid their dues." Distrust for the cartpetbagger is a legacy of territorial days that is still alive. Newcomers tend to divide their loyalties between their adopted state and "back home." There is also an attitude among some of the many retirees now living in the state not to support measures they might never see to completion, and also to vote against measures that might increase their taxes.

CHANGING DEMOGRAPHICS

Changing demographics and time partially solve this dilemma. The newcomers are the numerical majority and they will eventually become Arizonans, if not this generation, then definitely the next. And they will eventually influence actively the future course of the state. Traditional concerns reflected by public opinion polls rank education, family, social services, and crime. Of course, superseding these concerns is the ongoing budget crisis. Governmental action always involves an increase in expenditures. Increased expenditures should lead to an increase in revenues, something the state has been reluctant to address in recent years. Ultimately, the question is whether Arizonans are willing to pay for what they want.

The 2000 Census counted 5,131,000 people living in Arizona, making it the twentieth most populated state. Of that number, 668,000 were age 65 or older, representing 13% of the total population. The 60 to 64 age group accounted for another 203,700 individuals, creating a 60 plus age group that reflected 17% of the statewide population. The Census also counted 304,000 people who were age 75 or older.

The 45 to 60 age group contained 866,600 individuals, and these individuals are obviously moving into the 60 plus age group on an annual basis. Due to ever increasing longevity, this movement will swell the ranks of the senior population considerably in the near future. The Arizona Department of Economic Security has predicted that by 2020 approximately 1,756,000 Arizonians will be age 65 or older, accounting for 24% of the projected population by that date Along with Florida, Arizona leads the nation as a retirement state.

Increased numbers results in increased political power. In 2000, the voters in Proposition 104 froze property tax rates for specified low-income level seniors. And although all privately held real property in Arizona is subject to taxation, Proposition 105 passed in 2000, exempted cemetery plots from property taxes. Meanwhile, Proposition 204 allowed for the expansion of eligibility for Arizona's Health Care Cost Containment System (health care for low income people), to be financed out of Arizona's estimated $3.2 billion tobacco settlement funds. This money is to be paid out over twenty-five years, and will also be earmarked for funding those programs that have been insufficiently funded through lottery proceeds. Yet the state was overly optimistic in projecting both funds and costs. Further, future lottery earnings have been pledged to cover current economic shortfall.

Although most retirees bring a lifetime of accumulated savings to their retirement haven, currently estimated to add $400 million annually to the states' economy, catastrophic health costs could quickly erode away their savings, leaving them in need of state services. In any event major expenses are eminent: increased health care costs, protective services, managed health care facilities, recreational programs, and senior centers, to name a few. Related issues involve segregated communities for retirees, and in some instances, varying degrees of tax exemptions for these communities. Seniors are living longer, are healthier, and are more active. They are increasingly more active politically. They possess the right to vote, exercise that right, and by sheer strength of numbers will increasingly become a political force in the state.

At the opposite end of the generational spectrum, there exists a growing number of childbearing couples moving to the state. Additionally, the birth rates of traditionally oriented populations, of which Arizona is amply blessed, are higher than national averages. Parents will increasingly demand more and better schools, a variety of family aid programs, enhanced safety, and more concern for environmental issues, to name a few. All of these translate into dollars. According to the 2000 Census, 30% of Arizona's population is under nineteen years of age.

Arizona has been making progress in these areas. Statistics can be used for any purpose. In dollars per capita spent on certain programs, Arizona tends to rank in the bottom half nationally. Yet in percentage increase of dollars spent on the same programs Arizona tends to rank near the top. And this is indicative of measured movement to recognize and resolve issues facing the state. The reader is directed to Arizona Department of Economic Security Annual Report for much informative data on the states' performance.[1] Unfortunately, the budget crisis fiscal 2007 forward and the Special Legislative Sessions of fiscal 2010, have drastically reversed and in some instances obliterated earlier progress.

---

[1] Contact: DES, Office of Policy, Planning and Project Control at (602) 542-2106, or view the state web site.

ENVIRONMENTAL ISSUES

Environmental concerns are very real in the modern world. The debate over pollution, global warming, deforestation, etc., has been well publicized. Residents of Arizona during the pre Columbian era left little mark on the environment. Their numbers were relatively small and their lifestyle was in harmony with nature. With the massive influx of people, with urbanization and industrialization, with a Now Generation attitude, there is serious concern for the future of the state, where the desert environment itself compounds the problem. There is such a thing as natural pollution, and desert environments are abundantly possessed of it. Low humidity and limited rainfall, coupled with sparse vegetation, allow for considerable airborne particles (a positive side effect is a beautiful sunset). Agriculture is more polluting than in areas of abundant rainfall; the dust cloud generated by one tractor is visible for miles. Construction, anything that disturbs the environment, appears to pollute exponentially. Various regulations and procedures are used to reduce the problem, but none have actually resolved it.

This is in addition to standard automobile and industrial pollution. Thermal inversion often traps these particulates in urban areas located in desert valleys. The Valley of the Sun, wherein the greater Phoenix area is located, is a prime example. Fortunately, many industries in Arizona are high tech "clean" industries, but pollution from automobiles and diesel trucks, as growth outdistances freeway construction, continues to be a problem. The state is struggling with these issues in its urban areas.

Other environmental issues result from irrigation, the importation of plants and landscaping themes that require ample quantities of it, and the proliferation of swimming pools and golf courses, that coincidentally raise the humidity. The introduction of non indigenous plants, although attractive to the eye, only add to the pollen problem. And the paving of the desert provides a prime example of heat island effect. Current night time low temperatures run consistently higher than average or normal lows. The issue really is: can we learn to live with the environment, or will we remain insistent on changing it?

Many of the characteristics bringing people to the state, the pristine desert environment, the favorable climate, and the scenic beauty, are at risk. Deserts cannot support heavy use without heroic intervention, and if damaged they heal slowly or not at all. A desert is an extremely fragile ecosystem. Destroy it and it may never recover, or, it may take a lifetime to recover. When unthinking individuals destroy a stately saguaro by using it for target practice, they may very well be destroying in minutes what nature took a century to create. There is a limit to how much the desert can withstand. Already there is the beginning of limited access to some highly popular sites. Picturesque Slide Rock is occasionally closed due to high bacterial count. Access to Sabino Canyon is by tram or on foot; discussion over prohibiting private automobiles in Grand Canyon National Park is currently underway. Popular hiking trails in urban areas are sometimes closed for repair and maintenance.

Even in the high country, where the air is pure, the press of urbanites escaping the desert heat is taking a toll on the environment. Building requirements in the high country are becoming more stringent. Forest fires, often manmade, are an ever present danger. Human miscalculation places a tremendous strain on government, as search and rescue operations are both commonplace and expensive.

Much of Arizona is designated wilderness area. The state tries to enforce its protected species legislation. It tries to protect people from themselves and allow for enjoying the natural beauty of the state without destroying it. It is a most difficult balancing act. Yet, Arizona voters have sent a conflicting message to their government. In the 2000 election, propositions mandating urban growth planning, relating to wildlife management, and a state trust lands and conservation initiative, were all defeated. Apparently Arizona's love for its environment has its limitations.

No discussion of a desert environment can exclude the topic of water. There both is and is not enough water to accommodate Arizona's phenomenal growth. The region where most of the states' population live averages around 7" of rainfall annually. Some parts of the lower Sonoran Desert average less; mountainous regions do somewhat better. But there is no question that Arizona is a desert. Prior to the twentieth century rivers were either trickles and pools or roaring walls of water that quickly disappeared. Massive water conservation efforts such as the Salt River Project and the Central Arizona Project, plus the building of numerous other dams and reservoirs, retained the water when it did come and directed it to where it was needed. The watersheds that funnel into Arizona's few rivers provide massive quantities of water. But nature can be fickle and droughts do occur, so concern for the future must always be present.

Agriculture currently accounts for better than 80% of water usage in Arizona. If the rate of urban growth continues, and water is used as it is currently, competition between agriculture and urbanization will occur. Strong vested interests and deep seated cultural attitudes would make for a most difficult situation. In both California and Nevada water demands of urban centers won out over agriculture and ranching. A healthy economic climate requires a win-win resolution.

Water usage cannot be separated from economic concerns. It is one thing to be critical of the ever increasing number of golf courses in Arizona, but the golfing industry employs 17,000 and brings over $1 billion in revenues to the state each year. People want their swimming pools, their green belts, and their plush landscaping. These things constitute the externals of the lifestyle being sought in the Southwest. They are accustomed to water on demand.

Much of our drinking water comes from deep wells. The water table has been dropping at alarming rates. The state has in place a plan to restore and preserve our underground water supply, but again, the underground reservoir was created in geological time. Programs for conservation, zeroscaping, low yield faucets and toilets, selective use of gray water for irrigation, are all being implemented. Water is a limited natural resource, to be treated with respect. But the basic problem with water is a political problem. Leading state legislators are divided on the issue. Some seek a comprehensive long-term water conservation plan. Others see little need to do much of anything. Both sides do a lot of talking. The urgent drought conditions of 2004 were diminished temporarily as reservoirs were filled by the heavy rains of 2005. But this was followed by below average rain 2006–2009, while 2010 looks more promising. Rainfall averages are just that—averages.

EDUCATION

Arizona has not ranked well historically among the states in the category of education, but the state has made substantial progress in recent decades, particularly the

Nineties. For the better part of the states' history there existed no ground swell of need expressed for a well developed statewide educational system. Agriculture, mining, and ranching did not seem to require a formal education. It really needs to be emphasized, to put Arizona's position in perspective, that Arizona has become a very different place in an extremely short time. In 1940 the entire population of the state was under one half million. Phoenix counted a population of 65,000. By 1950, after the wartime defense boom, the population of Phoenix approximated 100,000. The percentage of people living in rural areas versus urban areas has transposed itself over the last fifty years, radically changing expectations of government.

Three major developments have changed the manner in which the population views education. One, the state is experiencing phenomenal economic growth, and a significant percentage of new jobs are information age jobs, requiring considerable education. Two, a majority of the people moving into the state come from areas that have had well developed educational systems of long standing, and there is an expectation of same in their adopted state. Three, there now exists a tremendous amount of public data with which to compare oneself.

The 2008 K-12 budget earmarked $4.4 billion and another $1.1 billion for the state universities. Under threat of heavy fines by the United States District Court the state legislature allocated $40 million for additional English language instruction. The legislature has approved full day kindergarten funding and start up funds for a Phoenix based medical school. Another educational enactment provided business tax credits for donations to private schools for scholarships, termed "school choice."

Educational budgets take a major hit whenever there is an economic downturn. The reason is simple. The educational budget is the largest state expenditure, has the greatest critical mass, and is therefore susceptible to nibbling away. The fiscal 2009 and 2010 budgets reduced K-12 spending $272 million and university funding by $90 million. Full day funded kindergarten was cut back to half day and numerous new initiatives were put on hold. Further cuts in the K-12 budgets are unlikely due to MOE requirements, even though it constitutes 47% of the general fund budget.

A positive recent development has been the development of the Arizona Instrument to Measure Standards, better known as the AIMS test. An initiative of former State Superintendent of Public Instruction Lisa Graham Keegan, the program requires periodic testing of students for grade advancement, and ultimately, to qualify to graduate from high school. Controversy has arisen over AIMS in that an alarming number of students are not passing, particularly the math portion of the test. Since Arizona already witnesses a significant high school drop out rate, the fear is that failure to pass the test will only serve to further increase the drop out rate. Due to the high rate of students not passing the AIMS test for high school graduation, the state legislature voted to disregard test results if students had successfully passed the courses the content of which they failed on the AIMS test.

One national study ranked states from "smart" to "dumb." Rankings were based on state comparisons of pupil expenditure, reading and math proficiency, graduation rates and average class size, none of which necessarily is an indication of smartness or dumbness. Arizona ranked 48th in the study. Certainly that ranking is highly arguable, but it does indicate that Arizona has a challenge. The Goldwater Institute has announced that improvement in educational attainment is painfully slow. As of 2007 one half of Arizona's fourth graders scored beloe "basic" in reading. This refers to basic literacy achievement by age 10. According to United States census figures 2008 16.3% of Arizona residents 25 years of age or order lack a high school diploma. Currently, 23,000 Arizona high school students drop out each year. Only 30% of Arizona high school graduates start college; 15% of that number actually complete a 4 year degree. How does this equate for high paying jobs or the ability to attract new industry?

Shock waves ruminated through Arizona in 2000 when, according to one study, the state was given the distinction of being the worst state in which to raise children. The study took into account school dropout rate, the number of children living in poverty (22% according to the 2000 Census), availability of social programs, programs for children, etc., in reaching its conclusions. Whether Arizona deserves to be ranked at the bottom is arguable. What is certain, however, is that the state has some distance to climb into the upper third.

In 1994, the state authorized the creation of charter schools as one way of filling in gaps in the educational system. Charter schools are publicly funded private schools that must display evidence of enhanced student performance in order to continue. During the 2006–2007 academic year, 84,404 students attended Arizona's 469 charter schools. The Center for Educational Reform has awarded Arizona high marks for its charter school system, based on the strength of the law that created it and the supervision of the Arizona State Board for Charter Schools. Approximately 8% of Arizona's public school enrollment is to be found in charter schools.

Yet a front page headline in the *Arizona Republic,* dated May 22, 2001, claimed that Arizona had the highest high school dropout rate in the nation (the text of the article listed a tie with Nevada for this dubious honor). The rate listed was 17%.

Higher education has done well in the state, bearing in mind the University of Arizona was founded two hundred fifty years after the founding of Harvard College. The Thunderbird School of International Management is ranked number one in the nation for its area of specialization. The Maricopa Community College District is a recognized national leader. The three state universities now serve over 110,000 students; a number of faculty, departments and programs have received national acclaim. There are more than 250 post secondary institutions in the state. This figures includes trade and technical schools, private and public degree granting colleges and universities, and the state community college system. There are approximately 350,000 students enrolled in colleges and universities throughout the state. 23.5% of Arizona's population past the age of 25 possess a four year degree or higher.

The biggest state educational concern is that of keeping students in school. Some Arizona employers have claimed there is a lack of sufficiently skilled individuals to perform basic jobs. 24% of Arizona adults have not graduated from high school, and among adult Hispanics the percentage is double. Without a basic education employment opportunities simply do not exist. There are monumental socioeconomic implications to be derived from this data.

The biggest problem concerns how to keep students in school. Twenty-four percent of Arizona adults have not graduated high school, and a report prepared by the Arizona

Hispanic Chamber of Commerce, entitled *Datos*, estimates that 48% of adult Hispanics have not completed high school.[2] There are monumental socioeconomic implications to be derived from this data.

ECONOMIC DEVELOPMENT ISSUES

The economic base of the state and its educational emphasis are inextricably intertwined. Historically, the Arizona economy was based on copper, cattle, and cotton, to which was eventually added, climate. The Arizona Mining Association lists the state as the leading mining state in the nation, with $5 billion in annual production. The Arizona Cotton Growers Association lists the state as number two in the production of Pima cotton.

But Arizona is moving in the direction of a more diversified economy. The Napolitano administration is actively pursuing development in the bio tech industry.

According to the *Western Blue Chip Economic Forecast,* Arizona is number two among the states in non-farm economic growth (2004) and is projected to maintain that position. The Government Performance Project report entitled "Grading the States, 2005," gave the state a rating of "B" for overall government management, citing in particular, the states' handling of budget issues. Only seven states received a higher ranking in the report. At the same time the state government is losing public employees (11% voluntarily left government employment during 2003). The report does not cite reasons, but in general, public sector jobs have not

---

[2]These figures should not be confused with high school graduation rates, which currently approximate 81%.

kept pace with private sector jobs. The report also noted that the infrastructure of the state was not keeping pace with population growth.

At the opening of the new century Arizona was tied with Nevada for the lowest unemployment rate in the nation. As of April, 2008, the unemployment rate was 3.8%, one of the lowest in the nation. But over the preceding twelve months the job growth rate has been a negative 4.9%. Personal income is rising faster than the national average, but individual annual income remains below the national average. The service area, which includes information age jobs as well as recreation, amusement and hotels, accounted for 26% of Arizona jobs in 2004. Arizona construction ranked number four among the states in growth, accounting for 8% of all non-farm jobs. High tech industries account for almost half of all manufacturing jobs. Only two high tech companies are among the top ten employers in Arizona. The largest single private sector employer in the state is Wal-Mart. Four other retailers are in the top ten list.

Too much reliance on a single industry can have dire economic consequences. During the year following 9/11 Arizona tourism dropped 22%. Since tourists spend money, and since the state relies heavily on sales tax as a revenue source, the state took a major financial hit. Currently (mid 2005) tourism is a $12 billion industry.

High technology manufacturing adds $33 billion annually to the economy. Since much of this is defense and communications related, it should not be negatively impacted. Agriculture and mining, once combined with cattle, to provide the economic mainstay of the state, now only account for 2.2% of all jobs. Agricultural jobs pay rather poorly, whereas the highly dangerous mining jobs, pay reasonably well. Certain industries take full advantage of available cheap labor from across the Mexican border, thereby holding down the overall wage scale.

In October, 2000, the Corporation for Enterprise Development conferred a mixed rating on Arizona. The state received high marks for creating new jobs promoting business growth. But it received low marks for its poverty levels, for income disparity, and for educational funding. It is to be noted that 12% of Arizona's families ranked below the poverty level, while almost 13% have incomes of $100,000 or above. These figures have changed very little. As of 2005 Arizona ranks 46th among the states in real per capita personal income.

As of the end of 2007 Arizona per capita personal income was $32,411. Personal income growth was the smallest among the fifty states in 2007, largely the result of the collapse of the housing market, but possibly also due to the tough Employer Sanctions Law that has driven some workers and even a few small businesses out of the state.

The Washington based Corporation for Enterprise Development is a non profit organization that annually rates all fifty states according to seventy indicators. These indicators are understandably challenged by states that do not fare well in the ratings.

In the two years following December 2007, Arizona lost 9.8% of its workforce, a total of 280,000 jobs. Many were due to a collapsing construction industry that had driven much of the earlier boom. Fast jobs means less purchasing power and has a trickle effect on the economy, as retailers, entertainment outlets, and restaurants consequently reduce their work force. Projections for a quick rebound in the job market, necessary for the recovery of economic health in the state, are not particularly bright.

Chart 13-1

How did we get here?

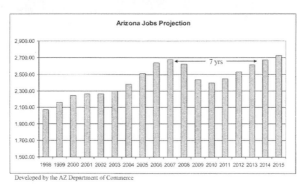

Arizona Jobs Projection

Developed by the AZ Department of Commerce

January 08, 2010   Office of Governor Janice K. Brewer

Arizona has been a major benefactor of NAFTA. During the first three years of its existence, Arizona exports to Canada and Mexico have increased by 55%. Mexico is Arizona's largest trade partner. High tech exports to Asia have been a major factor in Arizona's hot economy, but the financial crisis in that part of the world is beginning to have a major impact on that portion of the state's export business.

Mature American magazine has listed Prescott, Scottsdale, and Tucson in the top five of best places to retire in the Untied States. While retirees help swell the population growth figures for the state, mention should also be made of annual winter visitors who are estimated to add another $1 billion to the states' economy. Rising gasoline and airfare costs could seriously impact this resource.

Construction has been a very bright spot for the Arizona economy. For a number of years it could not keep pace with the demand and home prices escalated. Unfortunately, a considerable portion of the demand turned out to be a speculative "bubble." In 2006 alone the average price of a home in the greater Phoenix area increased by 47%. Part of the increase was due to the demand generated by population growth, but a large part was also due to real estate speculation. A number of investors bought with the intention of immediately selling or "flipping" and reap an instantaneous profit. For a time such was the case. One financial analyst likened the real estate market to the day trading that rocked the stock market several years ago. At issue is affordability. Rising prices remove home buying from the reach of many prospective buyers. Arizona wages are below the national average and fewer individuals, especially first time home buyers, could qualify for traditional home mortgages. So creative financing entered the market—the sub-prime fiasco. Hit especially hard has been the "starter home" communities, but the mortgage mess has had a ripple effect throughout the real estate market. Arizona is experiencing considerable home foreclosures.

Population growth helps fuel the construction industry, expands the financial services sector, and adds to retail sales. It also puts a strain on the existing infrastructure which always seems to be in a state of becoming. Numerous sources have ranked Arizona quite favorably as a place to do business, start a business, or to advance one's career. But then came the economic meltdown and Arizona's immigration policies.

Arizona ranks above the national average in the commission of crimes, but it also ranks near the top for expenditures for crime prevention, and the state incarceration rate is also above the national average. Juvenile violent crime ranks slightly below the national average. Part of the crime rate can be attributed to the two Arizona interpretation outlined at the beginning of this chapter. The gap between rich and poor is widening in this state, and this is not without profound ramifications. Part of the crime rate can also be attributed to the high transitional population in Arizona. With boom era growth the state can hardly be classified as a stable area. It is in transition and there is a price to be paid for change.

Arizonians drive slightly more than the national average, but in traffic deaths per miles driven, it ranks near the top. In 1990 Arizona ranked 39th among the states in least number of fatal traffic accidents. As of 2005 it had dropped to 47th. Red light running, excessive speed and tailgating are the principle factors. Yet legislation was introduced during the 2005 session to raise some state speed limits to 80 mph; fortunately, it failed. Part of this can be attributed to the large number of visiting drivers in the state who might not be familiar with local driving issues. But it is also due to congestion, impatience, carelessness, road rage, and seemingly never ending road construction. It should be noted, too, that many miles of Arizona's roads are mountainous, or isolated monotonous stretches given to road hypnosis or primitive and/or unimproved.

IMPLICATIONS OF CENSUS 2000

Arizona is a culturally diverse state. According to the 2000 Census, the white population of the state is 3,873,611, comprising 75.5% of the total population. This population is overwhelmingly urbanized. The African-American population is 158,873, or 3.1% of the total population. It, too, is overwhelmingly urbanized, and resides primarily in Maricopa County. The Asian-American population is 98.969, or 1.5%

of the population, and it is also highly urbanized. The Hispanic population is widely dispersed. Lower income Hispanics tend to live in rural areas or in barrios. Upper income Hispanics are more generally dispersed, urbanized, and tend to live in those communities that reflect their economic status. Hispanics account for 1,295,617 individuals, or 25.3% of the population. Hispanics may be of any race. Native Americans number 255,879. This translates as 5% of the population, and almost exclusively resides on reservations. Approximately two-thirds of Arizona's Native population resides in Apache, Coconino, and Navajo counties. The Census provided for a new designation in 2000, that being Multi-Race. 146,526 Arizonians identified with this designation, representing 2.9% of the population. Minorities now account for 36.2% of Arizona's population.

Of note is the age distribution of certain groups. 38% of Hispanics, 39% of Native Americans, and 32% of African-Americans, are under the age of 18. Only 21% of non-Hispanic whites are under the age of 18. This strongly indicates increased minority presence in years to come. The male and female mix is fairly even for all groups. The average age in the state is 34, which is close to the national average. Hispanics are the youngest average age group in America, and were it not for the presence of large numbers of seniors in the state, would drive down the average age of the state considerably. 59.9% of the state population resides in Maricopa County, which contains the greater Phoenix metropolitan area. The county now has a population of over three million people. Added to Pima County, home of the greater Tucson metropolitan area, and the percentage of total state population becomes 76.3%. This leaves 23.7% of the population to be divided up among the remaining thirteen counties, which by comparison, are quite rural.

An editorial in the *Arizona Republic* concerning Proposition 201, passage of which abolished legal cockfighting in the state, pointed out that the underlying substantive issue in the proposition was not cockfighting. The issue was one of conflicting values between rural, or Old Arizona, and the highly urbanized New Arizona. By sheer force of numbers, the New Arizona will eventually win out.

According to the United Health Federation, in 2004 Arizona ranked 23rd as a healthy state. The state was ranked 32nd by the same organization in 2003. The reason for the improvement is state government support of public health and recent efforts to improve Child Protective Services. Yet drug and alcohol dependency is above the national average (5.3% for Arizona and 4.8 nationally), prenatal care is absent in 31.3% of pregnancies, and children living below the poverty line stands at 19.1%. There remains a substantial underclass in the state.

These conditions are partly due to Arizona's obsession with being a "business friendly" state. The term translates into low business taxes, minimal regulation and cheap wages. Low taxes results in low funding of state social welfare programs, which in turn, results in Arizona ranking poorly in many state comparison categories. Enhanced living standard is not fueling the economy; population growth minus quality of life issues is doing it. As numerous articles in the *Arizona Republic* have indicated, the economy of Arizona is booming, unless one looks closely beneath its surface.

IMMIGRATION

A highly significant issue concerns illegal immigration. Arizona is the remaining principle corridor for illegals to enter the United States from the south. Arizona possesses a significant population of Hispanic origin (approximately 30%), mostly from Mexico, and most are United States citizens. There remains a constant illegal crossing of the international border by individuals who are seeking economic opportunities in the United States. Most of these individuals are from Mexico, but the countries of Central America are well represented.

It is to be noted that the Treaty of Guadalupe–Hidalgo (1848) and the Gadsden Purchase Treaty (1853) conferred United States citizenship on the Mexican inhabitants of the regions acquired if they did not declare to the contrary within one year. So many modern day Mexican-Americans can trace their legal lineage back over a century and a half.

It is also to be noted that "issues" with immigrant groups have always been part of American "nativist and attitudes." Irish, Italian, Chinese, Puerto Rican, and many other groups, were all at one time or another viewed as detrimental to the interest of America. Arguments of diminished wages, increased crime, the corruption of American culture have been present since the foundation of the republic. Unique regarding the current immigration issue, however, is the immediate proximity of the border.

Immigration was mainly a non-issue before the 20th century. A major reason was the lack of population in Mexico. Around the 1880's there was a significant spike in the Mexican birth rate, which would result in a greatly expanded population looking for work around 1900. This led to some incidents. Also, the policies of Porfirio Diaz dispossessed many Mexican small farmers. The Ejido movement consolidated small farmers into large rancheros, at the expense of many small farmers. Pressure brought many to the United States seeking employment in the area in which they were most skilled. In the World War I era Goodyear Rubber moved part of its operation to Arizona and encouraged citrus growers to convert to cotton production (cotton was then being used to reinforce rubber tires and to provide the covering for aircraft of the day). The call went out to 30,000 Mexican agricultural workers, resulting in labor camps such as Litchfield Park.

Between the world wars Mexicans were unwelcomed again. The disillusionment and the isolationistic tendencies of the United States during the twenties saw only the white Anglo Saxon Protestant as a worthy addition to the country. With the depression, the competition for jobs rendered a variety of immigrant groups undesirable. At one point President Herbert Hoover blamed the depression on cheap Mexican labor destroying American jobs. Still, a little progress for Arizona's Hispanic minority was achieved through various New Deal recovery programs during the 1930's.

The 1940's brought massive changes, some good and some not so good. The United States government had tremendous labor needs during World War II. The Emergency Labor Program of 1942, also known as the bracero program called for Mexico to send 220,000 farm workers to the United States. Later, an additional request was made for 68,000 railroad workers. In exchange the U.S. would guarantee non-discriminatory wages (fixed at 30 cents an hour) and promised a "bonus" for those braceros who stayed for the duration of the war. The federal government then "opened" the border. As word spread throughout Mexico of what was then regarded as a good wage, workers poured into the United States. The American government then claimed it could not distinguish between braceros and other workers. Some of the higher wage guarantees remained in place due to the extreme shortage in the wartime labor force; the bracero bonuses, however, were never paid. The border remained open until 1954 in order to attract cheap labor for the postwar economic boom. Bracero contracts officially ended in 1964.

The Servicemen Readjustment Act of 1944 (G.I. Bill) to some extent aided all minorities. The sixties ushered in an era of protest. Yuma resident Cesar Chavez organized the National Farm Workers Association in 1962 that led to the "no uvas" boycott. By 1969 the term "chicano/a" had come into existence. A growing pride was festering in Mexican-American communities that were becoming increasingly urbanized.

In the seventies the postwar economic boom ended, and with it came a return to American "nativism." Immigrants had become a problem again. A highly touted solution to the issue of illegals was the Immigration Reform and Control Act of the Reagan Administration. Principle among its provisions was the granting of amnesty to those illegals seeking to make their status legal. But more than two decades later the issue remains. The economy of the United States attracted job seekers, some legal and many not. How many? No one really knows. How does one accurately count illegals?

There are two sides to the issue. From the perspective of the illegals and their supporters, they are merely seeking economic opportunities that are not available to them in their respective homelands. They generally take the lowest paid jobs and provide essential services for the rest of society. Most are law-biding individuals who are seeking a better life for themselves and their families. Opponents see them as illegally taking jobs, driving down the wage scale and avoiding the paying of taxes in the process. And since federal law mandates that anyone in the United States is entitled to certain basic benefits they can receive health care and education at taxpayer expense. This is a federal issue, calling sensible immigration and work permits laws, but there are major ramifications for the state. It is estimated that 4000 illegals cross through Cabeza Prieta National Wildlife Refuge each week. The 56 mile border region is patrolled by four rangers. In the Tucson border sector the Border Patrol apprehended 35,704 individuals during the month of January 2005. It also seized 35,000 pounds of marijuana. (Drug dealers also cross the border). Ranchers along the border tell stories of destroyed fences, contaminated water, slaughtered cattle, abandoned vehicles and human waste, on their property. The pristine desert environment itself is under siege.

Overall control by the federal government appears to be quite ineffectual. So locals have taken up the "defense" of the border, creating such movements as the Minutemen who, at their own expense patrolled the Naco region of the border to stop the illegal flow. The activity received considerable negative publicity in the national press but enjoyed the support of a majority of Arizonians (57%).

Led in large measure by State Senator Russell Pearce, Arizona has taken the national lead in state legislation concerning illegal immigration. And some additional legislation on the subject has been the result of voter initiative. In 2000 voters banned bilingual education, federal court orders not withstanding. In 2004 the Arizona Taxpayers and Citizens Protection Act required proof of citizenship in order to vote and to receive any state funded services other than emergency.

In 2006 proof of citizenship was required to qualify for in-state tuition at Arizona's universities. Bail was denied for illegal's accused of crimes. Civil lawsuits brought by illegal's were banned. English was established as the official language of the state. The year also witnessed passage of a tough employer sanction law, requiring employers to verify the citizenship status of their employees. The law has had some negative impact on Arizona's economy, but its supporters believe the price is worth paying. Data indicates that Arizonians approve of the measures in the 60–70% range.

Exact impact of illegals in the economy is impossible to determine, either positively or negatively. Hard data simply does not exist. And both sides on the issue tend to overstate their claims. Some data suggest illegals commit less crime than the general population, if for no other reason than to avoid drawing attention to themselves. Most of the crime is in some way related to the drug cartels. Most illegals do pay taxes. Via fake social security numbers they pay income and social security taxes. Those in the economic underground still contribute to the economy by paying sales and other taxes. According to the Department of Homeland Security Arizona's undocumented as of January 2008, was 560,000, and dropped to 460,000 by January 2009. How you count people for which no record exist is for the reader to determine.

The Immigration Act of 2010 is the latest effort by the state to control illegal immigration. The law makes it a state crime for a non United States citizen to fail to carry alien registration papers. It makes it a crime to pick up day labors or be picked up if the process in anyway impedes the flow of traffic. It makes it a state crime to knowingly transport, conceal or protect an illegal. All of these crimes are misdemeanor level offenses to be tried in limited jurisdiction courts. Charges of profiling were immediately raised. A subsequent amendment to the law prohibits law enforcement officials from considering race, color or national origins except to the extent allowed by the United States and Arizona Constitutions. Immigration status can only be pursued after "stop, detention, arrest" for violation of an existing law. As of the time of this writing, Arizona's new immigration law is under investigation by the federal government, and multiple law suits have been filed challenging it.

For several years the Maricopa County Sheriff's Department, via its Immigration Interdiction Unit, has conducted sweeps through targeted communities hoping to round up illegal immigrants. The program is highly controversial and has helped polarize the state.

State Senator Pearce has already announced his proposed immigration legislation for the next session: to deny birth certificates to the offspring of illegal residents born in Arizona. The stated purpose: to make Arizona a hostile environment for illegals.

Illegals fill an essential slot in the labor force. There is no comprehensive and reasonable federal law that deals with the issue. Ultimately, it is only the federal government that has the authority to create such a law. If and when that happens there will be massive implications for Arizona.

The information presented in this chapter is intended to provide the reader with a greater appreciation for the diverse interests of the citizens of this state. While statistics are reported as averages or percentages, individuals relate to them quite differently. Personal political orientation and cultural socialization reflect one's perceived status regarding these figures. The nineteenth century political cartoon character Mr. Dooley is attributed with the saying: "all politics is local." To this we might add: "all politics is personal."

The reality is that most people in Arizona are urban dwellers who work at skilled jobs that require some degree of education and training. Almost one half of urban households have two wage earners. Most live in neighborhoods of like interests, comparable incomes, and in some instances, racial or ethnic similarity, although upward mobility and sheer force of population growth are beginning to challenge the latter. Arizona is a collection of ghettos, barrios, neighborhoods, or the old, the young, the rich, the poor, of singles, of families. It is a collection of what the futurists refer to as "urban villages." With the exception of employment opportunity, most do not stray too far from their "urban village."

Politicians and government officials try to appeal to each constituency and obtain for it some governmental advantage. In viewing Arizona government and politics, it is important to keep in mind that ninety legislators, elected executive officers, state administrators, and county and local officials, are all trying to balance the needs, demands, interests, and resources of a diverse and changing population.

CHAPTER SUMMARY

✓ There is a significant contrast between rural and urban Arizona.

✓ Newcomers to the state are slow to politically socialize, generally maintaining loyalties and interests of "back home."

✓ Arizona is a prime destination for retirees and winter visitors, and this results in a considerable senior population.

✓ Environmental issues are of great concern but solutions and behaviors are often contradictory.

✓ Water usage in Arizona tends to ignore the fact that the state is a desert, as is evidence by the abundance of swimming pools and golf courses.

✓ Although there has been considerable progress, Arizona continues to rank poorly in educational funding.

✓ The economy has become quite diversified, but there continues to be a disproportionate number of service industry jobs.

✓ Increasingly Arizona is a culturally diversified state.

✓ Arizona minorities exhibit high birth rates, indicated further increases of minority population for the immediate future.

✓ Arizona prides itself on its low taxes but this also means low funding of many services that some regard as being essential.

CONSTITUTION
of the
STATE OF ARIZONA

Table of Contents   **Page**

HISTORICAL NOTES

The Constitution of Arizona, in its original form, was adopted in the afternoon of December 9, 1910, as the Constitutional Convention by which the instrument was drafted concluded sixty-one days of earnest labor. Forty of the fifty-two delegates composing the body voted approval of the instrument, while twelve voiced opposition to its provisions—chiefly those establishing the Initiative, Referendum and Recall. Nevertheless, one of the members voting "no" appended his signature to the document.

Formulation of the Constitution was authorized by an Enabling Act of Congress which received the President's signature on June 20, 1910, after an historic struggle waged by the people of Arizona over more than a quarter of a century, for the right of local self-government and Arizona's recognition as a member of the Union of States.

Conclusion of the labors of the Constitutional Convention did not, however, automatically admit Arizona into the Union. That long sought end still depended upon ratification of the Constitution by the people of Arizona, and, in compliance with unusual requirements of the Enabling Act, its approval by the Congress and the President, or approval by the President in the event of the failure of Congress to act at the ensuing session of that body.

At an election held February 9, 1911, the people of Arizona ratified the Constitution by a vote of 12,187 to 3,302, and the Sixty-second Congress, after a protracted debate, adopted a resolution of approval. This, however, was on August 15, 1911, vetoed by President William H. Taft, who gave as a primary reason his unalterable opposition to the provision for the recall, by the people, of public officers, including judicial officers. A second resolution was thereupon adopted by Congress and approved by the President, which fixed as the price of statehood the holding of an election at which the people of Arizona should adopt an amendment removing judicial officers from the provision of the recall. The demand was complied with at an election held December 12, 1911, 14,963 votes being cast in favor of removal of the offending provision and 1,890 against. The significance of the vote was not that the people of Arizona opposed the recall of the judiciary but that they favored statehood. At the first election following that desired consummation, the provision was restored to its original form by a vote of 16,272 to 3,705.

On February 14, 1912, President Taft issued a proclamation declaring Arizona an equal State of the Union, thus giving effect to the Constitution amended at his behest.

CONSTITUTION
of the
STATE OF ARIZONA
PREAMBLE

We, the people of the State of Arizona, grateful to Almighty God for our liberties, do ordain this Constitution.

ARTICLE I
STATE BOUNDARIES

§ 1. Designation of boundaries

The boundaries of the State of Arizona shall be as follows, namely: Beginning at a point on the Colorado River twenty English miles below the junction of the Gila and Colorado Rivers, as fixed by the Gadsden Treaty between the United States and Mexico, being in latitude thirty-two degrees, twenty-nine minutes, forty-four and forty-five one-hundredths seconds north and longitude one hundred fourteen degrees, forty-eight minutes, forty-four and fifty-three one-hundredths seconds west of Greenwich; thence along and with the international boundary line between the United States and Mexico in a southeastern direction to Monument Number 127 on said boundary line in latitude thirty-one degrees, twenty minutes north; thence east along and with said parallel of latitude, continuing on said boundary line to an intersection with the meridian of longitude one hundred nine degrees, two minutes, fifty-nine and twenty-five one-hundredths seconds west, being identical with the southwestern corner of New Mexico; thence north along and with said meridian of longitude and the west boundary of New Mexico to an intersection with the parallel of latitude thirty-seven degrees north, being the common corner of Colorado, Utah, Arizona, and New Mexico; thence west along and with said parallel of latitude and the south boundary of Utah to an intersection with the meridian of longitude one hundred fourteen degrees, two minutes, fifty-nine and twenty-five one-hundredths seconds west, being on the east boundary line of the state of Nevada; thence south along and with said meridian of longitude and the east boundary of said state of Nevada, to the center of the Colorado River; thence down the mid- channel of said Colorado River in a southern direction along and with the east boundaries of Nevada, California, and the Mexican Territory of Lower California, successively, to the place of beginning.

Added, election Sept. 11, 1956, effective Oct. 1, 1956.

§ 2. Alteration of state boundaries
Section 2.   The legislature, in cooperation with the properly constituted authority of any adjoining state, is empowered to change, alter, and redefine the state boundaries, such change, alteration and redefinition to become effective only upon approval of the congress of the United States.

ARTICLE II
DECLARATION OF RIGHTS

§ 1. Fundamental principles, recurrence to
Section 1.   A frequent recurrence to fundamental principles is essential to the security of individual rights and the perpetuity of free government.

§ 2. Political power; purpose of government
Section 2.   All political power is inherent in the people, and governments derive their just powers from the consent of the governed, and are established to protect and maintain individual rights.

§ 2.1. Victims' Bill of Rights
Section 2.1.   (A) To preserve and protect victims' rights to justice and due process, a victim of crime has a right:
1.   To be treated with fairness, respect, and dignity, and to be free from intimidation, harassment, or abuse, throughout the criminal justice process.
2.   To be informed, upon request, when the accused or convicted person is released from custody or has escaped.
3.   To be present at and, upon request, to be informed of all criminal proceedings where the defendant has the right to be present.
4.   To be heard at any proceeding involving a post-arrest release decision, a negotiated plea, and sentencing.
5.   To refuse an interview, deposition, or other discovery request by the defendant, the defendant's attorney, or other person acting on behalf of the defendant.
6.   To confer with the prosecution, after the crime against the victim has been charged, before trial or before any disposition of the case and to be informed of the disposition.

7.   To read pre-sentence reports relating to the crime against the victim when they are available to the defendant.

8.   To receive prompt restitution from the person or persons convicted of the criminal conduct that caused the victim's loss or injury.

9.   To be heard at any proceeding when any post-conviction release from confinement is being considered.

10.   To a speedy trial or disposition and prompt and final conclusion of the case after the conviction and sentence.

11.   To have all rules governing criminal procedure and the admissibility of evidence in all criminal proceedings protect victims' rights and to have these rules be subject to amendment or repeal by the legislature to ensure the protection of these rights.

12.   To be informed of victims' constitutional rights.

(B)   A victim's exercise of any right granted by this section shall not be grounds for dismissing any criminal proceeding or setting aside any conviction or sentence.

(C)   "Victim" means a person against whom the criminal offense has been committed or, if the person is killed or incapacitated, the person's spouse, parent, child or other lawful representative, except if the person is in custody for an offense or is the accused.

(D)   The legislature, or the people by initiative or referendum, have the authority to enact substantive and procedural laws to define, implement, preserve and protect the rights guaranteed to victims by this section, including the authority to extend any of these rights to juvenile proceedings.

(E)   The enumeration in the constitution of certain rights for victims shall not be construed to deny or disparage others granted by the legislature or retained by victims.

Added, election Nov. 6, 1990, effective Nov. 27, 1990.

§ 3.   Supreme law of the land
Section 3.   The Constitution of the United States is the supreme law of the land.

§ 4.   Due process of law
Section 4.   No person shall be deprived of life, liberty, or property without due process of law.

§ 5.   Right of petition and of assembly
Section 5.   The right of petition, and of the people peaceably to assemble for the common good, shall never be abridged.

§ 6. Freedom of speech and press
Section 6.   Every person may freely speak, write, and publish on all subjects, being responsible for the abuse of that right.

§ 7. Oaths and affirmations
Section 7.   The mode of administering an oath, or affirmation, shall be such as shall be most consistent with and binding upon the conscience of the person to whom such oath, or affirmation, may be administered.

§ 8. Right to privacy
Section 8.   No person shall be disturbed in his private affairs, or his home invaded, without authority of law.

§ 9. Irrevocable grants of privileges, franchises or immunities
Section 9.   No law granting irrevocably any privilege, franchise, or immunity shall be enacted.

§ 10. Self-incrimination; double jeopardy
Section 10.   No person shall be compelled in any criminal case to give evidence against himself, or be twice put in jeopardy for the same offense.

§ 11. Administration of justice
Section 11.   Justice in all cases shall be administered openly, and without unnecessary delay.

§ 12. Liberty of conscience; appropriations for religious purposes prohibited; religious freedom
Section 12.   The liberty of conscience secured by the provisions of this constitution shall not be so construed as to excuse acts of licentiousness, or justify practices inconsistent with the peace and safety of the state. No public money or property shall be appropriated for or applied to any religious worship, exercise, or instruction, or the support of any religious establishment. No religious qualification shall be required for any public office or employment, nor shall any person be incompetent as a witness or juror in consequence of his opinion on matters of religion, nor be questioned touching his religious belief in any court of justice to affect the weight of his testimony.

§ 13. Equal privileges and immunities
Section 13.   No law shall be enacted granting to any citizen, class of citizens, or corporation other than municipal, privileges or

immunities which, upon the same terms, shall not equally belong to all citizens or corporations.

§ 14. Habeas corpus
Section 14.   The privilege of the writ of habeas corpus shall not be suspended by the authorities of the state.

§ 15. Excessive bail; cruel and unusual punishment
Section 15.   Excessive bail shall not be required, nor excessive fines imposed, nor cruel and unusual punishment inflicted.

§ 16. Corruption of blood; forfeiture of estate
Section 16.   No conviction shall work corruption of blood, or forfeiture of estate.

§ 17. Eminent domain; just compensation for private property taken; public use as judicial question
Section 17.   Private property shall not be taken for private use, except for private ways of necessity, and for drains, flumes, or ditches, on or across the lands of others for mining, agricultural, domestic, or sanitary purposes. No private property shall be taken or damaged for public or private use without just compensation having first been made, paid into court for the owner, secured by bond as may be fixed by the court, or paid into the state treasury for the owner on such terms and conditions as the legislature may provide, and no right of way shall be appropriated to the use of any corporation other than municipal, until full compensation therefor be first made in money, or ascertained and paid into court for the owner, irrespective of any benefit from any improvement proposed by such corporation, which compensation shall be ascertained by a jury, unless a jury be waived as in other civil cases in courts of record, in the manner prescribed by law. Whenever an attempt is made to take private property for a use alleged to be public, the question whether the contemplated use be really public shall be a judicial question, and determined as such without regard to any legislative assertion that the use is public.

Amended, election Nov. 3, 1970, effective Nov. 27, 1970.

§ 18. Imprisonment for debt
Section 18.   There shall be no imprisonment for debt, except in cases of fraud.

§ 19. Bribery or illegal rebating; witnesses; self-incrimination no defense
Section 19.   Any person having knowledge or possession of facts that tend to establish the guilt of any other person or corporation charged with bribery or illegal rebating, shall not be excused from giving testimony or producing evidence, when legally called upon to do so, on the ground that it may tend to incriminate him under the laws of the state; but no person shall be prosecuted or subject to any penalty or forfeiture for, or on account of, any transaction, matter, or thing concerning which he may so testify or produce evidence.

§ 20. Military power subordinate to civil power
Section 20.   The military shall be in strict subordination to the civil power.

§ 21. Free and equal elections
Section 21.   All elections shall be free and equal, and no power, civil or military, shall at any time interfere to prevent the free exercise of the right of suffrage.

§ 22. Bailable offenses
Section 22.   All persons charged with crime shall be bailable by sufficient sureties, except for:
1.   Capital offenses when the proof is evident or the presumption great.
2.   Felony offenses, committed when the person charged is already admitted to bail on a separate felony charge and where the proof is evident or the presumption great as to the present charge.
3.   Felony offenses if the person charged poses a substantial danger to any other person or the community, if no conditions of release which may be imposed will reasonably assure the safety of the other person or the community and if the proof is evident or the presumption great as to the present charge.

Amended, election Nov. 3, 1970, effective Nov. 27, 1970; election Nov. 2, 1982, effective Nov. 30, 1982.

§ 23. Trial by jury; number of jurors specified by law
Section 23.   The right of trial by jury shall remain inviolate. Juries in criminal cases in which a sentence of death or imprison-

ment for thirty years or more is authorized by law shall consist of twelve persons. In all criminal cases the unanimous consent of the jurors shall be necessary to render a verdict. In all other cases, the number of jurors, not less than six, and the number required to render a verdict, shall be specified by law.

Amended, election Nov. 7, 1972, effective Dec. 1, 1972.

§ 24. Rights of accused in criminal prosecutions
Section 24.   In criminal prosecutions, the accused shall have the right to appear and defend in person, and by counsel, to demand the nature and cause of the accusation against him, to have a copy thereof, to testify in his own behalf, to meet the witnesses against him face to face, to have compulsory process to compel the attendance of witnesses in his own behalf, to have a speedy public trial by an impartial jury of the county in which the offense is alleged to have been committed, and the right to appeal in all cases; and in no instance shall any accused person before final judgment be compelled to advance money or fees to secure the rights herein guaranteed.

§ 25. Bills of attainder; ex post facto laws; impairment of contract obligations
Section 25.   No bill or attainder, ex post facto law, or law impairing the obligation of a contract, shall ever be enacted.

§ 26. Bearing arms
Section 26.   The right of the individual citizen to bear arms in defense of himself or the state shall not be impaired, but nothing in this section shall be construed as authorizing individuals or corporations to organize, maintain, or employ an armed body of men.

§ 27. Standing army; quartering soldiers
Section 27.   No standing army shall be kept up by this state in time of peace, and no soldier shall in time of peace be quartered in any house without the consent of its owner, nor in time of war except in the manner prescribed by law.

§ 28. Treason
Section 28.   Treason against the state shall consist only in levying war against the state, or adhering to its enemies, or in giving them aid and comfort. No person shall be convicted of treason

unless on the testimony of two witnesses to the same overt act, or confession in open court.

§ 29. Hereditary emoluments, privileges or powers; perpetuities or entailments

Section 29.   No hereditary emoluments, privileges, or powers shall be granted or conferred, and no law shall be enacted permitting any perpetuity or entailment in this state.

§ 30. Indictment or information; preliminary examination

Section 30.   No person shall be prosecuted criminally in any court of record for felony or misdemeanor, otherwise than by information or indictment; no person shall be prosecuted for felony by information without having had a preliminary examination before a magistrate or having waived such preliminary examination.

§ 31. Damages for death or personal injuries

Section 31.   No law shall be enacted in this state limiting the amount of damages to be recovered for causing the death or injury of any person.

§ 32. Constitutional provisions mandatory

Section 32.   The provisions of this constitution are mandatory, unless by express words they are declared to be otherwise.

§ 33. Reservation of rights

Section 33.   The enumeration in this constitution of certain rights shall not be construed to deny others retained by the people.

§ 34. Industrial pursuits by the state and municipal corporations

Section 34.   The state of Arizona and each municipal corporation within the state of Arizona shall have the right to engage in industrial pursuits.

Added, election Nov. 5, 1912, effective Dec. 5, 1912.

ARTICLE III
DISTRIBUTION OF POWERS

The powers of the government of the State of Arizona shall be divided into three separate departments, the Legislative, the Executive, and the Judicial; and, except as provided in this Constitution, such departments shall be separate and distinct, and no one of such departments shall exercise the powers properly belonging to either of the others.

ARTICLE IV
LEGISLATIVE DEPARTMENT

PART 1. INITIATIVE AND REFERENDUM

§ 1. Legislative authority; initiative and referendum

Section 1.　　(1) [**Senate; house of representatives; reservation of power to people**] The legislative authority of the state shall be vested in a legislature, consisting of a senate and a house of representatives, but the people reserve the power to propose laws and amendments to the constitution and to enact or reject such laws and amendments at the polls, independently of the legislature; and they also reserve, for use at their own option, the power to approve or reject at the polls any act, or item, section, or part of any act, of the legislature.

(2)　　[**Initiative power**] The first of these reserved powers is the initiative. Under this power ten per centum of the qualified electors shall have the right to propose any measure, and fifteen per centum shall have the right to propose any amendment to the constitution.

(3)　　[**Referendum power; emergency measures; effective date of acts**] The second of these reserved powers is the referendum. Under this power the legislature, or five per centum of the qualified electors, may order the submission to the people at the polls of any measure, or item, section, or part of any measure, enacted by the legislature, except laws immediately necessary for the preservation of the public peace, health, or safety, or for the support and maintenance of the departments of the state government and state institutions; but to allow opportunity for referendum petitions, no act passed by the legislature shall be operative for ninety days after the close of the session of the legislature enacting such measure, except such as require earlier operation to preserve the public peace, health, or safety, or to provide appropriations for the support and maintenance of the departments of the state and of state institutions; provided, that no such emergency measure shall be considered passed by the legislature unless it shall state in a separate section why it is necessary that it shall become imme- diately operative, and shall be approved by the affirmative votes of two- thirds of the members elected to each house of the legis- lature, taken by roll call of ayes and nays, and also approved by the governor; and should such measure be vetoed by the governor, it shall not become a law unless it shall be approved by the votes of three- fourths of the members elected to each house of the legis- lature, taken by roll call of ayes and nays.

(4)   **[Initiative and referendum petitions; filing]** All peti- tions submitted under the power of the initiative shall be known as initiative petitions, and shall be filed with the secretary of state not less than four months preceding the date of the election at which the measures so proposed are to be voted upon. All peti- tions submitted under the power of the referendum shall be known as referendum petitions, and shall be filed with the secretary of state not more than ninety days after the final adjournment of the session of the legislature which shall have passed the measure to which the referendum is applied. The filing of a referendum petition against any item, section, or part of any measure shall not prevent the remainder of such measure from becoming operative.

(5)   **[Effective date of initiative and referendum measures]** Any measure or amendment to the constitution proposed under the initiative, and any measure to which the referendum is applied, shall be referred to a vote of the qualified electors, and shall become law when approved by a majority of the votes cast thereon and upon proclamation of the governor, and not otherwise.

(6)   **(A) Veto of initiative or referendum.** The veto power of the governor shall not extend to an initiative measure approved by a majority of the votes cast thereon or to a referendum meas- ure decided by a majority of the votes cast thereon.

(6)   **(B) Legislature's power to repeal initiative or refer- endum.** The legislature shall not have the power to repeal an initia- tive measure approved by a majority of the votes cast thereon or to repeal a referendum measure decided by a majority of the votes cast thereon.

(6)   **(C) Legislature's power to amend initiative or refer- endum.** The legislature shall not have the power to amend an initia- tive measure approved by a majority of the votes cast thereon, or to amend a referendum measure decided by a majority of the votes cast thereon, unless the amending legislation furthers the purposes

of such measure and at least three-fourths of the members of each house of the legislature, by a roll call of ayes and nays, vote to amend such measure.

(6)   **(D) Legislature's power to appropriate or divert funds created by initiative or referendum.** The legislature shall not have the power to appropriate or divert funds created or allocated to a specific purpose by an initiative measure approved by a majority of the votes cast thereon, or by a referendum measure decided by a majority of the votes cast thereon, unless the appropriation or diversion of funds furthers the purposes of such measure and at least three-fourths of the members of each house of the legislature, by a roll call of ayes and nays, vote to appropriate or divert such funds.

(7)   [**Number of qualified electors**] The whole number of votes cast for all candidates for governor at the general election last preceding the filing of any initiative or referendum petition on a state or county measure shall be the basis on which the number of qualified electors required to sign such petition shall be computed.

(8)   [**Local, city, town or county matters**] The powers of the initiative and the referendum are hereby further reserved to the qualified electors of every incorporated city, town, and county as to all local, city, town, or county matters on which such incorporated cities, towns, and counties are or shall be empowered by general laws to legislate. Such incorporated cities, towns, and counties may prescribe the manner of exercising said powers within the restrictions of general laws. Under the power of the initiative fifteen per centum of the qualified electors may propose measures on such local, city, town or county matters, and ten per centum of the electors may propose the referendum on legislation enacted within and by such city, town, or county. Until provided by general law, said cities and towns may prescribe the basis on which said percentages shall be computed.

(9)   [**Form and contents of initiative and of referendum petitions; verification**] Every initiative or referendum petition shall be addressed to the secretary of state in the case of petitions for or on state measures, and to the clerk of the board of supervisors, city clerk, or corresponding officer in the case of petitions for or on county, city, or town measures; and shall contain the declaration of each petitioner, for himself, that he is a qualified elector of the state (and in the case of petitions for or on city, town, or county measures, of the city, town, or county affected), his post office address, the street

and number, if any, of his residence, and the date on which he signed such petition. Each sheet containing petitioners' signatures shall be attached to a full and correct copy of the title and text of the measure so proposed to be initiated or referred to the people, and every sheet of every such petition containing signatures shall be verified by the affidavit of the person who circulated said sheet or petition, setting forth that each of the names on said sheet was signed in the presence of the affiant and that in the belief of the affiant each signer was a qualified elector of the state, or in the case of a city, town, or county measure, of the city, town, or county affected by the measure so proposed to be initiated or referred to the people.

(10)   [**Official ballot**] When any initiative or referendum petition or any measure referred to the people by the legislature shall be filed, in accordance with this section, with the secretary of state, he shall cause to be printed on the official ballot at the next regular general election the title and number of said measure, together with the words "Yes" and "No" in such manner that the electors may express at the polls their approval or disapproval of the measure.

(11)   [**Publication of measures**] The text of all measures to be submitted shall be published as proposed amendments to the constitution are published, and in submitting such measures and proposed amendments the secretary of state and all other officers shall be guided by the general law until legislation shall be especially provided therefor.

(Method of publication superseded by A.R.S. § 19-123.)

(12)   [**Conflicting measures or constitutional amendments**] If two or more conflicting measures or amendments to the constitution shall be approved by the people at the same election, the measure or amendment receiving the greatest number of affirmative votes shall prevail in all particulars as to which there is conflict.

(13)   [**Canvass of votes; proclamation**] It shall be the duty of the secretary of state, in the presence of the governor and the chief justice of the supreme court, to canvass the votes for and against each such measure or proposed amendment to the constitution within thirty days after the election, and upon the completion of the canvass the governor shall forthwith issue a proclamation, giving the whole number of votes cast for and against each measure or proposed amendment, and declaring such measures or amendments as are approved by a majority of those voting thereon to be law.

(14)   [**Reservation of legislative power**] This section shall not

252

be construed to deprive the legislature of the right to enact any measure except that the legislature shall not have the power to adopt any measure that supersedes, in whole or in part, any initiative measure approved by a majority of the votes cast thereon or any referendum measure decided by a majority of the votes cast thereon unless the superseding measure furthers the purposes of the initiative or referendum measure and at least three-fourths of the members of each house of the legislature, by a roll call of ayes and nays, vote to supersede such initiative or referendum measure.

(15) **Legislature's right to refer measure to the people.** Nothing in this section shall be construed to deprive or limit the legislature of the right to order the submission to the people at the polls of any measure, item, section, or part of any measure.

(16) **[Self-executing]** This section of the constitution shall be, in all respects, self-executing.

Amended, election November 3, 1914, effective December 14, 1914; amended, election Nov. 3, 1998, effective December 10, 1998.

Section 2.   Section 1 hereof shall apply retroactively to all initiative and referendum measures decided by the voters at and after the November 1998 general election.

Added, election Nov. 3, 1998, effective December 10, 1998. The text of Arizona Constitution article 4, part 1, § 1, (section 2) is numbered exactly as Proposition 105 was submitted to the voters.

§ 2. Penalty for violation of initiative and referendum provisions

Section 2.   The legislature shall provide a penalty for any wilful violation of any of the provisions of the preceding section.

PART 2. THE LEGISLATURE

§ 1. Senate; house of representatives; members; special session upon petition of members; congressional and legislative boundaries; citizen commissions

Section 1.   (1) The senate shall be composed of one member elected from each of the thirty legislative districts established pursuant to this section.

The house of representatives shall be composed of two members elected from each of the thirty legislative districts established pursuant to this section.

(2) Upon the presentation to the governor of a petition bearing the signatures of not less than two-thirds of the members of each house, requesting a special session of the legislature and designating the date of convening, the governor shall promptly call a special session to assemble on the date specified. At a special session so called the subjects which may be considered by the legislature shall not be limited.

(3) By February 28 of each year that ends in one, an independent redistricting commission shall be established to provide for the redistricting of congressional and state legislative districts. The independent redistricting commission shall consist of five members. No more than two members of the independent redistricting commission shall be members of the same political party. Of the first four members appointed, no more than two shall reside in the same county. Each member shall be a registered Arizona voter who has been continuously registered with the same political party or registered as unaffiliated with a political party for three or more years immediately preceding appointment, who is committed to applying the provisions of this section in an honest, independent and impartial fashion and to upholding public confidence in the integrity of the redistricting process. Within the three years previous to appointment, members shall not have been appointed to, elected to, or a candidate for any other public office, including precinct committeeman or committeewoman but not including school board member or officer, and shall not have served as an officer of a political party, or served as a registered paid lobbyist or as an officer of a candidate's campaign committee.

(4) The commission on appellate court appointments shall nominate candidates for appointment to the independent redistricting commission, except that, if a politically balanced commission exists whose members are nominated by the commission on appellate court appointments and whose regular duties relate to the elective process, the commission on appellate court appointments may delegate to such existing commission (hereinafter called the commission on appellate court appointments' designee) the duty of nominating members for the independent redistricting commission, and all other duties assigned to the commission on appellate court appointments in this section.

(5) By January 8 of years ending in one, the commission on appellate court appointments or its designee shall establish a pool of persons who are willing to serve on and are qualified for appoint-

ment to the independent redistricting commission. The pool of candidates shall consist of twenty-five nominees, with ten nominees from each of the two largest political parties in Arizona based on party registration, and five who are not registered with either of the two largest political parties in Arizona.

(6)   Appointments to the independent redistricting commission shall be made in the order set forth below. No later than January 31 of years ending in one, the highest ranking officer elected by the Arizona house of representatives shall make one appointment to the independent redistricting commission from the pool of nominees, followed by one appointment from the pool made in turn by each of the following: the minority party leader of the Arizona house of representatives, the highest ranking officer elected by the Arizona senate, and the minority party leader of the Arizona senate. Each such official shall have a seven-day period in which to make an appointment. Any official who fails to make an appointment within the specified time period will forfeit the appointment privilege. In the event that there are two or more minority parties within the house or the senate, the leader of the largest minority party by statewide party registration shall make the appointment.

(7)   Any vacancy in the above four independent redistricting commission positions remaining as of March 1 of a year ending in one shall be filled from the pool of nominees by the commission on appellate court appointments or its designee. The appointing body shall strive for political balance and fairness.

(8)   At a meeting called by the secretary of state, the four independent redistricting commission members shall select by majority vote from the nomination pool a fifth member who shall not be registered with any party already represented on the independent redistricting commission and who shall serve as chair. If the four commissioners fail to appoint a fifth member within fifteen days, the commission on appellate court appointments or its designee, striving for political balance and fairness, shall appoint a fifth member from the nomination pool, who shall serve as chair.

(9)   The five commissioners shall then select by majority vote one of their members to serve as vice-chair.

(10)   After having been served written notice and provided with an opportunity for a response, a member of the independent redistricting commission may be removed by the governor, with the concurrence of two-thirds of the senate, for substantial neglect of duty,

gross misconduct in office, or inability to discharge the duties of office.

(11)   If a commissioner or chair does not complete the term of office for any reason, the commission on appellate court appointments or its designee shall nominate a pool of three candidates within the first thirty days after the vacancy occurs. The nominees shall be of the same political party or status as was the member who vacated the office at the time of his or her appointment, and the appointment other than the chair shall be made by the current holder of the office designated to make the original appointment. The appointment of a new chair shall be made by the remaining commissioners. If the appointment of a replacement commissioner or chair is not made within fourteen days following the presentation of the nominees, the commission on appellate court appointments or its designee shall make the appointment, striving for political balance and fairness. The newly appointed commissioner shall serve out the remainder of the original term.

(12)   Three commissioners, including the chair or vice-chair, constitute a quorum. Three or more affirmative votes are required for any official action. Where a quorum is present, the independent redistricting commission shall conduct business in meetings open to the public, with 48 or more hours public notice provided.

(13)   A commissioner, during the commissioner's term of office and for three years thereafter, shall be ineligible for Arizona public office or for registration as a paid lobbyist.

(14)   The independent redistricting commission shall establish congressional and legislative districts. The commencement of the mapping process for both the congressional and legislative districts shall be the creation of districts of equal population in a grid-like pattern across the state. Adjustments to the grid shall then be made as necessary to accommodate the goals as set forth below:

A.   Districts shall comply with the United States constitution and the United States voting rights act;

B.   Congressional districts shall have equal population to the extent practicable, and state legislative districts shall have equal population to the extent practicable;

C.   Districts shall be geographically compact and contiguous to the extent practicable;

D.   District boundaries shall respect communities of interest to the extent practicable;

E.   To the extent practicable, district lines shall use visible geographic features, city, town and county boundaries, and undivided census tracts;

F. To the extent practicable, competitive districts should be favored where to do so would create no significant detriment to the other goals.

(15) Party registration and voting history data shall be excluded from the initial phase of the mapping process but may be used to test maps for compliance with the above goals. The places of residence of incumbents or candidates shall not be identified or considered.

(16) The independent redistricting commission shall advertise a draft map of congressional districts and a draft map of legislative districts to the public for comment, which comment shall be taken for at least thirty days. Either or both bodies of the legislature may act within this period to make recommendations to the independent redistricting commission by memorial or by minority report, which recommendations shall be considered by the independent redistricting commission. The independent redistricting commission shall then establish final district boundaries.

(17) The provisions regarding this section are self-executing. The independent redistricting commission shall certify to the secretary of state the establishment of congressional and legislative - districts.

(18) Upon approval of this amendment, the department of administration or its successor shall make adequate office space available for the independent redistricting commission. The treasurer of the state shall make $6,000,000 available for the work of the independent redistricting commission pursuant to the year 2000 census. Unused monies shall be returned to the state's general fund. In years ending in eight or nine after the year 2001, the department of administration or its successor shall submit to the legislature a recommendation for an appropriation for adequate redistricting expenses and shall make available adequate office space for the operation of the independent redistricting commission. The legislature shall make the necessary appropriations by a majority vote.

(19) The independent redistricting commission, with fiscal oversight from the department of administration or its successor, shall have procurement and contracting authority and may hire staff and consultants for the purposes of this section, including legal representation.

(20) The independent redistricting commission shall have stand-

ing in legal actions regarding the redistricting plan and the adequacy of resources provided for the operation of the independent redistricting commission. The independent redistricting commission shall have sole authority to determine whether the Arizona attorney general or counsel hired or selected by the independent redistricting commission shall represent the people of Arizona in the legal defense of a redistricting plan.

(21)   Members of the independent redistricting commission are eligible for reimbursement of expenses pursuant to law, and a member's residence is deemed to be the member's post of duty for purposes of reimbursement of expenses.

(22)   Employees of the department of administration or its successor shall not influence or attempt to influence the district-mapping decisions of the independent redistricting commission.

(23)   Each commissioner's duties established by this section expire upon the appointment of the first member of the next redistricting commission. The independent redistricting commission shall not meet or incur expenses after the redistricting plan is completed, except if litigation or any government approval of the plan is pending, or to revise districts if required by court decisions or if the number of congressional or legislative districts is changed.

Amended election Nov. 5, 1918, effective Dec. 5, 1918; election Nov. 8, 1932, effective Nov. 28, 1932; election Nov. 2, 1948, effective Nov. 22, 1948; election Sep. 29, 1953, effective Oct. 31, 1953; election Sept. 9, 1958, effective Sept. 30, 1958; election Nov. 5, 1968, effective Dec. 4, 1968; election Nov. 3, 1970, effective Nov. 27, 1970; election Nov. 7, 1972, effective Dec. 1, 1972; amended, election Nov. 7, 2000, effective Dec. 7, 2000.

§ 2.   Qualifications of members of legislature

Section 2.   No person shall be a member of the legislature unless he shall be a citizen of the United States at the time of his election, nor unless he shall be at least twenty-five years of age, and shall have been a resident of Arizona at least three years and of the county from which he is elected at least one year before his election.

§ 3.   Sessions of legislature; special sessions; limitation of subjects for consideration

Section 3.   The sessions of the legislature shall be held annually at the capitol of the state, and shall commence on the second

Monday of January of each year. The governor may call a special session, whenever in his judgment it is advisable. In calling a special session, the governor shall specify the subjects to be considered, and at such special session no laws shall be enacted except such as relate to the subjects mentioned in the call.

Amended, election Sept. 12, 1950, effective Oct. 2, 1950.

§ 4. Disqualification for membership in legislature
Section 4.   No person holding any public office of profit or trust under the authority of the United States, or of this state, shall be a member of the legislature; provided, that appointments in the state militia and the offices of notary public, justice of the peace, United States commissioner, and postmaster of the fourth class, shall not work disqualification for membership within the meaning of this section.

§ 5. Ineligibility of members of legislature to other public offices
Section 5.   No member of the legislature, during the term for which he shall have been elected or appointed shall be eligible to hold any other office or be otherwise employed by the state of Arizona or, any county or incorporated city or town thereof. This prohibition shall not extend to the office of school trustee, nor to employment as a teacher or instructor in the public school system.

Amended, election November 8, 1938, effective December 14, 1938.

§ 6. Privilege from arrest; civil process
Section 6.   Members of the legislature shall be privileged from arrest in all cases except treason, felony, and breach of the peace, and they shall not be subject to any civil process during the session of the legislature, nor for fifteen days next before the commencement of each session.

§ 7. Freedom of debate
Section 7.   No member of the legislature shall be liable in any civil or criminal prosecution for words spoken in debate.

§ 8. Organization; officers; rules of procedure
Section 8.   Each house, when assembled, shall choose its own officers, judge of the election and qualification of its own members, and determine its own rules of procedure.

§ 9. Quorum; compelling attendance; adjournment
Section 9.   The majority of the members of each house shall constitute a quorum to do business, but a smaller number may meet, adjourn from day to day, and compel the attendance of absent members, in such manner and under such penalties as each house may prescribe. Neither house shall adjourn for more than three days, nor to any place other than that in which it may be sitting, without the consent of the other.

§ 10. Journal of proceedings; roll call
Section 10.   Each house shall keep a journal of its proceedings, and at the request of two members the ayes and nays on roll call on any question shall be entered.

§ 11. Disorderly behavior; expulsion of members
Section 11.   Each house may punish its members for disorderly behavior, and may, with the concurrence of two-thirds of its members, expel any member.

§ 12. Procedure on bills; approval or disapproval by governor
Section 12.   Every bill shall be read by sections on three different days, unless in case of emergency, two-thirds of either house deem it expedient to dispense with this rule. The vote on the final passage of any bill or joint resolution shall be taken by ayes and nays on roll call. Every measure when finally passed shall be presented to the governor for his approval or disapproval.

Amended, election Nov. 7, 1972, effective Dec. 1, 1972.

§ 13. Subject and title of bills
Section 13.   Every act shall embrace but one subject and matters properly connected therewith, which subject shall be expressed in the title; but if any subject shall be embraced in an act which shall not be expressed in the title, such act shall be void only as to so much thereof as shall not be embraced in the title.

§ 14. Legislation by reference prohibited
Section 14.   No act or section thereof shall be revised or amended by mere reference to the title of such act, but the act or section as amended shall be set forth and published at full length.

§ 15. Passage of bills by majority; signing of bills
Section 15.   A majority of all members elected to each house

shall be necessary to pass any bill, and all bills so passed shall be signed by the presiding officer of each house in open session.

§ 16. Right to protest
Section 16.   Any member of the legislature shall have the right to protest and have the reasons of his protest entered on the journal.

§ 17. Extra compensation prohibited; increase or decrease of compensation during term of office
Section 17.   The legislature shall never grant any extra compensation to any public officer, agent, servant or contractor, after the services shall have been rendered or the contract entered into, nor shall the compensation of any public officer, other than a justice of the peace, be increased or diminished during his term of office; provided, however, that when any legislative increase or decrease in compensation of the members of any court or the clerk thereof, or of any board or commission composed of two or more officers or persons whose respective terms of office are not coterminous, has heretofore or shall hereafter become effective as to any member or clerk of such court, or any member of such board or commission, it shall be effective from such date as to each thereof.

Amended, election Nov. 4, 1930, effective Dec. 1, 1930; election Sept. 29, 1953, effective Oct. 31, 1953.

§ 18. Suits against state
Section 18.   The legislature shall direct by law in what manner and in what courts suits may be brought against the state.

§ 19. Local or special laws
Section 19.   No local or special laws shall be enacted in any of the following cases, that is to say:
1.   Granting divorces.
2.   Locating or changing county seats.
3.   Changing rules of evidence.
4.   Changing the law of descent or succession.
5.   Regulating the practice of courts of justice.
6.   Limitation of civil actions or giving effect to informal or invalid deeds.
7.   Punishment of crimes and misdemeanors.
8.   Laying out, opening, altering, or vacating roads, plats, streets, alleys, and public squares.
9.   Assessment and collection of taxes.
10.   Regulating the rate of interest on money.

11.   The conduct of elections.

12.   Affecting the estates of deceased persons or of minors.

13.   Granting to any corporation, association, or individual, any special or exclusive privileges, immunities, or franchises.

14.   Remitting fines, penalties, and forfeitures.

15.   Changing names of persons or places.

16.   Regulating the jurisdiction and duties of justices of the peace.

17.   Incorporation of cities, towns, or villages, or amending their charters.

18.   Relinquishing any indebtedness, liability, or obligation to this state.

19.   Summoning and empanelling of juries.

20.   When a general law can be made applicable.

§ 20. Appropriation bills
Section 20.   The general appropriation bill shall embrace nothing but appropriations for the different departments of the state, for state institutions, for public schools, and for interest on the public debt. All other appropriations shall be made by separate bills, each embracing but one subject.

§ 21. Term limits of members of state legislature
Section 21.   The members of the first legislature shall hold office until the first Monday in January, 1913. The terms of office of the members of succeeding legislatures shall be two years. No state Senator shall serve more than four consecutive terms in that office, nor shall any state Representative serve more than four consecutive terms in that office. This limitation on the number of terms of consecutive service shall apply to terms of office beginning on or after January 1, 1993. No Legislator, after serving the maximum number of terms, which shall include any part of a term served, may serve in the same office until he has been out of office for no less than one full term.

Amended, election Nov. 3, 1992, effective Nov. 23, 1992.

§ 22. Juvenile justice; certain chronic and violent juvenile offenders prosecuted as adults; community alternatives for certain juvenile offenders; public proceedings and records
Section 22.   In order to preserve and protect the right of the people to justice and public safety, and to ensure fairness and account-

ability when juveniles engage in unlawful conduct, the legislature, or the people by initiative or referendum, shall have the authority to enact substantive and procedural laws regarding all proceedings and matters affecting such juveniles. The following rights, duties, and powers shall govern such proceedings and matters:

(1)   Juveniles 15 years of age or older accused of murder, forcible sexual assault, armed robbery or other violent felony offenses as defined by statute shall be prosecuted as adults. Juveniles 15 years of age or older who are chronic felony offenders as defined by statute shall be prosecuted as adults. Upon conviction all such juveniles shall be subject to the same laws as adults, except as specifically provided by statute and by article 22, section 16 of this constitution. All other juveniles accused of unlawful conduct shall be prosecuted as provided by law. Every juvenile convicted of or found responsible for unlawful conduct shall make prompt restitution to any victims of such conduct for their injury or loss.

(2)   County attorneys shall have the authority to defer the prosecution of juveniles who are not accused of violent offenses and who are not chronic felony offenders as defined by statute and to establish community-based alternatives for resolving matters involving such juveniles.

(3)   All proceedings and matters involving juveniles accused of unlawful conduct shall be open to the public and all records of those proceedings shall be public records. Exceptions shall be made only for the protection of the privacy of innocent victims of crime, or when a court of competent jurisdiction finds a clear public interest in confidentiality.

Former Section 22 repealed, election Nov. 8, 1932, effective Nov. 28, 1932.
New Section 22 added, election Nov. 5, 1996, effective Dec. 6, 1996.

§ 23. Passes and purchase of transportation by public officers; in application to national guard

Section 23.   It shall not be lawful for any person holding public office in this state to accept or use a pass or to purchase transportation from any railroad or other corporation, other than as such transportation may be purchased by the general public; provided, that this shall not apply to members of the national guard of Arizona traveling under orders. The legislature shall enact laws to enforce this provision.

§ 24. Enacting clause of bills; initiative bills

Section 24. The enacting clause of every bill enacted by the legislature shall be as follows: "Be it enacted by the Legislature of the State of Arizona," or when the initiative is used: "Be it enacted by the People of the State of Arizona."

§ 25. Continuity of governmental operations in emergency

Section 25. The legislature, in order to insure continuity of state and local governmental operations in periods of emergency resulting from disasters caused by enemy attack, shall have the power and the immediate duty to:

1. Provide for prompt and temporary succession to the powers and duties of public offices, of whatever nature and whether filled by election or appointment, the incumbents of which may become unavailable for carrying on the powers and duties of such offices.

2. Adopt such other measures as may be necessary and proper for insuring the continuity of governmental operations.

In the exercise of the powers hereby conferred, the legislature shall in all respects conform to the requirements of this constitution except to the extent that in the judgment of the legislature so to do would be impracticable or would admit of undue delay.

Added, election Nov. 6, 1962, effective Nov. 26, 1962.

ARTICLE V
EXECUTIVE DEPARTMENT

§ 1. Term limits on Executive department and state officers; term lengths; election; residence and office at seat of government; duties

Section 1.   A. The executive department shall consist of the governor, secretary of state, state treasurer, attorney general, and superintendent of public instruction, each of whom shall hold office for a term of four years beginning on the first Monday of January, 1971 next after the regular general election in 1970. No member of the executive department shall hold that office for more than two consecutive terms. This limitation on the number of terms of consecutive service shall apply to terms of office beginning on or after January 1, 1993. No member of the executive department after serving the maximum number of terms, which shall include any

264

part of a term served, may serve in the same office until out of office for no less than one full term.

B.   The person having the highest number of the votes cast for the office voted for shall be elected, but if two or more persons have an equal and the highest number of votes for the office, the two houses of the legislature at its next regular session shall elect forthwith, by joint ballot, one of such persons for said office.

C.   The officers of the executive department during their terms of office shall reside at the seat of government where they shall keep their offices and the public records, books, and papers. They shall perform such duties as are prescribed by the constitution and as may be provided by law.

Amended, election Nov. 2, 1948, effective Nov. 22, 1948; amended, election Nov. 5, 1968, effective Dec. 4, 1968; amended, election Nov. 8, 1988, effective Dec. 5, 1988; amended, election Nov. 3, 1992, effective Nov. 23, 1992.

§ 2.   Eligibility to state offices
Section 2.   No person shall be eligible to any of the offices mentioned in section 1 of this article except a person of the age of not less than twenty-five years, who shall have been for ten years next preceding his election a citizen of the United States, and for five years next preceding his election a citizen of Arizona.

Amended, election Nov. 8, 1988, effective Dec. 5, 1988.

§ 3.   Governor, commander-in-chief of military forces
Section 3.   The governor shall be commander-in-chief of the military forces of the state, except when such forces shall be called into the service of the United States.

§ 4. Governor; powers and duties; special sessions of legislature; message and recommendations
Section 4.   The governor shall transact all executive business with the officers of the government, civil and military, and may require information in writing from the officers in the executive department upon any subject relating to the duties of their respective offices. He shall take care that the laws be faithfully executed. He may convene the legislature in extraordinary session. He shall communicate, by message, to the legislature at every session the condition of the state, and recommend such matters as he shall deem expedient.

5555555555555

55555555555555

An Introduction to Arizona History and Government

§ 5. Reprieves, commutations and pardons

Section 5.   The governor shall have power to grant reprieves, commutation, and pardons, after convictions, for all offenses except treason and cases of impeachment, upon such conditions and with such restrictions and limitations as may be provided by law.

§ 6. Death, resignation, removal or disability of governor; succession to office; impeachment, absence from state or temporary disability

Section 6.   In the event of the death of the governor, or his resignation, removal from office, or permanent disability to discharge the duties of the office, the secretary of state, if holding by election, shall succeed to the office of governor until his successor shall be elected and shall qualify. If the secretary of state be holding otherwise then by election, or shall fail to qualify as governor, the attorney general, the state treasurer, or the superintendent of public instruction, if holding by election, shall, in the order named, succeed to the office of governor. The taking of the oath of office as governor by any person specified in this section shall constitute resignation from the office by virtue of the holding of which he qualifies as governor. Any successor to the office shall become governor in fact and entitled to all of the emoluments, powers and duties of governor upon taking the oath of office.

In the event of the impeachment of the governor, his absence from the state, or other temporary disability to discharge the duties of the office, the powers and duties of the office of governor shall devolve upon the same person as in case of vacancy, but only until the disability ceases.

Amended, election Nov. 2, 1948, effective Nov. 22, 1948; election Nov. 5, 1968, effective Dec. 4, 1968.

§ 7. Presentation of bills to governor; approval; veto; filing with secretary of state; veto of items in appropriation bills; in application of veto power to referred bills

Section 7.   Every bill passed by the legislature, before it becomes a law, shall be presented to the governor. If he approve, he shall sign it, and it shall become a law as provided in this constitution. But if he disapprove, he shall return it, with his objections, to the house in which it originated, which shall enter the objections at large on the journal. If after reconsideration it again passes both houses by an aye and nay vote on roll call of two-thirds of the mem-

266

bers elected to each house, it shall become a law as provided in this constitution, notwithstanding the governor's objections. This section shall not apply to emergency measures as referred to in section 1 of the article of the legislative department.

If any bill be not returned within five days after it shall have been presented to the governor (Sunday excepted) such bill shall become a law in like manner as if he had signed it, unless the legislature by its final adjournment prevents its return, in which case it shall be filed with his objections in the office of the secretary of state within ten days after such adjournment (Sundays excepted) or become a law as provided in this constitution. After the final action by the governor, or following the adoption of a bill notwithstanding his objection, it shall be filed with the secretary of state.

If any bill presented to the governor contains several items of appropriations of money, he may object to one or more of such items, while approving other portions of the bill. In such case he shall append to the bill at the time of signing it, a statement of the item or items which he declines to approve, together with his reasons therefor, and such item or items shall not take effect unless passed over the governor's objections as in this section provided.

The veto power of the governor shall not extend to any bill passed by the legislature and referred to the people for adoption or rejection.

§ 8. Vacancies in office
Section 8.   When any office shall, from any cause, become vacant, and no mode shall be provided by the constitution or by law for filling such vacancy, the governor shall have the power to fill such vacancy by appointment.

§ 9. Powers and duties of state officers
Section 9.   The powers and duties of secretary of state, state treasurer, attorney general, and superintendent of public instruction shall be as prescribed by law.

Amended, election Nov. 5, 1968, effective Dec. 4, 1968.

§ 10. Repealed

Amended, election Nov. 4, 1980, effective Nov. 24, 1980; Repealed, election Nov. 3, 1992, effective Nov. 23, 1992.

§ 11. Canvass of election returns for state officers; certificates of election

Section 11.   The returns of the election for all state officers shall be canvassed, and certificates of election issued by the secretary of state, in such manner as may be provided by law.

§ 12. Commissions

Section 12.   All commissions shall issue in the name of the state, and shall be signed by the governor, sealed with the seal of the state, and attested by the secretary of state.

§ 13. Compensation of elective state officers; commission on salaries for elective state officers

Section 13.   The salaries of those holding elective state offices shall be as established by law from time to time, subject to the limitations of article 6, section 33 and to the limitations of article 4, part 2, section 17. Such salaries as are presently established may be altered from time to time by the procedure established in this section or as otherwise provided by law, except that legislative salaries may be altered only by the procedures established in this section.

A commission to be known as the commission on salaries for elective state officers is authorized to be established by the legislature. The commission shall be composed of five members appointed from private life, two of whom shall be appointed by the governor and one each by the president of the senate, the speaker of the house of representatives, and the chief justice. At such times as may be directed by the legislature, the commission shall report to the governor with recommendations concerning the rates of pay of elected state officers. The governor shall upon receipt of such report make recommendations to the legislature with respect to the exact rates of pay which he deems advisable for those offices and positions other than for the rates of pay of members of the legislature. Such recommendations shall become effective at a time established by the legislature after the transmission of the recommendation of the governor without aid of further legislative action unless, within such period of time, there has been enacted into law a statute which establishes rates of pay other than those proposed by the governor, or unless either house of the legislature specifically disapproves all or part of the governor's recommendation. The recommendations of the governor, unless disapproved or altered within the time provided by law, shall be effective; and any 1971 recommendations shall be effective as to all offices on the first Monday in January of 1973. In case of either a legislative enactment or disapproval by either house, the recommendations shall be effective only insofar as not altered or disapproved. The recommendations of the commission as to legislative salaries shall be certified by it to the secretary of state and the secretary of state shall submit to the qualified electors at the next regular general election the question, "Shall the recommendations of the commission on salaries for elective state officers concerning legislative salaries be accepted? Yes   No". Such recommendations if approved by the electors shall become effective at the beginning of the next regular legislative session without any other authorizing legislation. All recommendations which become effective under this section shall supersede all laws enacted prior to their effective date relating to such salaries.

Amended, election Nov. 3, 1970, effective Nov. 27, 1970.

ARTICLE VI
JUDICIAL DEPARTMENT

Former Article VI, consisting of sections 1-25, repealed, and new Article VI, consisting of sections 1-35, adopted by election, Nov. 8, 1960, effective Dec. 9, 1960.

§ 1.   Judicial power; courts
Section 1.   The judicial power shall be vested in an integrated judicial department consisting of a supreme court, such intermediate appellate courts as may be provided by law, a superior court, such courts inferior to the superior court as may be provided by law, and justice courts.

Added, election Nov. 8, 1960, effective Dec. 9, 1960.

§ 2.   Supreme court; composition; divisions; decisions, transactions of business
Section 2.   The supreme court shall consist of not less than five justices. The number of justices may be increased or decreased by law, but the court shall at all times be constituted of at least five justices.

The supreme court shall sit in accordance with rules adopted by it, either in banc or in divisions of not less than three justices, but the court shall not declare any law unconstitutional except when sitting in banc. The decisions of the court shall be in writing and the grounds stated.

The court shall be open at all times, except on nonjudicial days, for the transaction of business.

Added, election Nov. 8, 1960, effective Dec. 9, 1960.

§ 3. Supreme court; administrative supervision; chief justice

Section 3.   The supreme court shall have administrative supervision over all the courts of the state. The chief justice shall be elected by the justices of the supreme court from one of their number for a term of five years, and may be reelected for like terms. The vice chief justice shall be elected by the justices of the supreme court from one of their number for a term determined by the court. A member of the court may resign the office of chief justice or vice chief justice without resigning from the court.

The chief justice, or in his absence or incapacity, the vice chief justice, shall exercise the court's administrative supervision over all the courts of the state. He may assign judges of intermediate appellate courts, superior courts, or courts inferior to the superior court to serve in other courts or counties.

Added, election Nov. 8, 1960, effective Dec. 9, 1960; amended, election Nov. 5, 1974, effective Dec. 5, 1974.

§ 4. Supreme court; term of office

Section 4.   Justices of the supreme court shall hold office for a regular term of six years except as provided by this article.

Added, election Nov. 8, 1960, effective Dec. 9, 1960; amended, election Nov. 5, 1974, effective Dec. 5, 1974.

§ 5. Supreme court; jurisdiction; writs; rules; habeas corpus

Section 5.   The supreme court shall have:

1.   Original jurisdiction of habeas corpus, and quo warranto, mandamus, injunction and other extraordinary writs to state officers.

2.   Original and exclusive jurisdiction to hear and determine causes between counties concerning disputed boundaries and surveys thereof or concerning claims of one county against another.

3.   Appellate jurisdiction in all actions and proceedings except

civil and criminal actions originating in courts not of record, unless the action involves the validity of a tax, impost, assessment, toll, statute or municipal ordinance.

4. Power to issue injunctions and writs of mandamus, review, prohibition, habeas corpus, certiorari, and all other writs necessary and proper to the complete exercise of its appellate and revisory jurisdiction.

5. Power to make rules relative to all procedural matters in any court.

6. Such other jurisdiction as may be provided by law.

Each justice of the supreme court may issue writs of habeas corpus to any part of the state upon petition by or on behalf of a person held in actual custody, and may make such writs returnable before himself, the supreme court, appellate court or superior court, or judge thereof.

Added, election Nov. 8, 1960, effective Dec. 9, 1960.

§ 6. Supreme court; qualifications of justices

Section 6.   A justice of the supreme court shall be a person of good moral character and admitted to the practice of law in and a resident of the state of Arizona for ten years next preceding his taking office.

Added, election Nov. 8, 1960, effective Dec. 9, 1960.

§ 7. Supreme court; clerk and assistants; administrative director and staff

Section 7.   The supreme court shall appoint a clerk of the court and assistants thereto who shall serve at its pleasure, and who shall receive such compensation as may be provided by law.

The supreme court shall appoint an administrative director and staff to serve at its pleasure to assist the chief justice in discharging his administrative duties. The director and staff shall receive such compensation as may be provided by law.

Added, election Nov. 8, 1960, effective Dec. 9, 1960.

§ 8. Supreme court; publication of opinions

Section 8.   Provision shall be made by law for the speedy

publication of the opinions of the supreme court, and they shall be free for publication by any person.

Added, election Nov. 8, 1960, effective Dec. 9, 1960.

§ 9. Intermediate appellate courts

Section 9.   The jurisdiction, powers, duties and composition of any intermediate appellate court shall be as provided by law.

Added, election Nov. 8, 1960, effective Dec. 9, 1960.

§ 10. Superior court; number of judges

Section 10.   There shall be in each county at least one judge of the superior court. There shall be in each county such additional judges as may be provided by law, but not exceeding one judge for each thirty thousand inhabitants or majority fraction thereof. The number of inhabitants in a county for purposes of this section may be determined by census enumeration or by such other method as may be provided by law.

Added, election Nov. 8, 1960, effective Dec. 9, 1960.

§ 11. Superior court; presiding judges; duties

Section 11.   There shall be in each county a presiding judge of the superior court. In each county in which there are two or more judges, the supreme court shall appoint one of such judges presiding judge. Presiding judges shall exercise administrative supervision over the superior court and judges thereof in their counties, and shall have such other duties as may be provided by law or by rules of the supreme court.

Added, election Nov. 8, 1960, effective Dec. 9, 1960.

§ 12. Superior court; term of office

Section 12.   A. Judges of the superior court in counties having a population of less than two hundred fifty thousand persons according to the most recent United States census shall be elected by the qualified electors of their counties at the general election. They shall hold office for a regular term of four years except as provided by this section from and after the first Monday in January next succeeding their election, and until their successors are elected and qualify. The names of all candidates for judge of the superior court in such counties shall be placed on the regular ballot without partisan or other designation except the division and title of the office.

B.   The governor shall fill any vacancy in such counties by appointing a person to serve until the election and qualification of a successor. At the next succeeding general election following the appointment of a person to fill a vacancy, a judge shall be elected to serve for the remainder of the unexpired term.

Judges of the superior court in counties having a population of two hundred fifty thousand persons or more according to the most recent United States census shall hold office for a regular term of four years except as provided by this article.

Added, election Nov. 8, 1960, effective Dec. 9, 1960; amended, election Nov. 5, 1974, effective Dec. 5, 1974; amended, election Nov. 3, 1992, effective Nov. 23, 1992.

§ 13. Superior court; composition; salaries; judgments and proceedings; process

Section 13.   The superior courts provided for in this article shall constitute a single court, composed of all the duly elected or appointed judges in each of the counties of the state. The legislature may classify counties for the purpose of fixing salaries of judges or officers of the court.

The judgments, decrees, orders and proceedings of any session of the superior court held by one or more judges shall have the same force and effect as if all the judges of the court had presided.

The process of the court shall extend to all parts of the state.

Added, election Nov. 8, 1960, effective Dec. 9, 1960.

§ 14. Superior court; original jurisdiction

Section 14.   The superior court shall have original jurisdiction of:

1.   Cases and proceedings in which exclusive jurisdiction is not vested by law in another court.

2.   Cases of equity and at law which involve the title to or possession of real property, or the legality of any tax, impost, assessment, toll or municipal ordinance.

3.   Other cases in which the demand or value of property in controversy amounts to one thousand dollars or more, exclusive of interest and costs.

4.   Criminal cases amounting to felony, and cases of misdemeanor not otherwise provided for by law.
5.   Actions of forcible entry and detainer.
6.   Proceedings in insolvency.
7.   Actions to prevent or abate nuisance.
8.   Matters of probate.
9.   Divorce and for annulment of marriage.
10. Naturalization and the issuance of papers therefor.
11. Special cases and proceedings not otherwise provided for, and such other jurisdiction as may be provided by law.

Added, election Nov. 8, 1960, effective Dec. 9, 1960; amended, election Nov. 7, 1972, effective Dec. 1, 1972.

§ 15. Jurisdiction and authority in juvenile proceedings

Section 15.   The jurisdiction and authority of the courts of this state in all proceedings and matters affecting juveniles shall be as provided by the legislature or the people by initiative or referendum.

Added, election Nov. 8, 1960, effective Dec. 9, 1960. Section repealed, new Section added election Nov. 5, 1996, effective Dec. 6, 1996.

§ 16. Superior court; appellate jurisdiction

Section 16.   The superior court shall have appellate jurisdiction in cases arising in justice and other courts inferior to the superior court as may be provided by law.

Added, election Nov. 8, 1960, effective Dec. 9, 1960.

§ 17. Superior court; conduct of business; trial juries; jury trial; grand juries

Section 17.   The superior court shall be open at all times, except on nonjudicial days, for the determination of non-jury civil cases and the transaction of business. For the determination of civil causes and matters in which a jury demand has been entered, and for the trial of criminal causes, a trial jury shall be drawn and summoned from the body of the county, as provided by law. The right of jury trial as provided by this constitution shall remain inviolate, but trial by jury may be waived by the parties in any civil cause or by the parties with the consent of the court in any criminal cause. Grand juries shall be drawn and summoned only by order of the superior court.

Added, election Nov. 8, 1960, effective Dec. 9, 1960.

§ 18. Superior court; writs
Section 18.   The superior court or any judge thereof may issue writs of mandamus, quo warranto, review, certiorari, prohibition, and writs of habeas corpus on petition by or on behalf of a person held in actual custody within the county. Injunctions, attachments, and writs of prohibition and habeas corpus may be issued and served on legal holidays and non-judicial days.

Added, election Nov. 8, 1960, effective Dec. 9, 1960.

§ 19. Superior court; service of judge in another county
Section 19.   A judge of the superior court shall serve in another county at the direction of the chief justice of the supreme court or may serve in another county at the request of the presiding judge of the superior court thereof.

Added, election Nov. 8, 1960, effective Dec. 9, 1960.

§ 20. Retirement and service of retired justices and judges
Section 20.   The legislature shall prescribe by law a plan of retirement for justices and judges of courts of record, including the basis and amount of retirement pay, and requiring except as provided in section 35 of this article, that justices and judges of courts of record be retired upon reaching the age of seventy. Any retired justice or judge of any court of record who is drawing retirement pay may serve as a justice or judge of any court. When serving outside his county of residence, any such retired justice or judge shall receive his necessary traveling and subsistence expenses. A retired judge who is temporarily called back to the active duties of a judge is entitled to receive the same compensation and expenses as other like active judges less any amount received for such period in retirement benefits.

Added, election Nov. 8, 1960, effective Dec. 9, 1960; amended, election Nov. 5, 1974, effective Dec. 5, 1974.

§ 21. Superior court; speedy decisions
Section 21.   Every matter submitted to a judge of the superior court for his decision shall be decided within sixty days from the date of submission thereof. The supreme court shall by rule

provide for the speedy disposition of all matters not decided within such period.

Added, election Nov. 8, 1960, effective Dec. 9, 1960.

§ 22. Superior and other courts; qualifications of judges
Section 22.   Judges of the superior court, intermediate appellate courts or courts inferior to the superior court having jurisdiction in civil cases of one thousand dollars or more, exclusive of interest and costs, established by law under the provisions of section 1 of this article, shall be at least thirty years of age, of good moral character and admitted to the practice of law in and a resident of the state for five years next preceding their taking office.

Added, election Nov. 8, 1960, effective Dec. 9, 1960; amended, election Nov. 7, 1972. effective Dec. 1, 1972.

§ 23. Superior court; clerk
Section 23.   There shall be in each county a clerk of the superior court. The clerk shall be elected by the qualified electors of his county at the general election and shall hold office for a term of four years from and after the first Monday in January next succeeding his election. The clerk shall have such powers and perform such duties as may be provided by law or by rule of the supreme court or superior court. He shall receive such compensation as may be provided by law.

Added, election Nov. 8, 1960, effective Dec. 9, 1960.

§ 24. Superior court; court commissioners, masters and referees
Section 24.   Judges of the superior court may appoint court commissioners, masters and referees in their respective counties, who shall have such powers and perform such duties as may be provided by law or by rule of the supreme court. Court commissioners, masters and referees shall receive such compensation as may be provided by law.

Added, election Nov. 8, 1960, effective Dec. 9, 1960.

§ 25. Style of process; conduct of prosecutions in name of state
Section 25.   The style of process shall be "The State of Arizona", and prosecutions shall be conducted in the name of the state and by its authority.

Added, election Nov. 8, 1960, effective Dec. 9, 1960.

§ 26. Oath of office

Section 26.   Each justice, judge and justice of the peace shall, before entering upon the duties of his office, take and subscribe an oath that he will support the Constitution of the United States and the constitution of the state of Arizona, and that he will faithfully and impartially discharge the duties of his office to the best of his ability.

The oath of all judges of courts inferior to the superior court and the oath of justices of peace shall be filed in the office of the county recorder, and the oath of all other justices and judges shall be filed in the office of the secretary of state.

Added, election Nov. 8, 1960, effective Dec. 9, 1960.

§ 27. Charge to juries; reversal of causes for technical error

Section 27.   Judges shall not charge juries with respect to matters of fact, nor comment thereon, but shall declare the law. No cause shall be reversed for technical error in pleadings or proceedings when upon the whole case it shall appear that substantial justice has been done.

Added, election Nov. 8, 1960, effective Dec. 9, 1960.

§ 28. Justices and judges; dual office holding; political activity; practice of law

Section 28.   Justices and judges of courts of record shall not be eligible for any other public office or for any other public employment during their term of office, except that they may assume another judicial office, and upon qualifying therefor, the office formerly held shall become vacant. No justice or judge of any court of record shall practice law during his continuance in office, nor shall he hold any office in a political party or actively take part in any political campaign other than his own for his reelection or retention in office. Any justice or judge who files nomination papers for an elective office, other than for judge of the superior court or a court of record inferior to the superior court in a county having a population of less than two hundred fifty thousand persons according to the most recent United States census, forfeits his judicial office.

Added, election Nov. 8, 1960, effective Dec. 9, 1960; amended, election Nov. 5, 1974, effective Dec. 5, 1974; amended, election Nov. 3, 1992, effective Nov. 23, 1992.

§ 29. Repealed, election Nov. 3, 1970, effective Nov. 27, 1970

§ 30. Courts of record

Section 30.　　A. The supreme court, the court of appeals and the superior court shall be courts of record. Other courts of record may be established by law, but justice courts shall not be courts of record.

B.　　All justices and judges of courts of record, except for judges of the superior court and other courts of record inferior to the superior court in counties having a population of less than two hundred fifty thousand persons according to the most recent United States census, shall be appointed in the manner provided in § 37 of this article.

Added, election Nov. 8, 1960, effective Dec. 9, 1960; amended, election Nov. 5, 1974, effective Dec. 5, 1974; amended, election Nov. 3, 1992, effective Nov. 23, 1992.

§ 31. Judges pro tempore

Section 31.　　The legislature may provide for the appointment of members of the bar having the qualifications provided in § 22 of this article as judges pro tempore of courts inferior to the supreme court. When serving, any such person shall have all the judicial powers of a regular elected judge of the court to which he is appointed. A person so appointed shall receive such compensation as may be provided by law. The population limitation of § 10 of this article shall not apply to the appointment of judges pro tempore of the superior court.

Added, election Nov. 8, 1960, effective Dec. 9, 1960.

§ 32. Justices of the peace and inferior courts; jurisdiction, powers and duties; terms of office; salaries

Section 32.　　The number of justices of the peace to be elected in precincts shall be as provided by law. Justices of the peace may be police justices of incorporated cities and towns.

The jurisdiction, powers and duties of courts inferior to the superior court and of justice courts, and the terms of office of judges of such courts and justices of the peace shall be as provided by law. The legislature may classify counties and precincts for the purpose of fixing salaries of judges of courts inferior to the superior court and of justices of the peace.

The civil jurisdiction of courts inferior to the superior court and of justice courts shall not exceed the sum of ten thousand dollars, exclusive of interest and costs. Criminal jurisdiction shall be limited to misdemeanors. The jurisdiction of such courts shall not encroach upon the jurisdiction of courts of record but may be made concurrent therewith, subject to the limitations provided in this section.

Added, election Nov. 8, 1960, effective Dec. 9, 1960. Amended, election Nov. 6, 1990, effective Nov. 27, 1990.

§ 33. Change by legislature in number of justices or judges; reduction of salary during term of office

Section 33.　　No change made by the legislature in the number of justices or judges shall work the removal of any justice or judge from office. The salary of any justice or judge shall not be reduced during the term of office for which he was elected or appointed.

Added, election Nov. 8, 1960, effective Dec. 9, 1960.

§ 34. Absence of judicial officer from state

Section 34.　　Any judicial officer except a retired justice or judge who absents himself from the state for more than sixty consecutive days shall be deemed to have forfeited his office, but the governor may extend the leave of absence for such time as reasonable necessity therefor exists.

Added, election Nov. 8, 1960, effective Dec. 9, 1960.

§ 35. Continuance in office; continued existence of offices; application of prior statute and rules

Section 35.　　A. All justices, judges, justices of the peace and officers of any court who are holding office as such by election or appointment at the time of the adoption of this section shall serve or continue in office for the respective terms for which they are so elected or for their respective unexpired terms, and until their successors are elected or appointed and qualify or they are retained in office pursuant to section 38 of this article; provided, however, that any justice or judge elected at the general election at which this section is adopted shall serve for the term for which he is so elected. The continued existence of any office heretofore legally established or held shall not be abolished or repealed by the adoption of this article. The statutes and rules relating to the authority, jurisdiction, practice and procedure of courts, judicial officers and offices in force at the time of the adoption of this article and not inconsistent herewith, shall, so far as applicable, apply to and govern such courts, judicial officers and offices until amended or repealed.

B.   All judges of the superior court holding office by appointment or retention in counties with a population of two hundred fifty thousand persons or more according to the most recent United States census at the time of the adoption of this amendment to this section shall serve or continue in office for the respective terms for which they were appointed. Upon an incumbent vacating the office of judge of the superior court, whether by failing to file a declaration for retention, by rejection by the qualified electors of the county or resignation, the appointment shall be pursuant to section 37 of this article.

Added, election Nov. 8, 1960, effective Dec. 9, 1960; amended, election Nov. 5, 1974, effective Dec. 5, 1974; amended, election Nov. 3, 1992, effective Nov. 23, 1992.

§ 36. Commissions on appellate and trial court appointments and terms, appointments and vacancies on such commissions

Section 36   A. There shall be a nonpartisan commission on appellate court appointments which shall be composed of the chief justice of the supreme court, who shall be chairman, five attorney members, who shall be nominated by the board of governors of the state bar of Arizona and appointed by the governor with the advice and consent of the senate in the manner prescribed by law, and ten nonattorney members who shall be appointed by the governor with the advice and consent of the senate in the manner prescribed by law. At least ninety days prior to a term expiring or within twenty-one days of a vacancy occurring for a nonattorney member on the commission for appellate court appointments, the governor shall appoint a nominating committee of nine members, not more than five of whom may be from the same political party. The makeup of the committee shall, to the extent feasible, reflect the diversity of the population of the state. Members shall not be attorneys and shall not hold any governmental office, elective or appointive, for profit. The committee shall provide public notice that a vacancy exists and shall solicit, review and forward to the governor all applications along with the committee's recommendations for appointment.

Attorney members of the commission shall have resided in the state and shall have been admitted to practice before the supreme court for not less than five years. Not more than three attorney members shall be members of the same political party and not more than two attorney members shall be residents of any one county. Nonattorney members shall have resided in the state for not less than five years and shall not be judges, retired judges or admitted to practice before the supreme court. Not more than five nonattorney members shall be members of the same political party. Not more than two nonattorney members shall be residents of any one county. None of the attorney or nonattorney members of the commission shall hold any governmental office, elective or appointive, for profit, and no attorney member shall be eligible for appointment to any judicial office of the state until one year after he ceases to be a member. Attorney members of the commission shall serve staggered four-year terms, and nonattorney members shall serve staggered four-year terms. Vacancies shall be filled for the unexpired terms in the same manner as the original appointments.

B.   No person other than the chief justice shall serve at the same time as a member of more than one judicial appointment commission.

C.   In making or confirming appointments to the appellate court commission, the governor, the senate and the state bar shall endeavor to see that the commission reflects the diversity of Arizona's population.

In the event of the absence or incapacity of the chairman the supreme court shall appoint a justice thereof to serve in his place and stead.

D.   Prior to making recommendations to the governor as hereinafter provided, the commission shall conduct investigations, hold public hearings and take public testimony. An executive session as prescribed by rule may be held upon a two-thirds vote of the members of the commission in a public hearing. Final decisions as to recommendations shall be made without regard to political affiliation in an impartial and objective manner. The commission shall consider the diversity of the state's population, however the primary consideration shall be merit. Voting shall be in a public hearing. The expenses of meetings of the commission and the attendance of members thereof for travel and subsistence shall be paid from the general fund of the state as state officers are paid, upon claims approved by the chairman.

E.   After public hearings the supreme court shall adopt rules of procedure for the commission on appellate court appointments.

F.   Notwithstanding the provisions of subsection A, the initial appointments for the five additional nonattorney members and the two additional attorney members of the commission shall be designated by the governor for staggered terms as follows:

1.   One appointment for a nonattorney member shall be for a one-year term.

2.   Two appointments for nonattorney members shall be for a two-year term.

3.   Two appointments for nonattorney members shall be for a three-year term.

4.   One appointment for an attorney member shall be for a one-year term.

5.   One appointments for an attorney member shall be for a two-year term.

G.   The members currently serving on the commission may continue to serve until the expiration of their normal terms. All subsequent appointments shall be made as prescribed by this section.

Added, election Nov. 5, 1974, effective Dec. 5, 1974; amended, election Nov. 2, 1976, effective Nov. 22, 1976; amended, election Nov. 3, 1992, effective Nov. 23, 1992.

§ 37. Judicial vacancies and appointments; initial terms; residence; age

Section 37.   A. Within sixty days from the occurrence of a vacancy in the office of a justice or judge of any court of record, except for vacancies occurring in the office of a judge of the superior court or a judge of a court of record inferior to the superior court, the commission on appellate court appointments, if the vacancy is in the supreme court or an intermediate appellate court of record, shall submit to the governor the names of not less than three persons nominated by it to fill such vacancy, no more than two of whom shall be members of the same political party unless there are more than four such nominees, in which event not more than sixty per centum of such nominees shall be members of the same political party.

B.   Within sixty days from the occurrence of a vacancy in the office of a judge of the superior court or a judge of a court of record inferior to the superior court except for vacancies occurring in the office of a judge of the superior court or a judge of a court of record inferior to the superior court in a county having a population of less than two hundred fifty thousand persons according to the most recent united states census, the commission on trial court appointments for the county in which the vacancy occurs shall submit to the governor the names of not less than three persons nominated by it to fill such vacancy, no more than two of whom shall be members of the same political party unless there are more than four such nominees, in which event no more than sixty per centum of such nominees shall be members of the same political party. A nominee shall be under sixty-five years of age at the time his name is submitted to the governor. Judges of the superior court shall be subject to retention or rejection by a vote of the qualified electors of the county from which they were appointed at the general election in the manner provided by section 38 of this article.

C.   A vacancy in the office of a justice or a judge of such courts of record shall be filled by appointment by the governor without regard to political affiliation from one of the nominees whose names shall be submitted to him as hereinabove provided. In making the appointment, the governor shall consider the diversity of the state's population for an appellate court appointment and the diversity of the county's population for a trial court appointment, however the primary consideration shall be merit. If the governor does not appoint one of such nominees to fill such vacancy within sixty days after their names are submitted to the governor by such commission, the chief justice of the supreme court forthwith shall appoint on the basis of merit alone without regard to political affiliation one of such nominees to fill such vacancy. If such commission does not, within sixty days after such vacancy occurs, submit the names of nominees as hereinabove provided, the governor shall have the power to appoint any qualified person to fill such vacancy at any time thereafter prior to the time the names of the nominees to fill such vacancy are submitted to the governor as hereinabove provided. Each justice or judge so appointed shall initially hold office for a term ending sixty days following the next regular general election after the expiration of a term of two years in office. Thereafter, the terms of justices or judges of the supreme court and the superior court shall be as provided by this article.

D.   A person appointed to fill a vacancy on an intermediate appellate court or another court of record now existing or hereafter established by law shall have been a resident of the counties or county in which that vacancy exists for at least one year prior to his appointment, in addition to possessing the other required qualifications. A nominee shall be under sixty-five years of age at the time his name is submitted to the governor.

Added, election Nov. 5, 1974, effective Dec. 5, 1974; amended, election Nov. 3, 1992, effective Nov. 23, 1992.

§ 38. Declaration of candidacy; form of judicial ballot, rejection and retention; failure to file declaration

Section 38.   A. A justice or judge of the supreme court or an intermediate appellate court shall file in the office of the secretary of state, and a judge of the superior court or other court of record including such justices or judges who are holding office as such by election or appointment at the time of the adoption of this section except for judges of the superior court and other courts of record inferior to the superior court in counties having a population of less than two hundred fifty thousand persons, according to the United States census, shall file in the office of the clerk of the board of supervisors of the county in which he regularly sits and resides, not less than sixty nor more than ninety days prior to the regular general election next preceding the expiration of his term of office, a declaration of his desire to be retained in office, and the secretary of state shall certify to the several boards of supervisors the appropriate names of the candidate or candidates appearing on such declarations filed in his office.

B.   The name of any justice or judge whose declaration is filed as provided in this section shall be placed on the appropriate official ballot at the next regular general election under a nonpartisan designation and in substantially the following form:

Shall _____, (Name of Justice or Judge) of the _____ Court be retained in Office? Yes _____

No _____ (Mark X after one).

C.   If a majority of those voting on the question votes "No," then, upon the expiration of the term for which such justice or judge was serving, a vacancy shall exist, which shall be filled as provided by this article. If a majority of those voting on the question votes "Yes," such justice or judge shall remain in office for another term, subject to removal as provided by this constitution.

D.   The votes shall be counted and canvassed and the result declared as in the case of state and county elections, whereupon a certificate of retention or rejection of the incumbent justice or judge shall be delivered to him by the secretary of state or the clerk of the board of supervisors, as the case may be.

E.   If a justice or judge fails to file a declaration of his desire to be retained in office, as required by this section, then his office shall become vacant upon expiration of the term for which such justice or judge was serving.

Added, election Nov. 5, 1974, effective Dec. 5, 1974; amended, election Nov. 3, 1992, effective Nov. 23, 1992.

§ 39. Retirement of justices and judges; vacancies

Section 39.   On attaining the age of seventy years a justice or judge of a court of record shall retire and his judicial office shall be vacant, except as otherwise provided in section 35 of this article. In addition to becoming vacant as provided in this section, the office of a justice or judge of any court of record becomes vacant upon his death or his voluntary retirement pursuant to statute or his voluntary resignation, and also, as provided in section 38 of this article, upon the expiration of his term next following a general election at which a majority of those voting on the question of his retention vote in the negative or for which general election he is required, but fails, to file a declaration of his desire to be retained in office.

This section is alternative to and cumulative with the methods of removal of judges and justices provided in parts 1 and 2 of article 8 and article 6.1 of this constitution.

Added, election Nov. 5, 1974, effective Dec. 5, 1974.

§ 40. Option for counties with less than two hundred fifty thousand persons

Section 40.   Notwithstanding any provision of this article to the contrary, any county having a population of less than two hundred fifty thousand persons, according to the most recent United States census, may choose to select its judges of the superior court or of courts of record inferior to the superior court as if it had a population of two hundred fifty thousand or more persons. Such choice shall be determined by vote of the qualified electors of such county voting on the question at an election called for such purpose by resolution of the board of supervisors of such county. If such qualified electors approve, the provisions of sections 12, 28, 30, 35 through 39, 41 and 42 shall apply as if such county had a population of two hundred fifty thousand persons or more.

Added, election Nov. 5, 1974, effective Dec. 5, 1974; amended, election Nov. 3, 1992, effective Nov. 23, 1992.

§ 41. Superior court divisions; commission on trial court appointments; membership; terms

A.   Except as otherwise provided, judges of the superior court in counties having a population of two hundred fifty thousand persons or more according to the most recent United States census shall hold office for a regular term of four years.

B.   There shall be a nonpartisan commission on trial court appointments for each county having a population of two hundred fifty thousand persons or more according to the most recent United States census which shall be composed of the following members:

1.   The chief justice of the supreme court, who shall be the chairman of the commission. In the event of the absence or incapacity of the chairman the supreme court shall appoint a justice thereof to serve in his place and stead.

2.   Five attorney members, none of whom shall reside in the same supervisorial district and not more than three of whom shall be members of the same political party, who are nominated by the board of governors of the state bar of Arizona and who are appointed by the governor subject to confirmation by the senate in the manner prescribed by law.

3.   Ten nonattorney members, no more than two of whom shall reside in the same supervisorial district.

C.   At least ninety days prior to a term expiring or within twenty-one days of a vacancy occurring for a nonattorney member on the commission for trial court appointments, the member of the board of supervisors from the district in which the vacancy has occurred shall appoint a nominating committee of seven members who reside in the district, not more than four of whom may be from the same political party. The make-up of the committee shall, to the extent feasible, reflect the diversity of the population of the district. Members shall not be attorneys and shall not hold any governmental office, elective or appointive, for profit. The committee shall provide public notice that a vacancy exists and shall solicit, review and forward to the governor all applications along with the committee's recommendations for appointment. The governor shall appoint two persons from each supervisorial district who shall not be of the same political party, subject to confirmation by the senate in the manner prescribed by law.

D.   In making or confirming appointments to trial court commissions, the governor, the senate and the state bar shall endeavor to see that the commission reflects the diversity of the county's population.

E.   Members of the commission shall serve staggered four year terms, except that initial appointments for the five additional nonattorney members and the two additional attorney members of the commission shall be designated by the governor as follows:

1.   One appointment for a nonattorney member shall be for a one-year term.

2.   Two appointments for nonattorney members shall be for a two-year term.

3.   Two appointments for nonattorney members shall be for a three-year term.

4.   One appointment for an attorney member shall be for a one-year term.

5.   One appointment for an attorney member shall be for a two-year term.

F.   Vacancies shall be filled for the unexpired terms in the same manner as the original appointments.

G.   Attorney members of the commission shall have resided in this state and shall have been admitted to practice in this state by the supreme court for at least five years and shall have resided in the supervisorial district from which they are appointed for at least one year. Nonattorney members shall have resided in this state for at least five years, shall have resided in the supervisorial district for at least one year before being nominated and shall not be judges, retired judges nor admitted to practice before the supreme court. None of the attorney or nonattorney members of the commission shall hold any governmental office, elective or appointive, for profit and no attorney member is eligible for appointment to any judicial office of this state until one year after membership in the commission terminates.

H.   No person other than the chief justice shall serve at the same time as a member of more than one judicial appointment commission.

I.   The commission shall submit the names of not less than three individuals for nomination for the office of the superior court judge pursuant to section 37 of this article.

J.   Prior to making recommendations to the governor, the commission shall conduct investigations, hold public hearings and take public testimony. An executive session as prescribed by rule may be held upon a two-thirds vote of the members of the commission in a public hearing. Final decisions as to recommendations shall be made without regard to political affiliation in an impartial and objective manner. The commission shall consider the diversity of the county's population and the geographical distribution of the residences of the judges throughout the county, however the primary consideration shall be merit. Voting shall be in a public hearing. The expenses of meetings of the commission and the attendance of members thereof for travel and subsistence shall be paid from the general fund of the state as state officers are paid, upon claims approved by the chairman.

K.   After public hearings the supreme court shall adopt rules of procedure for the commission on trial court appointments.

L.   The members of the commission who were appointed pursuant to section 36 of this article prior to the effective date of this section may continue to serve until the expiration of their normal terms. All subsequent appointments shall be made as prescribed by this section.

Added, election Nov. 3, 1992, effective Nov. 23, 1992.

§ 42. Retention evaluation of justices and judges

The supreme court shall adopt, after public hearings, and administer for all justices and judges who file a declaration to be retained in office, a process, established by court rules for evaluating judicial performance. The rules shall include written performance standards and performance reviews which survey opinions of persons who have knowledge of the justice's or judge's performance. The public shall be afforded a full and fair opportunity for participation in the evaluation process through public hearings, dissemination of evaluation reports to voters and any other methods as the court deems advisable.

Added, election Nov. 3, 1992, effective Nov. 23, 1992.

ARTICLE VI.I
COMMISSION ON JUDICIAL CONDUCT

Added by election Nov. 3, 1970, effective Nov. 27, 1970.

§ 1. Composition; appointment; term; vacancies

Section 1.   A.   A commission on judicial conduct is created to be composed of eleven persons consisting of two judges of the court of appeals, two judges of the superior court, one justice of the peace and one municipal court judge, who shall be appointed by the supreme court, two members of the state bar of Arizona, who shall be appointed by the governing body of such bar association, and three citizens who are not judges, retired judges nor members of the state bar of Arizona, who shall be appointed by the governor subject to confirmation by the senate in the manner prescribed by law.

B.   Terms of members of the commission shall be six years, except that initial terms of two members appointed by the supreme court and one member appointed by the state bar of Arizona for terms which begin in January, 1991 shall be for two years and initial terms of one member appointed by the supreme court and one member appointed by the state bar of Arizona for terms which begin in January, 1991 shall be for four years. If a member ceases to hold the position that qualified him for appointment his membership on the commission terminates. An appointment to fill a vacancy for an unexpired term shall be made for the remainder of the term by the appointing power of the original appointment.

Added, election Nov. 3, 1970, effective Nov. 27, 1970; amended, election Nov. 2, 1976, effective Nov. 22, 1976; amended, election Nov. 8, 1988, effective Dec. 5, 1988.

§ 2. Disqualification of judge

Section 2.   A judge is disqualified from acting as a judge, without loss of salary, while there is pending an indictment or an information charging him in the United States with a crime punishable as a felony under Arizona or federal law, or a recommendation to the supreme court by the commission on judicial conduct for his suspension, removal or retirement.

Added, election Nov. 3, 1970, effective Nov. 27, 1970; amended, election Nov. 8, 1988, effective Dec. 5, 1988.

§ 3. Suspension or removal of judge

Section 3.   On recommendation of the commission on judicial conduct, or on its own motion, the supreme court may suspend a judge from office without salary when, in the United States, he pleads guilty or no contest or is found guilty of a crime punishable as a felony under Arizona or federal law or of any other crime that involves moral turpitude under such law. If his conviction is reversed the suspension terminates, and he shall be paid his salary for the period of suspension. If he is suspended and his conviction becomes final the supreme court shall remove him from office.

Added, election Nov. 3, 1970, effective Nov. 27, 1970; amended, election Nov. 8, 1988, effective Dec. 5, 1988.

§ 4. Retirement of judge

Section 4.   A. On recommendation of the commission on judicial conduct, the supreme court may retire a judge for disability that seriously interferes with the performance of his duties and is or is likely to become permanent, and may censure, suspend without pay or remove a judge for action by him that constitutes wilful misconduct in office, wilful and persistent failure to perform his duties, habitual intemperance or conduct prejudicial to the administration of justice that brings the judicial office into disrepute.
B.   A judge retired by the supreme court shall be considered to have retired voluntarily. A judge removed by the supreme court is ineligible for judicial office in this state.

Added, election Nov. 3, 1970, effective Nov. 27, 1970; amended, election Nov. 8, 1988, effective Dec. 5, 1988.

§ 5. Definitions and rules implementing article

Section 5.   The term "judge" as used in this article shall apply to all justices of the peace, judges in courts inferior to the superior court as may be provided by law, judges of the superior court, judges of the court of appeals and justices of the supreme court.

The supreme court shall make rules implementing this article and providing for confidentiality of proceedings. A judge who is a member of the commission or supreme court shall not participate as a member in any proceedings hereunder involving his own censure, suspension, removal or involuntary retirement.

Added, election Nov. 3, 1970, effective Nov. 27, 1970; amended, election Nov. 8, 1988, effective Dec. 5, 1988.

§ 6. Article self-executing
Section 6.   The provisions of this article shall be self-executing.

Added, election Nov. 3, 1970, effective Nov. 27, 1970.

ARTICLE VII
SUFFRAGE AND ELECTIONS

§ 1. Method of voting; secrecy
Section 1.   All elections by the people shall be by ballot, or by such other method as may be prescribed by law; provided, that secrecy in voting shall be preserved.

§ 2. Qualifications of voters; disqualification
Section 2.   A.   No person shall be entitled to vote at any general election, or for any office that now is, or hereafter may be, elective by the people, or upon any question which may be submitted to a vote of the people, unless such person be a citizen of the United States of the age of eighteen years or over, and shall have resided in the state for the period of time preceding such election as prescribed by law, provided that qualifications for voters at a general election for the purpose of electing presidential electors shall be as prescribed by law. The word "citizen" shall include persons of the male and female sex.

B.   The rights of citizens of the United States to vote and hold office shall not be denied or abridged by the state, or any political division or municipality thereof, on account of sex, and the right to register, to vote and to hold office under any law now in effect, or which may hereafter be enacted, is hereby extended to, and conferred upon males and females alike.

C.   No person who is adjudicated an incapacitated person shall be qualified to vote at any election, nor shall any person convicted of treason or felony, be qualified to vote at any election unless restored to civil rights.

Amended, election Nov. 5, 1912, effective Dec. 12, 1912; election Nov. 6, 1962, effective Nov. 26, 1962; amended election Nov. 7, 2000, effective Dec. 7, 2000.

§ 3. Voting residence of federal employees and certain others

Section 3.   For the purpose of voting, no person shall be deemed to have gained or lost a residence by reason of being present or absent while employed in the service of the United States, or while a student at any institution of learning, or while kept at any institution or other shelter at public expense, or while confined in any public jail or prison.

Amended, election Nov. 7, 2000, effective Dec. 7, 2000.

§ 4. Privilege of electors from arrest

Section 4.   Electors shall in all cases, except treason, felony, or breach of the peace, be privileged from arrest during their attendance at any election, and in going thereto and returning therefrom.

§ 5. Military duty on day of election

Section 5.   No elector shall be obliged to perform military duty on the day of an election, except in time of war or public danger.

§ 6. Residence of military personnel stationed within state

Section 6.   No soldier, seaman, or marine, in the army or navy of the United States shall be deemed a resident of this state in consequence of his being stationed at any military or naval place within this state.

§ 7. Highest number of votes received as determinative of person elected

Section 7.   In all elections held by the people in this state, the person, or persons, receiving the highest number of legal votes shall be declared elected.

Amended, election Nov. 8, 1988, effective Dec. 5, 1988; amended, election Nov. 3, 1992, effective Nov. 23, 1992.

§ 8. Qualifications for voters at school elections

Section 8.   Qualifications for voters at school elections shall be as are now, or as may hereafter be, provided by law.

§ 9. Advisory vote
Section 9.   For the purpose of obtaining an advisory vote of the people, the legislature shall provide for placing the names of candidates for United States senator on the official ballot at the general election next preceding the election of a United States senator.

§ 10. Direct primary election law
Section 10.   The legislature shall enact a direct primary election law, which shall provide for the nomination of candidates for all elective state, county, and city offices, including candidates for United States Senator and for Representative in Congress. Any person who is registered as no party preference or independent as the party preference or who is registered with a political party that is not qualified for representation on the ballot may vote in the primary election of any one of the political parties that is qualified for the ballot.

Amended, election Nov. 3, 1998, effective December 10, 1998.

§ 11. General elections; date
Section 11.   There shall be a general election of representatives in congress, and of state, county, and precinct officers on the first Tuesday after the first Monday in November of the first even numbered year after the year in which Arizona is admitted to statehood and biennially thereafter.

§ 12. Registration and other laws
Section 12.   There shall be enacted registration and other laws to secure the purity of elections and guard against abuses of the elective franchise.

§ 13. Submission of questions upon bond issues or special assessments
Section 13.   Questions upon bond issues or special assessments shall be submitted to the vote of real property tax payers, who shall also in all respects be qualified electors of this state, and of the political subdivision thereof affected by such question.

Amended, election Nov. 4, 1930, effective Dec. 1, 1930.

§ 14. Fee for placing candidate's name on ballot
Section 14.   No fee shall ever be required in order to have the name of any candidate placed on the official ballot for any election or primary.

§ 15. Qualifications for public office

Section 15.   Every person elected or appointed to any elective office of trust or profit under the authority of the state, or any political division or any municipality thereof, shall be a qualified elector of the political division or municipality in which such person shall be elected.

Amended, election Nov. 5, 1912, effective Dec. 12, 1912; election Nov. 2, 1948, effective Nov. 22, 1948; election Nov. 7, 1972, effective Dec. 1, 1972.

§ 16. Campaign contributions and expenditures; publicity

Section 16.   The legislature, at its first session, shall enact a law providing for a general publicity, before and after election, of all campaign contributions to, and expenditures of campaign committees and candidates for public office.

§ 17. Vacancy in congress

Section 17.   There shall be a primary and general election as prescribed by law, which shall provide for nomination and election of a candidate for United States senator and for representative in congress when a vacancy occurs through resignation or any other cause.

Added, election Nov. 6, 1962, effective Nov. 26, 1962.

§ 18. Term limits on ballot appearances in congressional elections

Section 18.   The name of any candidate for United States Senator from Arizona shall not appear on the ballot if, by the end of the current term of office, the candidate will have served (or, but for resignation, would have served) in that office for two consecutive terms, and the name of a candidate for United States Representative from Arizona shall not appear on the ballot if, by the end of the current term of office, the candidate will have served (or, but for resignation, would have served) in that office for three consecutive terms. Terms are considered consecutive unless they are at least one full term apart. Any person appointed or elected to fill a vacancy in the United States Congress who serves at least one half of a term of office shall be considered to have served a term in that office for purposes of this section. For purposes of this section, terms beginning before January 1, 1993 shall not be considered.

Added, election Nov. 3, 1992, effective Nov. 23, 1992.

ARTICLE VIII
REMOVAL FROM OFFICE

PART 1. RECALL OF PUBLIC OFFICERS

§ 1. Officers subject to recall; petitioners
Section 1.   Every public officer in the state of Arizona, holding an elective office, either by election or appointment, is subject to recall from such office by the qualified electors of the electoral district from which candidates are elected to such office. Such electoral district may include the whole state. Such number of said electors as shall equal twenty-five per centum of the number of votes cast at the last preceding general election for all of the candidates for the office held by such officer, may by petition, which shall be known as a recall petition, demand his recall.

Amended, election Nov. 5, 1912, effective Dec. 12, 1912.

§ 2. Recall petitions; contents; filing; signatures; oath
Section 2.   Every recall petition must contain a general statement, in not more than two hundred words, of the grounds of such demand, and must be filed in the office in which petitions for nominations to the office held by the incumbent are required to be filed. The signatures to such recall petition need not all be on the one sheet of paper, but each signer must add to his signature the date of his signing said petition, and his place of residence, giving his street and number, if any, should he reside in a town or city. One of the signers of each sheet of such petition, or the person circulating such sheet, must make and subscribe an oath on said sheet, that the signatures thereon are genuine.

§ 3. Resignation of officer; special election
Section 3.   If such officer shall offer his resignation it shall be accepted, and the vacancy shall be filled as may be provided by law. If he shall not resign within five days after a recall petition is filed as provided by law, a special election shall be ordered to be held as provided by law, to determine whether such officer shall be recalled. On the ballots at such election shall be printed the reasons as set forth in the petition for demanding his recall, and, in not more than two hundred words, the officer's justification of his course in

office. He shall continue to perform the duties of his office until the result of such election shall have been officially declared.

Amended, election Nov. 5, 1974, effective Dec. 5, 1974.

§ 4. Special election; candidates; results; qualification of successor

Section 4.   Unless the incumbent otherwise requests, in writing, the incumbent's name shall be placed as a candidate on the official ballot without nomination. Other candidates for the office may be nominated to be voted for at said election. The candidate who receives the highest number of votes shall be declared elected for the remainder of the term. Unless the incumbent receives the highest number of votes, the incumbent shall be deemed to be removed from office, upon qualification of the successor. In the event that the successor shall not qualify within five days after the result of said election shall have been declared, the said office shall be vacant, and may be filled as provided by law.

Amended, election Nov. 8, 1988, effective Dec. 5, 1988; amended, election Nov. 3, 1992, effective Nov. 23, 1992.

§ 5. Recall petitions; restrictions and conditions

Section 5.   No recall petition shall be circulated against any officer until he shall have held his office for a period of six months, except that it may be filed against a member of the legislature at any time after five days from the beginning of the first session after his election. After one recall petition and election, no further recall petition shall be filed against the same officer during the term for which he was elected, unless petitioners signing such petition shall first pay into the public treasury which has paid such election expenses, all expenses of the preceding election.

§ 6. Application of general election laws; implementary legislation

Section 6.   The general election laws shall apply to recall elections in so far as applicable. Laws necessary to facilitate the operation of the provisions of this article shall be enacted, including provision for payment by the public treasury of the reasonable special election campaign expenses of such officer.

PART 2. IMPEACHMENT

§ 1. Power of impeachment in house of representatives; trial by senate

Section 1.   The house of representatives shall have the sole power of impeachment. The concurrence of a majority of all the members shall be necessary to an impeachment. All impeachments shall be tried by the senate, and, when sitting for that purpose, the senators shall be upon oath or affirmation to do justice according to law and evidence, and shall be presided over by the chief justice of the supreme court. Should the chief justice be on trial, or otherwise disqualified, the senate shall elect a judge of the supreme court to preside.

§ 2. Conviction; grounds for impeachment; judgment; liability to trial

Section 2.   No person shall be convicted without a concurrence of two-thirds of the senators elected. The governor and other state and judicial officers, except justices of courts not of record, shall be liable to impeachment for high crimes, misdemeanors, or malfeasance in office, but judgment in such cases shall extend only to removal from office and disqualification to hold any office of honor, trust, or profit in the state. The party, whether convicted or acquitted, shall, nevertheless, be liable to trial and punishment according to law.

ARTICLE IX
PUBLIC DEBT, REVENUE, AND TAXATION

§ 1. Surrender of power of taxation; uniformity of taxes

Section 1.   The power of taxation shall never be surrendered, suspended or contracted away. Except as provided by section 18 of this article, all taxes shall be uniform upon the same class of property within the territorial limits of the authority levying the tax, and shall be levied and collected for public purposes only.

Amended, election Nov. 7, 2000, effective Dec. 7, 2000.

§ 2. Property subject to taxation; exemptions

Section 2.   (1)   There shall be exempt from taxation all federal, state, county and municipal property.

(2)   Property of educational, charitable, and religious associa-

tions or institutions not used or held for profit may be exempt from taxation by law.

(3)   Public debts, as evidenced by the bonds of Arizona, its counties, municipalities, or other subdivisions, shall also be exempt from taxation.

(4)   All household goods owned by the user thereof and used solely for noncommercial purposes shall be exempt from taxation, and such person entitled to such exemption shall not be required to take any affirmative action to receive the benefit of such exemption.

(5)   Stocks of raw or finished materials, unassembled parts, work in process or finished products constituting the inventory of a retailer or wholesaler located within the state and principally engaged in the resale of such materials, parts or products, whether or not for resale to the ultimate consumer, shall be exempt from taxation.

(6)   The legislature may exempt personal property that is used for agricultural purposes or in a trade or business from taxation in a manner provided by law, except that the exemption does not apply to any amount of the full cash value of the personal property of a taxpayer that exceeds fifty thousand dollars. The legislature may provide by law to increase the exempt amount according to annual variations in a designated national inflation index.

(7)   The legislature may exempt the property of cemeteries that are set apart and used to inter deceased human beings from taxation in a manner provided by law

(8)   There shall be further exempt from taxation the property of each honorably discharged airman, soldier, sailor, United States marine, member of revenue marine service, the coast guard, nurse corps or of any predecessor or of the component of auxiliary of any thereof, resident of this state, in the amount of:

(a)   One thousand five hundred dollars if the total assessment of such person does not exceed three thousand five hundred dollars.

(b)   One thousand dollars if the total assessment of such person does not exceed four thousand dollars.

(c)   Five hundred dollars if the total assessment of such person does not exceed four thousand five hundred dollars.

(d)   Two hundred fifty dollars if the total assessment of such person does not exceed five thousand dollars.

(e)   No exemption if the total assessment of such person exceeds five thousand dollars.

No such exemption shall be made for such person unless such person shall have served at least sixty days in the military or naval service of the United States during World War I or prior wars and shall have been a resident of this state prior to September 1, 1945.

(9)   There shall be further exempt from taxation as herein provided the property of each honorably discharged airman, soldier, sailor, United States marine, member of revenue marine service, the coast guard, nurse corps or of any predecessor or of the component of auxiliary of any thereof, resident of this state, where such person has a service-connected disability as determined by the United States veterans administration or its successor. No such exemption shall be made for such person unless he shall have been a resident of this state prior to September 1, 1945 or unless such person shall have been a resident of this state for at least four years prior to his original entry into service as an airman, soldier, sailor, United States marine, member of revenue marine service, the coast guard, nurse corps or of any predecessor or of the component of auxiliary of any thereof. The property of such person having a compensable service-connected disability exempt from taxation as herein provided shall be determined as follows:

(a)   If such person's service-connected disability as determined by the United States veterans administration or its successor is sixty per cent or less, the property of such person exempt from taxation shall be determined by such person's percentage of disability multiplied by the assessment of such person in the amount of:

(i)   One thousand five hundred dollars if the total assessment of such person does not exceed three thousand five hundred dollars.

(ii)   One thousand dollars if the total assessment of such person does not exceed four thousand dollars.

(iii)   Five hundred dollars if the total assessment of such person does not exceed four thousand five hundred dollars.

(iv)   Two hundred fifty dollars if the total assessment of such person does not exceed five thousand dollars.

(v)   No exemption if the total assessment of such person exceeds five thousand dollars.

(b)   If such person's service-connected disability as determined by the United States veterans administration or its successor is more than sixty per cent, the property of such person exempt from taxation shall be in the amount of:

(i)   One thousand five hundred dollars if the total assessment of such person does not exceed three thousand five hundred dollars.

(ii)   One thousand dollars if the total assessment of such person does not exceed four thousand dollars.

(iii)   Five hundred dollars if the total assessment of such person does not exceed four thousand five hundred dollars.

(iv)   Two hundred fifty dollars if the total assessment of such person does not exceed five thousand dollars.

(v)   No exemption if the total assessment of such person exceeds five thousand dollars.

(10)   There shall be further exempt from taxation the property of each honorably discharged airman, soldier, sailor, United States marine, member of revenue marine service, the coast guard, nurse corps or of any predecessor or of the component of auxiliary of any thereof, resident of this state, where such person has a non-service-connected total and permanent disability, physical or mental, as so certified by the United States veterans administration, or its successor, or such other certification as provided by law, in the amount of:

(a)   One thousand five hundred dollars if the total assessment of such person does not exceed three thousand five hundred dollars.

(b)   One thousand dollars if the total assessment of such person does not exceed four thousand dollars.

(c)   Five hundred dollars if the total assessment of such person does not exceed four thousand five hundred dollars.

(d)   Two hundred fifty dollars if the total assessment of such person does not exceed five thousand dollars.

(e)   No exemption if the total assessment of such person exceeds five thousand dollars.

No such exemption shall be made for such person unless he shall have served at least sixty days in the military or naval service of the United States during time of war after World War I and shall have been a resident of this state, prior to September 1, 1945.

(11)   There shall be further exempt from taxation the property of each widow, resident of the state, in the amount of:

(a)   One thousand five hundred dollars if the total assessment of such widow does not exceed three thousand five hundred dollars.

(b)   One thousand dollars if the total assessment of such widow does not exceed four thousand dollars.

(c)   Five hundred dollars if the total assessment of such widow does not exceed four thousand five hundred dollars.

(d)   Two hundred fifty dollars if the total assessment of such widow does not exceed five thousand dollars.

(e)   No exemption if the total assessment of such widow exceeds five thousand dollars.

In order to qualify for this exemption, the income from all sources of such widow, together with the income from all sources of all children of such widow residing with the widow in her residence in the year immediately preceding the year for which such widow applies for this exemption, shall not exceed:

1.   Seven thousand dollars if none of the widow's children under the age of eighteen years resided with her in such widow's residence; or

2.   Ten thousand dollars if one or more of the widow's children residing with her in such widow's residence was under the age of eighteen years, or was totally and permanently disabled, physically or mentally, as certified by competent medical authority as provided by law.

Such widow shall have resided with her last spouse in this state at the time of the spouse's death if she was not a widow and a resident of this state prior to January 1, 1969.

(12)   No property shall be exempt which has been conveyed to evade taxation. The total exemption from taxation granted to the property owned by a person who qualifies for any exemption in accordance with the terms of subsections (7), (8), (9) or (10) shall not exceed one thousand five hundred dollars. The provisions of this section shall be self-executing.

(13)   All property in the state not exempt under the laws of the United States or under this constitution or exempt by law under the provisions of this section shall be subject to taxation to be ascertained as provided by law.

Amended, election Nov. 6, 1928, effective Nov. 28, 1928; election Nov. 5, 1946, effective Nov. 25, 1946; election Nov. 3, 1964, effective Dec. 3, 1964; election Nov. 5, 1968, effective Dec. 4, 1968; election June 3, 1980, effective June 28, 1980; election Nov. 5, 1996, effective Dec. 6, 1996; amended, election Nov. 7, 2000, effective Dec. 7, 2000.

§ 2.1. Exemption from tax; property of widowers

Section 2.1.   There shall be further exempt from taxation the

property of each widower, resident of this state, in the amount of:
1.   One thousand five hundred dollars if the total assessment of such widower does not exceed three thousand five hundred dollars.
2.   One thousand dollars if the total assessment of such widower does not exceed four thousand dollars.
3.   Five hundred dollars if the total assessment of such widower does not exceed four thousand five hundred dollars.
4.   Two hundred fifty dollars if the total assessment of such widower does not exceed five thousand dollars.
5.   No exemption if the total assessment of such widower exceeds five thousand dollars.
In order to qualify for this exemption, the income from all sources of such widower, together with the income from all sources of all children of such widower residing with the widower in his residence in the year immediately preceding the year for which such widower applies for this exemption, shall not exceed:
1.   Seven thousand dollars if none of the widower's children under the age of eighteen years resided with him in such widower's residence; or
2.   Ten thousand dollars if one or more of the widower's children residing with him in such widower's residence was under the age of eighteen years, or was totally and permanently disabled, physically or mentally, as certified by competent medical authority as provided by law.
Such widower shall have resided with his last spouse in this state at the time of the spouse's death if he was not a widower and a resident of this state prior to January 1, 1969.
No property shall be exempt which has been conveyed to evade taxation. The total exemption from taxation granted to the property owned by a person who qualifies for any exemption in accordance with the terms of this section shall not exceed one thousand five hundred dollars. This section shall be self-executing.

Added, election June 3, 1980, effective June 18, 1980.

§ 2.2. Exemption from tax; property of persons who are disabled
Section 2.2   A.   There shall be further exempt from taxation the property of each person who, after age seventeen, has been medically certified as totally and permanently disabled, in the amount of:

1.   One thousand five hundred dollars if the total assessment of such person does not exceed three thousand five hundred dollars.
2.   One thousand dollars if the total assessment of such person does not exceed four thousand dollars.
3.   Five hundred dollars if the total assessment of such person does not exceed four thousand five hundred dollars.
4.   Two hundred fifty dollars if the total assessment of such person does not exceed five thousand dollars.
5.   No exemption if the total assessment of such person exceeds five thousand dollars. The legislature may by law prescribe criteria for medical certification of such disability.
B.   The income from all sources of the person who is disabled, the person's spouse and all of the persons's children who reside in the person's residence in the year immediately preceding the year for the person applies for this exemption shall not exceed:
1.   Seven thousand dollars if none of the person's children under the age of eighteen years resided in the person's residence; or
2.   Ten thousand dollars if one or more of the person's children residing in the residence was under the age of eighteen years or was totally and permanently disabled, physically or mentally, as certified by competent medical authority as provided by law.
C.   No property shall be exempt which has been conveyed to evade taxation. The total exemption from taxation granted to the property owned by a person who qualifies for any exemption in accordance with the terms of this section shall not exceed one thousand five hundred dollars. This section shall be self-executing.

Added, election June 3, 1980, effective June 28, 1980; amended, election Nov. 7, 2000, effective Dec. 7, 2000.

§ 2.3. Exemption from tax; increase in amount of exemptions, assessments and income

Section 2.3   The legislature may by law increase the amount of the exemptions, the total permissible amount of assessments or the permissible amount of income from all sources prescribed in §§ 2, 2.1 and 2.2 of this article.

Added, election June 3, 1980, effective June 28, 1980.

§ 3.   Annual tax; purposes; amount; tax laws; payment of taxes into state treasury

Section 3.   The legislature shall provide by law for an annual tax sufficient, with other sources of revenue, to defray the necessary ordinary expenses of the state for each fiscal year. And for the purpose of paying the state debt, if there be any, the legislature shall provide for levying an annual tax sufficient to pay the annual interest and the principal of such debt within twenty-five years from the final passage of the law creating the debt.

No tax shall be levied except in pursuance of law, and every law imposing a tax shall state distinctly the object of the tax, to which object only it shall be applied.

All taxes levied and collected for state purposes shall be paid into the state treasury in money only.

§ 4. Fiscal year; annual statement of receipts and expenditures; deficit
Section 4.   The fiscal year shall commence on the first day of July in each year. An accurate statement of the receipts and expenditures of the public money shall be published annually, in such manner as shall be provided by law. Whenever the expenses of any fiscal year shall exceed the income, the legislature may provide for levying a tax for the ensuing fiscal year sufficient, with other sources of income, to pay the deficiency, as well as the estimated expenses of the ensuing fiscal year.

§ 5. Power of state to contract debts; purposes; limit; restrictions
Section 5.   The state may contract debts to supply the casual deficits or failures in revenues, or to meet expenses not otherwise provided for; but the aggregate amount of such debts, direct and contingent, whether contracted by virtue of one or more laws, or at different periods of time, shall never exceed the sum of three hundred and fifty thousand dollars; and the money arising from the creation of such debts shall be applied to the purpose for which it was obtained or to repay the debts so contracted, and to no other purpose.

In addition to the above limited power to contract debts the state may borrow money to repel invasion, suppress insurrection, or defend the state in time of war; but the money thus raised shall be applied exclusively to the object for which the loan shall have been authorized or to the repayment of the debt thereby created. No money shall be paid out of the state treasury, except in the manner provided by law.

Constitution of the State of Arizona

§ 6. Local assessments and taxes
Section 6.   Incorporated cities, towns, and villages may be vested by law with power to make local improvements by special assessments, or by special taxation of property benefited. For all corporate purposes, all municipal corporations may be vested with authority to assess and collect taxes.

§ 7. Gift or loan of credit; subsidies; stock ownership; joint ownership
Section 7.   Neither the state, nor any county, city, town, municipality, or other subdivision of the state shall ever give or loan its credit in the aid of, or make any donation or grant, by subsidy or otherwise, to any individual, association, or corporation, or become a subscriber to, or a shareholder in, any company or corporation, or become a joint owner with any person, company, or corporation, except as to such ownerships as may accrue to the state by operation or provision of law or as authorized by law solely for investment of the monies in the various funds of the state.

Amended, election Nov. 3, 1998, effective December 10, 1998.

§ 8. Local debt limits; assent of taxpayers
Section 8.   (1)   No county, city, town, school district, or other municipal corporation shall for any purpose become indebted in any manner to an amount exceeding six per centum of the taxable property in such county, city, town, school district, or other municipal corporation, without the assent of a majority of the property taxpayers, who must also in all respects be qualified electors, therein voting at an election provided by law to be held for that purpose, the value of the taxable property therein to be ascertained by the last assessment for state and county purposes, previous to incurring such indebtedness; except, that in incorporated cities and towns assessments shall be taken from the last assessment for city or town purposes; provided, that under no circumstances shall any county or school district become indebted to an amount exceeding fifteen per centum of such taxable property, as shown by the last assessment roll thereof; and provided further, that any incorporated city or town, with such assent, may be allowed to become indebted to a larger amount, but not exceeding twenty per centum additional, for supplying such city or town with water, artificial light, or sewers, when the works for supplying such water, light, or sewers are or shall be owned and controlled by the municipal-

ity, and for the acquisition and development by the incorporated city or town of land or interests therein for open space preserves, parks, playgrounds and recreational facilities.
(2)   The provisions of § 18, subsections (3), (4), (5) and (6) of this article shall not apply to this section.

Amended, election Nov. 5, 1912, effective Dec. 12, 1912; election Nov. 7, 1972, effective Dec. 1, 1972; election June 3, 1980, effective June 28, 1980.

§ 8.1. Unified school district debt limit
Section 8.1.   (1) Notwithstanding the provisions of section 8 of this article a unified school district may become indebted to an amount not exceeding thirty per cent of the taxable property of the school district, as shown by the last assessment roll thereof. For purposes of this section, a unified school district is a single school district which provides education to the area within the district for grades kindergarten through twelve and which area is not subject to taxation by any other common or high school district.
(2)   The provisions of § 18, subsections (3), (4), (5) and (6) of this article shall not apply to this section.

Added, election Nov. 5, 1974, effective Dec. 5, 1974. Amended, election June 3, 1980, effective June 28, 1980.

§ 9. Statement of tax and objects
Section 9.   Every law which imposes, continues, or revives a tax shall distinctly state the tax and the objects for which it shall be applied; and it shall not be sufficient to refer to any other law to fix such tax or object.

§ 10. Aid of church, private or sectarian school, or public service corporation
Section 10.   No tax shall be laid or appropriation of public money made in aid of any church, or private or sectarian school, or any public service corporation.

§ 11. Taxing procedure; license tax on registered vehicles
Section 11.   From and after December 31, 1973, the manner, method and mode of assessing, equalizing and levying taxes in the state of Arizona shall be such as is prescribed by law.
From and after December 31, 1973, a license tax is hereby imposed on vehicles registered for operation upon the highways in Arizona, which license tax shall be in lieu of all ad valorem property taxes

on any vehicle subject to such license tax. Such license tax shall be collected as provided by law. To facilitate an even distribution of the registration of vehicles and the collection of the license tax imposed by this section, the legislature may provide for different times or periods of registration between and within the several classes of vehicles.

In the event that a vehicle is destroyed after the beginning of a registration year, the license tax paid for such year on such vehicle may be reduced as provided by law.

From and after December 31, 1973, mobile homes, as defined by law for tax purposes, shall not be subject to the license tax imposed under the provisions of this section but shall be subject to ad valorem property taxes on any mobile homes in the manner provided by law. Distribution of the proceeds derived from such tax shall be as provided by law.

From and after December 31, 1973, the legislature shall provide for the distribution of the proceeds from such license tax to the state, counties, school districts, cities and towns.

Amended, election Nov. 5, 1912, effective Dec. 12, 1912; election Nov. 5, 1940, effective Nov. 27, 1940; election Nov. 5, 1968, effective Dec. 4, 1968; election Nov. 7, 1972, effective January 1, 1974.

§ 12. Authority to provide for levy and collection of license and other taxes
Section 12.   The law-making power shall have authority to provide for the levy and collection of license, franchise, gross revenue, excise, income, collateral and direct inheritance, legacy, and succession taxes, also graduated income taxes, graduated collateral and direct inheritance taxes, graduated legacy and succession taxes, stamp, registration, production, or other specific taxes.

§ 13. Inventory tax on materials and products of manufacturers
Section 13.   No tax shall be levied on:
1.   Raw or unfinished materials, unassembled parts, work in process or finished products, constituting the inventory of a manufacturer or manufacturing establishment located within the state and principally engaged in the fabrication, production and manufacture of products, wares and articles for use, from raw or prepared materials, imparting thereto new forms, qualities, properties and combinations, which materials, parts, work in process or finished products are not consigned or billed to any other party.

2.   Livestock, poultry, aquatic animals and honeybees owned by a person who is principally engaged in agricultural production, subject to such conditions as may be prescribed by law.

Added, election Sept. 12, 1950, effective Oct. 2, 1950; amended, election Nov. 8, 1994, effective November 28, 1994.

§ 14. Use and distribution of vehicle, user, and gasoline and diesel tax receipts

Section 14.   No moneys derived from fees, excises, or license taxes relating to registration, operation, or use of vehicles on the public highways or streets or to fuels or any other energy source used for the propulsion of vehicles on the public highways or streets shall be expended for other than highway and street purposes including the cost of administering the state highway system and the laws creating such fees, excises, or license taxes, statutory refunds and adjustments provided by law, payment of principal and interest on highway and street bonds and obligations, expenses of state enforcement of traffic laws and state administration of traffic safety programs, payment of costs of publication and distribution of Arizona Highways Magazine, state costs of construction, reconstruction, maintenance or repair of public highways, streets or bridges, costs of rights of way acquisitions and expenses related thereto, roadside development, and for distribution to counties, incorporated cities and towns to be used by them solely for highway and street purposes including costs of rights of way acquisitions and expenses related thereto, construction, reconstruction, maintenance, repair, roadside development, of county, city and town roads, streets, and bridges and payment of principal and interest on highway and street bonds. As long as the total highway user revenues derived equals or exceeds the total derived in the fiscal year ending June 30, 1970, the state and any county shall not receive from such revenues for the use of each and for distribution to cities and towns, fewer dollars than were received and distributed in such fiscal year. This section shall not apply to moneys derived from the automobile license tax imposed under section 11 of article IX of the Constitution of Arizona. All moneys collected in accordance with this section shall be distributed as provided by law.

Added, election Nov. 4, 1952, effective Nov. 24, 1952. Amended, election Nov. 3, 1970, effective Nov. 27, 1970.

§ 15. License tax on aircraft
Section 15.   Commencing January 1, 1965, a license tax is imposed on aircraft registered for operation in Arizona, which license tax shall be in lieu of all ad valorem property taxes on any aircraft subject thereto, but nothing in this section shall be deemed to apply to:
1.   Regularly scheduled aircraft operated by an air line company for the primary purpose of carrying persons or property for hire in interstate, intrastate, or international transportation.
2.   Aircraft owned and held by an aircraft dealer solely for purposes of sale.
3.   Aircraft owned by a nonresident who operates aircraft for a period not in excess of ninety days in any one calendar year, provided that such aircraft are not engaged in any intrastate commercial activity.
4.   Aircraft owned and operated exclusively in the public service by the state or by any political subdivision thereof, or by the civil air patrol.
The amount, manner, method and mode of assessing, equalizing and levying such license tax and the distribution of the proceeds therefrom shall be prescribed by law.

Added, election Nov. 3, 1964, effective Dec. 3, 1964.

§ 16. Exemption of watercraft from ad valorem property taxes
Section 16.   Commencing January 1, 1967, all watercraft registered for operation in Arizona, excluding watercraft owned and operated for any commercial purpose, is exempt from ad valorem property taxes. Watercraft exempt from ad valorem property taxes shall be subject to or exempt from a license tax, as may be prescribed by law.
"Watercraft", used in this section, shall be defined as provided by law.

Added, election Nov. 8, 1966, effective Nov. 29, 1966.

§ 17. Economic estimates commission; appropriation limitation; powers and duties of commission
Section 17.   (1) The economic estimates commission shall be established by law, with a membership of not to exceed three members, and shall determine and publish prior to February 1 of each year the estimated total personal income for the following fiscal

year. By April 1 of each year the commission shall determine and publish a final estimate of the total personal income for the following fiscal year, which estimate shall be used in computing the appropriations limit for the legislature. For the purposes of this section, "total personal income" means the dollar amount that will be reported as total income by persons for the state of Arizona by the U.S. department of commerce or its successor agency.

(2)   For purposes of this section, "state revenues":

(a)   Include all monies, revenues, fees, fines, penalties, funds, tuitions, property and receipts of any kind whatsoever received by or for the account of the state or any of its agencies, departments, offices, boards, commissions, authorities, councils and institutions except as provided in this subsection.

(b)   Do not include:

(i)   Any amounts or property received from the issuance or incurrence of bonds or other lawful long-term obligations issued or incurred for a specific purpose. For the purpose of this subdivision long-term obligations shall not include warrants issued in the ordinary course of operation or registered for payment by the state.

(ii)   Any amounts or property received as payment of dividends or interest.

(iii)   Any amounts or property received by the state in the capacity of trustee, custodian or agent.

(iv)   Any amounts received from employers for deposit in the unemployment compensation fund or any successor fund.

(v)   Any amounts collected by the state for distribution to counties, cities and towns without specific restrictions on the use of the funds other than the restrictions included in § 14 of this article.

(vi)   Any amounts received as grants, aid, contributions or gifts of any type, except voluntary contributions or other contributions received directly or indirectly in lieu of taxes.

(vii)   Any amounts received as the proceeds from the sale, lease or redemption of property or as consideration for services or the use of property.

(viii)   Any amounts received pursuant to a transfer during a fiscal year from another agency, department, office, board, commission, authority, council or institution of the state which were included as state revenues for such fiscal year or which are excluded from state revenue under other provisions of this subsection.

(ix)   Any amounts attributable to an increase in the rates of tax subsequent to July 1, 1979 on vehicle users, gasoline and diesel fuel which were levied on July 1, 1979.

(x)   Any amounts received during a fiscal year as refunds, reimbursements or other recoveries of amounts appropriated which were applied against the appropriation limitation for such fiscal year or which were excluded from state revenues under other provisions of this subsection.

(3)   The legislature shall not appropriate for any fiscal year state revenues in excess of seven per cent of the total personal income of the state for that fiscal year as determined by the economic estimates commission. The limitation may be exceeded upon affirmative vote of two-thirds of the membership of each house of the legislature on each measure that appropriates amounts in excess of the limitation. If the legislature authorizes a specific dollar amount of appropriation for more than one fiscal year, for the purpose of measuring such appropriation against the appropriation limitation, the entire amount appropriated shall be applied against the limitation in the first fiscal year during which any expenditures are authorized, and in no other fiscal year.

(4)   In order to permit the transference of governmental functions or funding responsibilities between the federal and state governments and between the state government and its political subdivisions without abridging the purpose of this section to limit state appropriations to a percentage of total personal income, the legislature shall provide for adjustments of the appropriation percentage limitation consistent with the following principles:

(a)   If the federal government assumes all or any part of the cost of providing a governmental function which the state previously funded in whole or in part, the appropriation limitation shall be commensurately decreased.

(b)   If the federal government requires the state to assume all or any part of the cost of providing a governmental function the appropriation limitation shall be commensurately increased.

(c)   If the state assumes all or any part of the cost of providing a governmental function and the state requires the political subdivision, which previously funded all or any part of the cost of the function to commensurately decrease its tax revenues, the appropriation percentage limitation shall be commensurately increased.

(d)   If a political subdivision assumes all or any part of the cost of providing a governmental function previously funded in whole

311

or in part by the state, the appropriation percentage limitation shall be commensurately decreased.

Any adjustments made pursuant to this subsection shall be made for the first fiscal year of the assumption of the cost. Such adjustment shall remain in effect for each subsequent fiscal year.

Added, election Nov. 7, 1978, effective Nov. 29, 1978. Amended, election June 3, 1980, effective June 28, 1980.

§ 18. Residential ad valorem tax limits; limit on increase in values; definitions

Section 18.   (1) The maximum amount of ad valorem taxes that may be collected from residential property in any tax year shall not exceed one per cent of the property's full cash value as limited by this section.

(2)   The limitation provided in subsection (1) does not apply to:

(a)   Ad valorem taxes or special assessments levied to pay the principal of and interest and redemption charges on bonded indebtedness or other lawful long-term obligations issued or incurred for a specific purpose.

(b)   Ad valorem taxes or assessments levied by or for property improvement assessment districts, improvement districts and other special purpose districts other than counties, cities, towns, school districts and community college districts.

(c)   Ad valorem taxes levied pursuant to an election to exceed a budget, expenditure or tax limitation.

(3)   Except as otherwise provided by subsections (5), (6) and (7) of this section the value of real property and improvements and the value of mobile homes used for all ad valorem taxes except those specified in subsection (2) shall be the lesser of the full cash value of the property or an amount ten per cent greater than the value of property determined pursuant to this subsection for the prior year or an amount equal to the value of property determined pursuant to this subsection for the prior year plus one-fourth of the difference between such value and the full cash value of the property for current tax year, whichever is greater.

(4)   The legislature shall by law provide a method of determining the value, subject to the provisions of subsection (3), of new property.

(5)   The limitation on increases in the value of property pre-

scribed in subsection (3) does not apply to equalization orders that the legislature specifically exempts by law from such limitation.

(6)   Subsection (3) does not apply to:

(a)   Property used in the business of patented or unpatented producing mines and the mills and the smelters operated in connection with the mines.

(b)   Producing oil, gas and geothermal interests.

(c)   Real property, improvements thereto and personal property used thereon used in the operation of telephone, telegraph, gas, water and electric utility companies.

(d)   Aircraft that is regularly scheduled and operated by an airline company for the primary purpose of carrying persons or property for hire in interstate, intrastate or international transportation.

(e)   Standing timber.

(f)   Property used in the operation of pipelines.

(g)   Personal property regardless of use except mobile homes.

(7)   A resident of this state who is sixty-five years of age or older may apply to the county assessor for a property valuation protection option on the person's primary residence, including not more than ten acres of undeveloped appurtenant land. The resident may apply for a property valuation protection option after residing in the primary residence for two years. If one person owns the property, the person's total income from all sources including nontaxable income shall not exceed four hundred per cent of the supplemental security income benefit rate established by section 1611 of the social security act. If the property is owned by two or more persons, including a husband and wife, at least one of the owners must be sixty-five years of age or older and the owners' combined total income from all sources including nontaxable income shall not exceed five hundred per cent of the supplemental security income benefit rate established by section 1611 of the social security act. The assessor shall review the owner's income qualifications on a triennial basis and shall use the owner's average total income during the previous three years for the review. If the county assessor approves a property valuation protection option, the value of the primary residence shall remain fixed at the full cash value in effect during the year the property valuation protection option is filed and as long as the owner remains eligible. To remain eligible, the county assessor shall require a qualifying resident to reapply for the property valuation protection option every

three years and shall send a notice of reapplication to qualifying residents six months before the three year reapplication requirement. If title to the property is conveyed to any person who does not qualify for the property valuation protection option, the property valuation protection option terminates, and the property shall revert to its current full cash value.

(8)   The legislature shall provide by law a system of property taxation consistent with the provisions of this section.

(9)   For purposes of this section:

(a)   "Owner" means the owner of record of the property and includes a person who owns the majority beneficial interest of a living trust.

(b)   "Primary residence" means all owner occupied real property and improvements to that real property in this state that is a single family home, condominium, townhouse, or an owner occupied mobile home and that is used for residential purposes.

Added, election June 3, 1980, effective June 28, 1980; amended, election Nov. 7, 2000, effective Dec. 7, 2000.

§ 19. Limitation on ad valorem tax levied; exceptions

Section 19.   (1) The maximum amount of ad valorem taxes levied by any county, city, town or community college district shall not exceed an amount two per cent greater than the amount levied in the preceding year.

(2)   The limitation prescribed by subsection (1) does not apply to:

(a)   Ad valorem taxes or special assessments levied to pay the principal of and the interest and redemption charges on bonded indebtedness or other lawful long-term obligations issued or incurred for a specific purpose.

(b)   Ad valorem taxes or assessments levied by or for property improvement assessment districts, improvement districts and other special purpose districts other than counties, cities, towns and community college districts.

(c)   Ad valorem taxes levied by counties for support of common, high and unified school districts.

(3)   This section applies to all tax years beginning after December 31, 1981.

(4)   The limitation prescribed by subsection (1) shall be increased each year to the maximum permissible limit, whether

or not the political subdivision actually levies ad valorem taxes to such amounts.

(5) The voters, in the manner prescribed by law, may elect to allow ad valorem taxation in excess of the limitation prescribed by this section.

(6) The limitation prescribed by subsection (1) of this section shall be increased by the amount of ad valorem taxes levied against property not subject to taxation in the prior year and shall be decreased by the amount of ad valorem taxes levied against property subject to taxation in the prior year and not subject to taxation in the current year. Such amounts of ad valorem taxes shall be computed using the rate applied to property not subject to this subsection.

(7) The legislature shall provide by law for the implementation of this section.

Added, election June 3, 1980, effective June 28, 1980.

§ 20. Expenditure limitation; adjustments; reporting

Section 20.   (1) The economic estimates commission shall determine and publish prior to April 1 of each year the expenditure limitation for the following fiscal year for each county, city and town. The expenditure limitations shall be determined by adjusting the amount of actual payments of local revenues for each such political subdivision for fiscal year 1979-1980 to reflect the changes in the population of each political subdivision and the cost of living. The governing board of any political subdivision shall not authorize expenditures of local revenues in excess of the limitation prescribed in this section, except as provided in subsections (2), (6) and (9) of this section.

(2) Expenditures in excess of the limitations determined pursuant to subsection (1) of this section may be authorized as follows:

(a) Upon affirmative vote of two-thirds of the members of the governing board for expenditures directly necessitated by a natural or man-made disaster declared by the governor. Any expenditures in excess of the expenditure limitation, as authorized by this paragraph, shall not affect the determination of the expenditure limitation pursuant to subsection (1) of this section in any subsequent years. Any expenditures authorized pursuant to this paragraph shall be made either in the fiscal year in which the disaster is declared or in the succeeding fiscal year.

(b)   Upon the affirmative vote of seventy per cent of the members of the governing board for expenditures directly necessitated by a natural or man-made disaster not declared by the governor, subject to the following:

(i)   The governing board reducing expenditures below the expenditure limitation determined pursuant to subsection (1) of this section by the amount of the excess expenditure for the fiscal year following a fiscal year in which excess expenditures were made pursuant to this paragraph; or

(ii)   Approval of the excess expenditure by a majority of the qualified electors voting either at a special election held by the governing board or at a regularly scheduled election for the nomination or election of the members of the governing board, in the manner provided by law. If the excess expenditure is not approved by a majority of the qualified electors voting, the governing board shall for the fiscal year which immediately follows the fiscal year in which the excess expenditures are made, reduce expenditures below the expenditure limitation determined pursuant to subsection (1) of this section by the amount of the excess expenditures. Any expenditures in excess of the expenditure limitation, as authorized by this paragraph, shall not affect the determination of the expenditure limitation pursuant to subsection (1) of this section in any subsequent years. Any expenditures pursuant to this paragraph shall be made either in the fiscal year in which the disaster occurs or in the succeeding fiscal year.

(c)   Upon affirmative vote of at least two-thirds of the members of the governing board and approval by a majority of the qualified electors voting either at a special election held by the governing board in a manner prescribed by law, or at a regularly scheduled election for the nomination or election of the members of the governing board. Such approval by a majority of the qualified electors voting shall be for a specific amount in excess of the expenditure limitation, and such approval must occur prior to the fiscal year in which the expenditure limitation is to be exceeded. Any expenditures in excess of the expenditure limitation, as authorized by this subdivision, shall not affect the determination of the expenditure limitation pursuant to subsection (1) of this section, in subsequent years.

(3)   As used in this section:

(a)   "Base limit" means the amount of actual payments of local revenues for fiscal year 1979-1980 as used to determine the expenditure limitation pursuant to subsection (1) of this section.

(b) "Cost of living" means either:

(i) The price of goods and services as measured by the implicit price deflator for the gross national product or its successor as reported by the United States department of commerce or its successor agency.

(ii) A different measure or index of the cost of living adopted at the direction of the legislature, by concurrent resolution, upon affirmative vote of two-thirds of the membership of each house of the legislature. Such measure or index shall apply for subsequent fiscal years, except it shall not apply for the fiscal year following the adoption of such measure or index if the measure or index is adopted after March 1 of the preceding fiscal year.

(c) "Expenditure" means any authorization for the payment of local revenues.

(d) "Local revenues" includes all monies, revenues, funds, fees, fines, penalties, tuitions, property and receipts of any kind whatsoever received by or for the account of a political subdivision or any of its agencies, departments, offices, boards, commissions, authorities, councils and institutions, except:

(i) Any amounts or property received from the issuance or incurrence of bonds or other lawful long-term obligations issued or incurred for a specific purpose, or collected or segregated to make payments or deposits required by a contract concerning such bonds or obligations. For the purpose of this subdivision long-term obligations shall not include warrants issued in the ordinary course of operation or registered for payment, by a political subdivision.

(ii) Any amounts or property received as payment of dividends or interest, or any gain on the sale or redemption of investment securities, the purchase of which is authorized by law.

(iii) Any amounts or property received by a political subdivision in the capacity of trustee, custodian or agent.

(iv) Any amounts received as grants and aid of any type received from the federal government or any of its agencies.

(v) Any amounts received as grants, aid, contributions or gifts of any type except amounts received directly or indirectly in lieu of taxes received directly or indirectly from any private agency or organization or any individual.

(vi) Any amounts received from the state which are included

317

within the appropriation limitation prescribed in § 17 of this article.

(vii)   Any amounts received pursuant to a transfer during a fiscal year from another agency, department, office, board, commission, authority, council or institution of the same political subdivision which were included as local revenues for such fiscal year or which are excluded from local revenue under other provisions of this section.

(viii)   Any amounts or property accumulated for the purpose of purchasing land, buildings or improvements or constructing buildings or improvements, if such accumulation and purpose have been approved by the voters of the political subdivision.

(ix)   Any amounts received pursuant to § 14 of this article which are greater than the amount received in fiscal year 1979- 1980.

(x)   Any amounts received in return for goods or services pursuant to a contract with another political subdivision, school district, community college district or the state, and expended by the other political subdivision, school district, community college district or the state pursuant to the expenditure limitation in effect when the amounts are expended by the other political subdivision, school district, community college district or the state.

(xi)   Any amounts expended for the construction, reconstruction, operation or maintenance of a hospital financially supported by a city or town prior to January 1, 1980.

(xii)   Any amounts or property collected to pay the principal of and interest on any warrants issued by a political subdivision and outstanding as of July 1, 1979.

(xiii)   Any amounts received during a fiscal year as refunds, reimbursements or other recoveries of amounts expended which were applied against the expenditure limitation for such fiscal year or which were excluded from local revenues under other provisions of this subsection.

(xiv)   Any amounts received collected by the counties for distribution to school districts pursuant to state law.

(e)   "Political subdivision" means any county, city or town. This definition applies only to this section and does not otherwise modify the commonly accepted definition of political subdivision.

(f)   "Population" means either:

(i)   The periodic census conducted by the United States department of commerce or its successor agency, or the annual update of such census by the department of economic security or its successor agency.

(ii)   A different measure or index of population adopted at the direction of the legislature, by concurrent resolution, upon affirmative vote of two-thirds of the membership of each house of the legislature. Such measure or index shall apply for subsequent fiscal years, except it shall not apply for the fiscal year following the adoption of such measure or index if the measure or index is adopted after March 1 of the preceding fiscal year.

(4)   The economic estimates commission shall adjust the base limit to reflect subsequent transfers of all or any part of the cost of providing a governmental function, in a manner prescribed by law. The adjustment provided for in this subsection shall be used in determining the expenditure limitation pursuant to subsection (1) of this section beginning with the fiscal year immediately following the transfer.

(5)   The economic estimates commission shall adjust the base limit to reflect any subsequent annexation, creation of a new political subdivision, consolidation or change in the boundaries of a political subdivision, in a manner prescribed by law. The adjustment provided for in this subsection shall be used in determining the expenditure limitation pursuant to subsection (1) of this section beginning with the fiscal year immediately following the annexation, creation of a new political subdivision, consolidation or change in the boundaries of a political subdivision.

(6)   Any political subdivision may adjust the base limit by the affirmative vote of two-thirds of the members of the governing board or by initiative, in the manner provided by law, and in either instance by approval of the proposed adjustment by a majority of the qualified electors voting at a regularly scheduled general election or at a nonpartisan election held for the nomination or election of the members of the governing board. The impact of the modification of the expenditure limitation shall appear on the ballot and in publicity pamphlets, as provided by law. Any adjustment pursuant to this subsection, of the base limit shall be used in determining the expenditure limitation pursuant to subsection (1) of this section beginning with the fiscal year immediately following the approval, as provided by law.

(7)   The legislature shall provide for expenditure limitations for such special districts as it deems necessary.

(8)   The legislature shall establish by law a uniform reporting system for all political subdivisions or special districts subject to an expenditure limitation pursuant to this section to insure compliance with this section. The legislature shall establish by law sanc-

tions and penalties for failure to comply with this section.

(9)   Subsection (1) of this section does not apply to a city or town which at a regularly scheduled election for the nomination or election of members of the governing board of the city or town adopts an expenditure limitation pursuant to this subsection different from the expenditure limitation prescribed by subsection (1) of this section. The governing board of a city or town may by a two-thirds vote provide for referral of an alternative expenditure limitation or the qualified electors may by initiative, in the manner provided by law, propose an alternative expenditure limitation. In a manner provided by law, the impact of the alternative expenditure limitation shall be compared to the impact of the expenditure limitation prescribed by subsection (1) of this section, and the comparison shall appear on the ballot and in publicity pamphlets. If a majority of the qualified electors voting on such issue vote in favor of the alternative expenditure limitation, such limitation shall apply to the city or town. If more than one alternative expenditure limitation is on the ballot and more than one alternative expenditure limitation is approved by the voters, the alternative expenditure limitation receiving the highest number of votes shall apply to such city or town. If an alternative expenditure limitation is adopted, it shall apply for the four succeeding fiscal years. Following the fourth succeeding fiscal year, the expenditure limitation prescribed by subsection (1) of this section shall become the expenditure limitation for the city or town unless an alternative expenditure limitation is approved as provided in this subsection. If a majority of the qualified electors voting on such issue vote against an alternative expenditure limitation, the expenditure limitation prescribed pursuant to subsection (1) of this section shall apply to the city or town, and no new alternative expenditure limitation may be submitted to the voters for a period of at least two years. If an alternative expenditure limitation is adopted pursuant to this subsection, the city or town may not conduct an override election provided for in section 19, subsection (4) of this article, during the time period in which the alternative expenditure limitation is in effect.

(10)   This section does not apply to any political subdivision until the fiscal year immediately following the first regularly scheduled election after July 1, 1980 for the nomination or election of the members of the governing board of such political subdivision, except that

a political subdivision, prior to the fiscal year during which the spending limitation would first become effective, may modify the expenditure limitation prescribed pursuant to subsection (1) of this section, by the provisions prescribed by subsections (2) and (6) of this section, or may adopt an alternative expenditure limitation pursuant to subsection (9) of this section.

A county may conduct a special election to exceed the expenditure limitation prescribed pursuant to subsection (1) of this section for the fiscal years 1982-1983 and 1983-1984, on the first Tuesday after the first Monday in November in 1981.

(11)   "City", as used in this article, means city or charter city.

Added, election June 3, 1980, effective June 28, 1980; amended, election Nov. 3, 1992, effective Nov. 23, 1992.

§ 21. Expenditure limitation; school districts and community college districts; adjustments; reporting

Section 21.   (1) The economic estimates commission shall determine and publish prior to April 1 of each year the expenditure limitation for the following fiscal year for each community college district. The expenditure limitations shall be determined by adjusting the amount of expenditures of local revenues for each such district for fiscal year 1979-1980 to reflect the changes in the student population of each district and the cost of living. The governing board of any community college district shall not authorize expenditures of local revenues in excess of the limitation prescribed in this section, except in the manner provided by law.

(2)   The economic estimates commission shall determine and publish prior to May 1 of each year the aggregate expenditure limitation for all school districts for the following fiscal year. The aggregate expenditure limitation shall be determined by adjusting the total amount of expenditures of local revenues for all school districts for fiscal year 1979-1980 to reflect the changes in student population in the school districts and the cost of living. The aggregate expenditures of local revenues for all school districts shall not exceed the limitation prescribed in this section, except as provided in subsection (3) of this section.

(3)   Expenditures in excess of the limitation determined pursuant to subsection (2) of this section may be authorized for a single fiscal year upon affirmative vote of two-thirds of the mem-

bership of each house of the legislature.

(4)   As used in this section:

(a)   "Cost of living" means either:

(i)   The price of goods and services as measured by the implicit price deflator for the gross national product or its successor as reported by the United States department of commerce, or its successor agency.

(ii)   A different measure or index of the cost of living adopted at the direction of the legislature, by concurrent resolution, upon affirmative vote of two-thirds of the membership of each house of the legislature. Such measure or index shall apply for subsequent fiscal years, except it shall not apply for the fiscal year following the adoption of such measure or index if the measure or index is adopted after March 1 of the preceding fiscal year.

(b)   "Expenditure" means any amounts budgeted to be paid from local revenues as prescribed by law.

(c)   "Local revenues" includes all monies, revenues, funds, property and receipts of any kind whatsoever received by or for the account of a school or community college district or any of its agencies, departments, offices, boards, commissions, authorities, councils and institutions, except:

(i)   Any amounts or property received from the issuance or incurrence of bonds, or other lawful long-term obligations issued or incurred for a specific purpose, or any amounts or property collected or segregated to make payments or deposits required by a contract concerning such bonds or obligations. For the purpose of this subdivision long-term obligations shall not include warrants issued in the ordinary course of operation or registered for payment, by a political subdivision.

(ii)   Any amounts or property received as payment of dividends and interest, or any gain on the sale or redemption of investment securities, the purchase of which is authorized by law.

(iii)   Any amounts or property received by a school or community college district in the capacity of trustee, custodian or agent.

(iv)   Any amounts received as grants and aid of any type received from the federal government or any of its agencies except school assistance in federally affected areas.

(v)   Any amounts or property received as grants, gifts, aid or contributions of any type except amounts received directly or indirectly in lieu of taxes received directly or indirectly from any private agency or organization, or any individual.

(vi)   Any amounts received from the state for the purpose of purchasing land, buildings or improvements or constructing buildings or improvements.

(vii)   Any amounts received pursuant to a transfer during a fiscal year from another agency, department, office, board, commission, authority, council or institution of the same community college or school district which were included as local revenues for such fiscal year or which are excluded from local revenue under other provisions of this subsection.

(viii)   Any amounts or property accumulated by a community college district for the purpose of purchasing land, buildings or improvements or constructing buildings or improvements.

(ix)   Any amounts received in return for goods or services pursuant to a contract with another political subdivision, school district, community college district or the state and expended by the other political subdivision, school district, community college district or the state pursuant to the expenditure limitation in effect when the amounts are expended by the other political subdivision, school district, community college district or the state.

(x)   Any amounts received as tuition or fees directly or indirectly from any public or private agency or organization or any individual.

(xi)   Any ad valorem taxes received pursuant to an election to exceed the limitation prescribed by § 19 of this article or for the purposes of funding expenditures in excess of the expenditure limitations prescribed by subsection (7) of this section.

(xii)   Any amounts received during a fiscal year as refunds, reimbursements or other recoveries of amounts expended which were applied against the expenditure limitation for such fiscal year or which were excluded from local revenues under other provisions of this subsection.

(d)   For the purpose of subsection (2) of this section, the following items are also excluded from local revenues:

(i)   Any amounts received as the proceeds from the sale, lease or rental of school property as authorized by law.

(ii)   Any amounts received from the capital levy as authorized by law.

(iii)   Any amounts received from the acquisition, operation, or maintenance of school services of a commercial nature which are entirely or predominantly self-supporting.

(iv)   Any amounts received for the purpose of funding expenditures authorized in the event of destruction of or damage to the facilities of a school district as authorized by law.

(e)   "Student population" means the number of actual, full-time or the equivalent of actual full-time students enrolled in the school district or community college district determined in a manner prescribed by law.

(5)   The economic estimates commission shall adjust the amount of expenditures of local revenues in fiscal year 1979-1980, as used to determine the expenditure limitation pursuant to subsections (1) and (2) of this section, to reflect subsequent transfers of all or any part of the cost of providing a governmental function, in a manner prescribed by law. The adjustment provided for in this subsection shall be used in determining the expenditure limitation pursuant to subsections (1) and (2) of this section beginning with the fiscal year immediately following the transfer.

(6)   The economic estimates commission shall adjust the amount of expenditures of local revenues in fiscal year 1979-1980, as used to determine the expenditure limitation pursuant to subsection (1) of this section, to reflect any subsequent annexation, creation of a new district, consolidation or change in the boundaries of a district, in a manner prescribed by law. The adjustment provided for in this subsection shall be used in determining the expenditure limitation pursuant to subsection (1) of this section beginning with the fiscal year immediately following the annexation, creation of a new district, consolidation or change in the boundaries of a district.

(7)   The legislature shall establish by law expenditure limitations for each school district beginning with the fiscal year beginning July 1, 1980. Expenditures by a school district in excess of such an expenditure limitation must be approved by a majority of the electors voting on the excess expenditures.

(8)   The legislature shall establish by law a uniform reporting system for districts to insure compliance with this section. The legislature shall establish by law sanctions and penalties for failure to comply with this section.

(9)   This section is not effective for any community college district until the fiscal year beginning July 1, 1981.

(10)   Subsections (2), (3), (5) and (6) of this section do not apply to school districts until the fiscal year beginning July 1, 1981.

Added, election June 3, 1980, effective June 28, 1980; amended, election Nov. 4, 1986, effective Dec. 16, 1986.

§ 22. Vote required to increase state revenues; application; exceptions

(A) An act that provides for a net increase in state revenues, as described in Subsection B is effective on the affirmative vote of two-thirds of the members of each house of the legislature. If the act receives such an affirmative vote, it becomes effective immediately on the signature of the governor as provided by Article IV, Part 1, Section 1. If the governor vetoes the measure, it shall not become effective unless it is approved by an affirmative vote of three-fourths of the members of each house of the legislature.

(B) The requirements of this section apply to any act that provides for a net increase in state revenues in the form of:

1. The imposition of any new tax.

2. An increase in a tax rate or rates.

3. A reduction or elimination of a tax deduction, exemption, exclusion, credit or other tax exemption feature in computing lax liability.

4. An increase in a statutorily prescribed state fee or assessment or an increase in a statutorily prescribed maximum limit for an administratively set fee.

5. The imposition of any new state fee or assessment or the authorization of any new administrative set fee.

6. The elimination of an exemption from a statutorily prescribed state fee or assessment.

7. A change in the allocation among the state, counties or cities of Arizona transaction privilege, severance, jet fuel and use, rental occupancy, or other taxes.

8. Any combination of the elements described in paragraphs 1 through 7.

(C) This section does not apply to:

1. The effects of inflation, increasing assessed valuation or any other similar effect that increases state revenue but in not caused by an affirmative act of the legislature.

2. Fees and assessments that are authorized by statute, but are not prescribed by formula, amount or limit, and are set by a state officer or agency.

3. Taxes, fees or assessments that are imposed by counties, cities, towns and other political subdivisions of this state.

(D) Each act to which this section applies shall include a separate provision describing the requirements for enactment prescribed by this section.

Added, election Nov. 3, 1992, effective Nov. 23, 1992.

ARTICLE X
STATE AND SCHOOL LANDS

§ 1. Acceptance and holding of lands by state in trust

Section 1. All lands expressly transferred and confirmed to the state by the provisions of the enabling act approved June 20, 1910, including all lands granted to the state and all lands heretofore granted to the territory of Arizona, and all lands otherwise acquired by the state, shall be by the state accepted and held in trust to be disposed of in whole or in part, only in manner as in the said enabling act and in this constitution provided, and for the several objects specified in the respective granting and confirmatory provisions. The natural products and money proceeds of any of said lands shall be subject to the same trusts and the lands producing the same.

§ 2. Unauthorized disposition of land or proceeds as breach of trust

Section 2. Disposition of any of said lands, or of any money or thing of value directly or indirectly derived therefrom, for any object other than that for which such particular lands (or the lands from which such money or thing of value shall have been derived) were granted or confirmed, or in any manner contrary to the provisions of the said enabling act, shall be deemed a breach of trust.

§ 3. Mortgage or other encumbrance; sale or lease at public auction

Section 3. No mortgage or other encumbrance of the said lands, or any part thereof, shall be valid in favor of any person or for any purpose or under any circumstances whatsoever. Said lands shall not be sold or leased, in whole or in part, except to the highest and best bidder at a public auction to be held at the county seat of the county wherein the lands to be affected, or the major portion thereof, shall lie, notice of which public auction shall first have been duly given by advertisement, which shall set forth the nature, time and place of the transaction to be had, with a full description of the lands to be offered, and be published once each week for not less than ten successive weeks in a newspaper of general circulation published regularly at the state capital, and in that newspaper of like circulation which shall then be regularly published nearest to the location of the lands so offered; nor shall any sale or contract for the sale of any timber or other natural product of such lands be made, save at the place, in the manner, and after the notice by publication provided for sales and leases of the lands themselves. Nothing herein, or elsewhere in article X contained, shall prevent:

1.   The leasing of any of the lands referred to in this article in such manner as the legislature may prescribe, for grazing, agricultural, commercial and homesite purposes, for a term of ten years or less, without advertisement;

2.   The leasing of any of said lands, in such manner as the legislature may prescribe, whether or not also leased for grazing and agricultural purposes, for mineral purposes, other than for the exploration, development, and production of oil, gas and other hydrocarbon substances, for a term of twenty years or less, without advertisement, or,

3.   The leasing of any of said lands, whether or not also leased for other purposes, for the exploration, development, and production of oil, gas and other hydrocarbon substances on, in or under said lands for an initial term of twenty (20) years or less and as long thereafter as oil, gas or other hydrocarbon substances may be procured therefrom in paying quantities, the leases to be made in any manner, with or without advertisement, bidding, or appraisement, and under such terms and provisions, as the legislature may prescribe, the terms and provisions to include a reservation of a royalty to the state of not less than twelve and one-half per cent of production.

Amended, election Nov. 5, 1940, effective Nov. 27, 1940; election Sept. 12, 1950, effective Oct. 2, 1950. See Enabling Act June 21, 1951, Ch. 120, 65 Stat. 51.

§ 4.   Sale or other disposal; appraisal; minimum price; credit; passing of title

Section 4.   All lands, lease-holds, timber, and other products of land, before being offered, shall be appraised at their true value, and no sale or other disposal thereof shall be made for a consideration less than the value so ascertained, nor in any case less than the minimum price hereinafter fixed, nor upon credit unless accompanied by ample security, and the legal title shall not be deemed to have passed until the consideration shall have been paid.

§ 5. Minimum price; relinquishment of lands to United States

Section 5.   No lands shall be sold for less than three dollars per acre, and no lands which are or shall be susceptible of irrigation under any projects now or hereafter completed or adopted by the United States under legislation for the reclamation of lands, or under any other project for the reclamation of lands, shall be sold at less than twenty-five dollars per acre; provided, that the state, at the request of the secretary of the interior, shall from time to time relinquish such of its lands to the United States as at any time are needed for irrigation works in connection with any such government project, and other lands in lieu thereof shall be selected from lands of the character named and in the manner prescribed in section twenty-four of the said enabling act.

§ 6. Lands reserved by United States for development of water power

Section 6.   No lands reserved and excepted of the lands granted to this state by the United States, actually or prospectively valuable for the development of water powers or power for hydro- electric use or transmission, which shall be ascertained and designated by the secretary of the interior within five years after the proclamation of the president declaring the admission of the state, shall be subject to any disposition whatsoever by the state or by any officer of the state, and any conveyance or transfer of such lands made within said five years shall be null and void.

§ 7. Establishment of permanent funds; segregation; investment and distribution of monies

Section 7.   A. A separate permanent fund shall be established for each of the several objects for which the said grants are made and confirmed by the enabling act to the state, and whenever any monies shall be in any manner derived from any of said lands, the same shall be deposited by the state treasurer in the permanent fund corresponding to the grant under which the particular land producing such monies was, by the enabling act, conveyed or confirmed.
B.   No monies shall ever be taken from one permanent fund for deposit in any other, or for any object other than that for which the land producing the same was granted or confirmed.

C.   All such monies shall be invested in safe interest-bearing securities and prudent equity securities consistent with the requirements of this section.

D.   The legislature shall establish a board of investment to serve as trustees of the permanent funds. The board shall provide for the management of the assets of the funds consistent with the following conditions:

1.   Not more than sixty per cent of a fund at cost may be invested in equities at any time.

2.   Equities that are eligible for purchase are restricted to stocks listed on any national stock exchange or eligible for trading through the United States national association of securities dealers automated quotation system, or successor institutions, except as may be prohibited by general criteria or by a restriction on investment in a specific security adopted pursuant to this subsection.

3.   Not more than five per cent of all of the funds combined at cost may be invested in equity securities issued by the same institution, agency or corporation, other than securities issued as direct obligations of and fully guaranteed by the United States government.

E.   In making investments under this section the state treasurer and trustees shall exercise the judgment and care under the prevailing circumstances that an institutional investor of ordinary prudence, discretion and intelligence exercises in managing large investments entrusted to it, not in regard to speculation, but in regard to the permanent disposition of monies, considering the probable safety of capital as well as the probable total rate of return over extended periods of time.

F.   The earnings, interest, dividends and realized capital gains and losses from investment of a permanent fund, shall be credited to that fund.

G.   The board of investment shall determine the amount of the annual distributions required by this section and allocate distributions pursuant to law. Beginning July 1, 2000 and except as otherwise provided in this section, the amount of the annual distribution from a permanent fund established pursuant to this section is the amount determined by multiplying the following factors:

1.   The average of the annual total rate of return for the immediately preceding five complete fiscal years less the average of the annual percentage change in the GDP price deflator, or a successor

index, for the immediately preceding five complete fiscal years. For purposes of this paragraph:
(a)   "Annual total rate of return" means the quotient obtained by dividing the amount credited to a fund pursuant to subsection F for a complete fiscal year, plus unrealized capital gains and losses, by the average monthly market value of the fund for that year.
(b)   "GDP price deflator" means the gross domestic price deflator reported by the United States department of commerce, bureau of economic analysis, or its successor agency.
2.   The average of the monthly market values of the fund for the immediately preceding five complete fiscal years.
H.   Notwithstanding any other provision of this section, the annual distribution from the permanent funds for fiscal years 1999-2000 through 2002-2003 shall be as follows:
1.   For fiscal year 1999-2000, the greater of five per cent of the average of the monthly market values of the funds for fiscal years 1994-1995 through 1998-1999 or the average of actual annual distributions for fiscal years 1994-1995 through 1998-1999.
2.   For fiscal years 2000-2001 through 2002-2003, the greater of the average of the actual annual distributions for the immediately preceding five complete fiscal years or the amount of the distribution required by subsection G.

Amended, election Nov. 3, 1998, effective Dec. 10, 1998.

§ 8.   Conformity of contracts with enabling act
Section 8.   Every sale, lease, conveyance, or contract of or concerning any of the lands granted or confirmed, or the use thereof or the natural products thereof made to this state by the said enabling act, not made in substantial conformity with the provisions thereof, shall be null and void.

§ 9.   Sale or lease; conditions; limitations; lease prior to adoption of constitution
Section 9.   All lands expressly transferred and confirmed to the state, by the provisions of the enabling act approved June 20, 1910, including all lands granted to the state, and all lands heretofore granted to the territory of Arizona, and all lands otherwise acquired by the state, may be sold or leased by the state in the manner, and on the conditions, and with the limitations, prescribed by the said enabling act and this constitution, and as may be further prescribed by law; provided, that the legislature shall provide for

the separate appraisement of the lands and of the improvements on school and university lands which have been held under lease prior to the adoption of this constitution, and for reimbursement to the actual bona fide residents or lessees of such lands upon which such improvements are situated, as prescribed by title 65, Civil Code of Arizona, 1901, and in such cases only as permit reimbursements to lessees in said title 65.

§ 10. Laws for sale or lease of state lands; protection of residents and lessees

Section 10.   The legislature shall provide by proper laws for the sale of all state lands or the lease of such lands, and shall further provide by said laws for the protection of the actual bona fide residents and lessees of said lands, whereby such residents and lessees of said lands shall be protected in their rights to their improvements (including water rights) in such manner that in case of lease to other parties the former lessee shall be paid by the succeeding lessee the value of such improvements and rights and actual bona fide residents and lessees shall have preference to a renewal of their leases at a reassessed rental to be fixed as provided by law.

Amended, election Nov. 5, 1918, effective Dec. 5, 1918.

§ 11. Maximum acreage allowed single purchaser

Section 11.   No individual, corporation or association shall be allowed to purchase more than one hundred sixty (160) acres of agricultural land or more than six hundred forty (640) acres of grazing land.

Amended, election Nov. 5, 1918, effective Dec. 5, 1918.

ARTICLE XI
EDUCATION

§ 1. Public school system; education of pupils who are hearing and vision impaired

Section 1.   A. The legislature shall enact such laws as shall provide for the establishment and maintenance of a general and uniform public school system, which system shall include:
1.   Kindergarten schools.
2.   Common schools.
3.   High schools.

4.   Normal schools.
5.   Industrial schools.
6.   Universities, which shall include an agricultural college, a school of mines, and such other technical schools as may be essential, until such time as it may be deemed advisable to establish separate state institutions of such character.
B.   The legislature shall also enact such laws as shall provide for the education and care of pupils who are hearing and vision impaired.

Amended, election Nov. 7, 2000, effective Dec. 7, 2000.

§ 2.   Conduct and supervision of school system

Section 2.   The general conduct and supervision of the public school system shall be vested in a state board of education, a state superintendent of public instruction, county school superintendents, and such governing boards for the state institutions as may be provided by law.

§ 3.   State board of education; composition; powers and duties; compensation

Section 3.   The state board of education shall be composed of the following members: the superintendent of public instruction, the president of a state university or a state college, three lay members, a member of the state junior college board, a superintendent of a high school district, a classroom teacher and a county school superintendent. Each member, other than the superintendent of public instruction, to be appointed by the governor with the consent of the senate in the manner prescribed by law. The powers, duties, compensation and expenses, and the terms of office of the board shall be such as may be prescribed by law.

Amended, election Nov. 3, 1964, effective Dec. 3, 1964; election Nov. 2, 1976, effective Nov. 22, 1976.

§ 4.   State superintendent of public instruction; board membership; powers and duties

Section 4.   The state superintendent of public instruction shall be a member, and secretary, of the state board of education, and, ex-officio, a member of any other board having control of public instruction in any state institution. His powers and duties shall be prescribed by law.

§ 5. Regents of university and other governing boards; appointments by governor; membership of governor on board of regents

Section 5.   The regents of the university, and the governing boards of other state educational institutions, shall be appointed by the governor with the consent of the senate in the manner prescribed by law, except that the governor shall be, ex-officio, a member of the board of regents of the university.

Amended, election Nov. 2, 1976, effective Nov. 22, 1976.

§ 6. Admission of students of both sexes to state educational institutions; tuition; common school system

Section 6.   The university and all other state educational institutions shall be open to students of both sexes, and the instruction furnished shall be as nearly free as possible.

The legislature shall provide for a system of common schools by which a free school shall be established and maintained in every school district for at least six months in each year, which school shall be open to all pupils between the ages of six and twenty-one years.

§ 7. Sectarian instruction; religious or political test or qualification

Section 7.   No sectarian instruction shall be imparted in any school or state educational institution that may be established under this constitution, and no religious or political test or qualification shall ever be required as a condition of admission into any public educational institution of the state, as teacher, student, or pupil; but the liberty of conscience hereby secured shall not be so construed as to justify practices or conduct inconsistent with the good order, peace, morality, or safety of the state, or with the rights of others.

§ 8. Permanent state school fund; source; apportionment of state funds

Section 8.   A. A permanent state school fund for the use of the common schools shall be derived from the sale of public school lands or other public lands specified in the enabling act approved June 20, 1910; from all estates or distributive shares of estates that may escheat to the state; from all unclaimed shares and dividends of any corporation incorporated under the laws of Arizona; and from all gifts, devises, or bequests made to the state for general educational purposes.

B.   The rental derived from school lands, with such other funds as may be provided by law shall be apportioned only for common and high school education in Arizona, and in such manner as may be prescribed by law.

Amended, election Nov. 3, 1964, effective Dec. 3, 1964; amended, election Nov. 3, 1998, effective December 10, 1998.

§ 9.   County school funds; size of fund; free schools
Section 9.   The amount of this apportionment shall become a part of the county school fund, and the legislature shall enact such laws as will provide for increasing the county fund sufficiently to maintain all the public schools of the county for a minimum term of six months in every school year. The laws of the state shall enable cities and towns to maintain free high schools, industrial schools, and commercial schools.

§ 10.   Source of revenue for maintenance of state educational institutions
Section 10.   The revenue for the maintenance of the respective state educational institutions shall be derived from the investment of the proceeds of the sale, and from the rental of such lands as have been set aside by the enabling act approved June 20, 1910, or other legislative enactment of the United States, for the use and benefit of the respective state educational institutions. In addition to such income the legislature shall make such appropriations, to be met by taxation, as shall insure the proper maintenance of all state educational institutions, and shall make such special appropriations as shall provide for their development and improvement.

ARTICLE XII
COUNTIES

§ 1.   Counties as bodies politic and corporate
Section 1.   Each county of the state, now or hereafter organized, shall be a body politic and corporate.

§ 2.   Counties of territory as counties of state
Section 2.   The several counties of the territory of Arizona as fixed by statute at the time of the adoption of this constitution are hereby declared to be the counties of the state until changed by law.

§ 3. County officers; election; term of office

Section 3.   There are hereby created in and for each organized county of the state the following officers who shall be elected by the qualified electors thereof: a sheriff, a county attorney, a recorder, a treasurer, an assessor, a superintendent of schools and at least three supervisors, each of whom shall be elected and hold his office for a term of four (4) years beginning on the first of January next after his election, which number of supervisors is subject to increase by law. The supervisors shall be nominated and elected from districts as provided by law.

The candidates for these offices elected in the general election of November 3, 1964 shall take office on the first day of January, 1965 and shall serve until the first day of January, 1969.

Amended, election Nov. 3, 1964, effective Dec. 3, 1964.

§ 4. County officers; duties, powers, and qualifications; salaries

Section 4.   The duties, powers, and qualifications of such officers shall be as prescribed by law. The board of supervisors of each county is hereby empowered to fix salaries for all county and precinct officers within such county for whom no compensation is provided by law, and the salaries so fixed shall remain in full force and effect until changed by general law.

§ 5. Charter committee; charter preparation; approval

Section 5.   A. The board of supervisors of any county with a population of more than five hundred thousand persons as determined by the most recent United States decennial or special census may call for an election to cause a charter committee to be elected by the qualified electors of that county at any time. Alternatively, the board of supervisors of any county with a population of more than five hundred thousand persons as determined by the most recent United States decennial or special census shall call for the election of the charter committee within ten days after receipt by the clerk of the board of supervisors of a petition that demands the election and that is signed by a number of qualified electors of the county at least equal to ten per cent of the total number of ballots cast for all candidates for governor or presidential electors in the county at the last preceding general election. The election shall be held at least one hundred days but not more than one hundred twenty days after the call for the election. Except as otherwise provided in this section, for elections held under this section or section 6 of this article, the manner of conducting and voting at an election, contesting an election, canvassing votes and certifying returns shall be the same, as nearly as practicable, as in elections for county officers.

B.   At the election a vote shall be taken to elect members of the charter committee who will function if further proceedings are authorized and the ballot shall contain the question of whether further proceedings toward adopting a charter shall be authorized pursuant to the call for the election. Unless a majority of the qualified electors voting on the question votes to authorize further proceedings, the election of members of the charter committee shall be invalidated and no further proceedings may be had except pursuant to a subsequent call pursuant to subsection A.

C.   The charter committee shall be composed of fifteen qualified electors of the county elected by supervisorial district with the same number serving from each district. A nomination petition for election to the charter committee shall be made available by the clerk of the board of supervisors and shall be signed by a number of qualified electors of the supervisorial district who are eligible to vote for the nominee at least equal to one per cent of the total number of ballots cast for all candidates for governor or presidential electors in the supervisorial district at the last preceding general election, and filed with the clerk not later than sixty days before the election. All qualified electors of the county, including all elected public officials, are eligible to seek election to the charter committee.

D.   Within one hundred eighty days after the election the charter committee shall prepare and submit a proposed charter for the county. The proposed charter shall be signed by a majority of the members of the committee and filed with the clerk of the board of supervisors, after which the charter committee shall be dissolved. The county shall then publish the proposed charter in the official newspaper of the county at least once a week for three consecutive weeks. The first publication shall be made within twenty days after the proposed charter is filed with the clerk of the board of supervisors.

E.   At least forty-five days but not more than sixty days after final publication, the proposed charter shall be submitted to the vote of the qualified electors of the county at a general or special election. If a general election will be held within ninety days after final publication, the charter shall be submitted at that general election. The full text of the proposed charter shall be printed in a publicity pamphlet and mailed to each household containing a registered voter at least eleven days before the charter election and the ballot may contain only a summary of the proposed charter provisions. the ballot shall contain a question regarding approval of the proposed charter and the questions pertaining to taxation authority and appointment of officers, if any, provided for in sections 7 and 8 of this article.

F.   If a majority of the qualified electors voting ratifies the proposed charter, a copy of the charter, together with a statement setting forth the submission of the charter to the qualified electors and its ratification by them, shall be certified by the clerk of the board of supervisors and shall be submitted to the governor for approval. The governor shall approve the charter within thirty days after its submission if it is not in conflict with, or states that in the event of a conflict is subject to, this constitution and the laws of this state. On approval, the charter becomes the organic law of the county, and certified copies of the charter shall be filed in the office of the secretary of state and with the clerk of the board of supervisors after being recorded in the office of the county recorder. Thereafter all courts shall take judicial notice of the charter.

Added, election Nov. 3, 1992, effective Nov. 23, 1992.

§ 6.   Amendment of charter
Section 6.   A charter shall set forth procedures for amendment of the charter. Proposed amendments shall be submitted to the qualified electors of the county at a general or special election and become effective if ratified by a majority of the qualified electors voting on the amendments and approved by the governor in the manner provided for in section 5 of this article.

Added, election Nov. 3, 1992, effective Nov. 23, 1992.

§ 7.   County charter provisions
Section 7.   A.   Charter counties continue to be political subdivisions of this state that exist to aid in the administration of this state's laws and for purposes of self-government. Except as otherwise provided in this article the powers of the legislature over

counties are not affected by this section and sections 5, 6, 8 and 9 of this article. Charter counties shall provide the same state mandated services and perform the same state mandated functions as non- charter counties. Charter counties may exercise, if provided by the charter, all powers over local concerns of the county consistent with, and subject to, the constitution and the laws of this state. In matters of strictly local municipal concern, charters adopted pursuant to article XIII shall control in any case of conflict with a county charter adopted pursuant to this article.

B.   If a county has framed and adopted a charter and the charter is approved by the governor as provided in this article, the county shall be governed by the terms of its charter and ordinances passed pursuant to its charter. If the charter has been framed, adopted and approved and any of its provisions are in conflict with any county ordinance, rule or regulation relating to local concerns of the counties in force at the time of the adoption and approval of the charter, the provisions of the charter prevail notwithstanding the conflict and operate as a repeal or suspension of the law to the extent of conflict, and the law is not thereafter operative as to such conflict.

C.   Notwithstanding article IX, section 1, if proposed and approved in the charter, a charter county may levy and collect:

1.   Taxes on a countywide basis to provide services on a countywide basis.

2.   Taxes on a specially designated area basis to provide services or special levels of service to that area. All taxes levied pursuant to this subsection shall be uniform upon the same class of property within the territorial limits of the county or the specially designated area and shall be levied and collected for public purposes only.

D.   The decision to include a charter provision authorizing taxation pursuant to subsection C, paragraph 1 or 2 of this section shall be placed on the ballot as separate questions at the election to ratify the charter and must be approved by a majority of the qualified electors voting at the election. The result of the voting on either provision authorizing taxation does not affect the result of the voting to ratify the charter. Charter provisions authorizing taxation pursuant to subsection C, paragraph 1 or 2 of this section may also be proposed by an amendment to the charter pursuant to section 6 of this article.

E.   If the authority to tax pursuant to subsection C, paragraph 2 of this section is approved for inclusion in the charter, any new tax proposed by the county under subsection C, paragraph 2 of this section shall be voted on by the qualified electors of the specially designated area. The tax must by ratified by a majority vote of the qualified electors voting at the election.

F.   A transaction privilege tax, use tax or similar tax levied by a county pursuant to subsection C, paragraph 1 of this section:

1.   May be imposed on only those business activities, or on the use, storage or consumption, which are subject to the comparable state transaction privilege tax, use tax or similar tax.

2.   Shall provide all exclusion and exemptions provided by, and administrative provisions consistent with, the comparable state transaction privilege tax, use tax or similar tax.

G.   All taxes levied under subsection F of this section shall not exceed an aggregate rate of two per cent when combined with existing taxes levied pursuant to title 42, chapter 8.3.

H.   If approved in the charter, a charter county may adopt fees and fee schedules for any county products and county service delivery it provides in the conduct of any official business. Notwithstanding any fee schedules or individual charges provided by state law, the governing body of a charter county may adopt an alternate fee schedule or individual charge. Any fee or charge established pursuant to this section shall be attributable to and defray or cover the current or future costs of the product or service delivery for which the fee or charge is assessed.

I.   Taxes raised under the authority of this section shall be subject to the provisions of the county property tax and expenditure limitations pursuant to article IX, sections 19 and 20.

Added, election Nov. 3, 1992, effective Nov. 23, 1992.

8.   Government and other powers

Section 8.   A. The county charter shall provide:

1.   For an elective governing body and its method of compensation, its powers, duties and responsibilities, its authority to delegate powers, the method of election and removal of members, the terms of office and the manner of filling vacancies in the governing body.

2.   For all officers established under section 3 of this article and article VI, section 23, and such additional officers as the

charter may provide for, their election or appointment, consolidation or segregation, method of compensation, powers, duties and responsibilities, authority to delegate powers and, if elected, the method of election and removal, terms of office and the manner of filling vacancies in such offices. If the charter provides for the attorney to remain an elective officer of the county, the charter may provide for an appointive office to carry out the civil representation needs of the county, its departments, agencies, boards, commissions, officials and employees. If the elective governing body provided for in the charter does not consist of the supervisors, the charter may provide for elimination of the office of supervisor. If the charter provides for the office of supervisor, the number of supervisors shall be not fewer than five or greater than nine. If the charter provides for the appointment or elimination of an officer established under section 3 of this article or article VI, section 23, or for an appointive office to carry out the civil representation needs of the county, those provisions shall include an effective date not earlier than the expiration of the term of office for the officer commencing in January immediately following the first general election at which the officer is elected following approval of the charter by the voters and shall be placed on the ballot as separate questions at the election to ratify the charter and must be approved by a majority of the qualified electors voting at the election. The result of the voting on any provisions authorizing appointment or elimination of officers does not affect the result of the voting to ratify the charter.

3.　　　For the performance of functions required by statute.

4.　　　For a periodic review of the charter provisions to be conducted at least once every ten years from the time of its ratification by the voters and the procedures for the periodic review.

B.　　　The county charter may provide for other elective and appointive offices.

Added, election Nov. 3, 1992, effective Nov. 23, 1992.

9.　Self-executing provision

Section 9.　　　The provisions of sections 5 through 8 of this article are self-executing, and no further legislation is required to make them effective.

Added, election Nov. 3, 1992, effective Nov. 23, 1992.

ARTICLE XIII
MUNICIPAL CORPORATIONS

§ 1. Incorporation and organization; classification

Section 1.　Municipal corporations shall not be created by special laws, but the legislature, by general laws, shall provide for the incorporation and organization of cities and towns and for the classification of such cities and towns in proportion to population, subject to the provisions of this article.

§ 2. Charter; preparation and proposal by board of freeholders; ratification and approval; amendment

Section 2.　Any city containing, now or hereafter, a population of more than three thousand five hundred may frame a charter for its own government consistent with, and subject to, the constitution and the laws of the state, in the following manner: a board of freeholders composed of fourteen qualified electors of said city may be elected at large by the qualified electors thereof, at a general or special election, whose duty it shall be, within ninety days after such election, to prepare and propose a charter for such city. Such proposed charter shall be signed in duplicate by the members of such board, or a majority of them, and filed, one copy of said proposed charter with the chief executive officer of such city and the other with the county recorder of the county in which said city shall be situated. Such proposed charter shall then be published in one or more newspapers published, and of general circulation, within said city for at least twenty-one days if in a daily paper, or in three consecutive issues if in a weekly paper, and the first publication shall be made within twenty days after the completion of the proposed charter. Within thirty days, and not earlier than twenty days, after such publication, said proposed charter shall be submitted to the vote of the qualified electors of said city at a general or special election. If a majority of such qualified electors voting thereon shall ratify such proposed charter, it shall thereupon be submitted to the governor for his approval, and the governor shall approve it if it shall not be in conflict with this constitution or with the laws of the state. Upon such approval said charter shall become the organic law of such city and supersede any charter then existing (and all amendments thereto), and all ordinances inconsistent with said new charter. A copy of such charter, certified by the chief executive officer, and authenticated by

the seal, of such city, together with a statement similarly certified and authenticated setting forth the submission of such charter to the electors and its ratification by them, shall, after the
approval of such charter by the governor, be made in duplicate and
filed, one copy in the office of the secretary of state and the other
in the archives of the city after being recorded in the office of said
county recorder. Thereafter all courts shall take judicial notice of
said charter.

The charter so ratified may be amended by amendments proposed
and submitted by the legislative authority of the city to the qualified electors thereof (or by petition as hereinafter provided), at a
general or special election, and ratified by a majority of the qualified electors voting thereon and approved by the governor as herein
provided for the approval of the charter.

§ 3. Election of board of freeholders
Section 3.   An election of such board of freeholders may
be called at any time by the legislative authority of any such
city. Such election shall be called by the chief executive officer
of any such city within ten days after there shall have been filed
with him a petition demanding such election, signed by a number of qualified electors residing within such city equal to twenty-
five per centum of the total number of votes cast at the next
preceding general municipal election. Such election shall be held
not later than thirty days after the call therefor. At such election
a vote shall be taken upon the question whether further proceedings toward adopting a charter shall be had in pursuance to the
call, and unless a majority of the qualified electors voting thereon
shall vote to proceed further, no further proceedings shall be had,
and all proceedings up to the time of said election shall be of
no effect.

§ 4. Franchises; approval of electors; term
Section 4.   No municipal corporation shall ever grant, extend,
or renew a franchise without the approval of a majority of the qualified electors residing within its corporate limits who shall vote
thereon at a general or special election, and the legislative body
of any such corporation shall submit any such matter for approval
or disapproval to such electors at any general municipal election,
or call a special election for such purpose at any time upon thirty
days' notice. No franchise shall be granted, extended, or renewed
for a longer time than twenty-five years.

§ 5. Right of municipal corporation to engage in business or enterprise

Section 5.   Every municipal corporation within this state shall have the right to engage in any business or enterprise which may be engaged in by a person, firm, or corporation by virtue of a franchise from said municipal corporation.

§ 6. Franchises; restrictions

Section 6.   No grant, extension, or renewal of any franchise or other use of the streets, alleys, or other public grounds, or ways, of any municipality shall divest the state or any of its subdivisions of its or their control and regulation of such use and enjoyment; nor shall the power to regulate charges for public services be surrendered; and no exclusive franchise shall ever be granted.

§ 7. Irrigation and other districts as political subdivisions

Section 7.   Irrigation, power, electrical, agricultural improvement, drainage, and flood control districts, and tax levying public improvement districts, now or hereafter organized pursuant to law, shall be political subdivisions of the state, and vested with all the rights, privileges and benefits, and entitled to the immunities and exemptions granted municipalities and political subdivisions under this constitution or any law of the state or of the United States; but all such districts shall be exempt from the provisions of sections 7 and 8 of article IX of this constitution.

Added, election Nov. 5, 1940, effective Nov. 27, 1940.

ARTICLE XIV
CORPORATIONS OTHER THAN MUNICIPAL

§ 1. "Corporation" defined; right to sue and suability

Section 1.   The term "corporation," as used in this article, shall be construed to include all associations and joint stock companies having any powers or privileges of corporations not possessed by individuals or co-partnerships, and all corporations shall have the right to sue and shall be subject to be sued, in all courts, in like cases as natural persons.

§ 2. Formation under general laws; change of laws; regulation

Section 2.   Corporations may be formed under general laws, but shall not be created by special acts. Laws relating to corporations may be altered, amended, or repealed at any time, and all corporations doing business in this state may, as to such business, be regulated, limited, and restrained by law.

§ 3. Existing charters
Section 3.   All existing charters under which a bona fide organization shall not have taken place and business commenced in good faith within six months from the time of the approval of this constitution shall thereafter have no validity.

§ 4. Restriction to business authorized by charter or law
Section 4.   No corporation shall engage in any business other than that expressly authorized in its charter or by the law under which it may have been or may hereafter be organized.

§ 5. Foreign corporations; transaction of business
Section 5.   No corporation organized outside of the limits of this state shall be allowed to transact business within this state on more favorable conditions than are prescribed by law for similar corporations organized under the laws of this state; and no foreign corporation shall be permitted to transact business within this state unless said foreign corporation is by the laws of the country, state, or territory under which it is formed permitted to transact a like business in such country, state, or territory.

§ 6. Stocks; bonds
Section 6.   No corporation shall issue stock, except to bona fide subscribers therefor or their assignees; nor shall any corporation issue any bond, or other obligation, for the payment of money, except for money or property received or for labor done. The stock of corporations shall not be increased, except in pursuance of a general law, nor shall any law authorize the increase of stock of any corporation without the consent of the person or persons holding the larger amount in value of the stock of such corporation, nor without due notice of the proposed increase having been given as may be prescribed by law. All fictitious increase of stock or indebtedness shall be void.

§ 7. Lease or alienation of franchise
Section 7.   No corporation shall lease or alienate any franchise so as to relieve the franchise, or property held thereunder, from the liabilities of the lessor, or grantor, lessee, or grantee, contracted or incurred in the operation, use, or enjoyment of such franchise or of any of its privileges.

§ 8. Filing of articles of incorporation; place of business; agent for service of process; venue

Section 8.   No domestic or foreign corporation shall do any business in this state without having filed its articles of incorporation or a certified copy thereof with the corporation commission, and without having one or more known places of business and an authorized agent, or agents, in the state upon whom process may be served. Suit may be maintained against a foreign corporation in the county where an agent of such corporation may be found, or in the county where the cause of action may arise.

§ 9. Eminent domain; taking corporate property and franchises for public use

Section 9.   The right of exercising eminent domain shall never be so abridged or construed as to prevent the state from taking the property and the franchises of incorporated companies and subjecting them to public use the same as the property of individuals.

§ 10. Elections for directors or managers

Section 10.   In all elections for directors or managers of any corporation, each shareholder shall have the right to cast as many votes in the aggregate as he shall be entitled to vote in said company under its charter multiplied by the number of directors or managers to be elected at such election; and each shareholder may cast the whole number of votes, either in person or by proxy, for one candidate, or distribute such votes among two or more such candidates; and such directors or managers shall not be elected otherwise.

§ 11. Liability of stockholders

Section 11.   [**Liability of stockholders**]. The shareholders or stockholders of every banking or insurance corporation or association shall be held individually responsible, equally and ratably, and not one for another, for all contracts, debts, and engagements of such corporation or association, to the extent of the amount of their stock therein, at the par value thereof, in addition to the amount invested in such shares or stock; provided, however, that the shareholders or stockholders of any banking corporation or association which is a member of the federal deposit insurance corporation or any successor thereto or other insuring instrumentality of the United States in accordance with the provisions of any applicable law of the United States of America, shall not be liable for any amount in addition to the amount already invested in such shares or stock.

Amended, election Sept. 11, 1956, effective Oct. 1, 1956.

§ 12. Officers of banking institutions; individual responsibility

Section 12.   Any president, director, manager, cashier, or other officer of any banking institution who shall receive, or assent to, the reception of any deposits after he shall have knowledge of the fact that such banking institution is insolvent or in failing circumstances shall be individually responsible for such deposits.

§ 13. Want of legal organization as a defense

Section 13.   No persons acting as a corporation under the laws of Arizona shall be permitted to set up, or rely upon, the want of a legal organization as a defense to any action which may be brought against them as a corporation, nor shall any person or persons who may be sued on a contract now or hereafter made with such corporation, or sued for any injury now or hereafter done to its property, or for a wrong done to its interests, be permitted to rely upon such want of legal organization in his or their defense.

§ 14. Legislative power to impose conditions

Section 14.   This article shall not be construed to deny the right of the legislative power to impose other conditions upon corporations than those herein contained.

§ 15. Monopolies and trusts

Section 15.   Monopolies and trusts shall never be allowed in this state and no incorporated company, co-partnership or association of persons in this state shall directly or indirectly combine or make any contract, with any incorporated company, foreign or domestic, through their stockholders or the trustees or assigns of such stockholders or with any co-partnership or association of persons, or, in any manner whatever, to fix the prices, limit the production, or regulate the transportation of any product or commodity. The legislature shall enact laws for the enforcement of this section by adequate penalties, and in the case of incorporated companies, if necessary for that purpose, may, as a penalty declare a forfeiture of their franchises.

§ 16. Records, books, and files; visitorial and inquisitorial powers of state
Section 16.   The records, books, and files of all public service corporations, state banks, building and loan associations, trust, insurance, and guaranty companies shall be at all times liable and subject to the full visitorial and inquisitorial powers of the state, notwithstanding the immunities and privileges secured in the declaration of rights of this constitution to persons, inhabitants, and citizens of this state.

§ 17. Fees; reports; licensing of foreign corporations
Section 17.   Provision shall be made by law for the payment of a fee to the state by every domestic corporation, upon the grant, amendment, or extension of its charter, and by every foreign corporation upon its obtaining a license to do business in this state; and also for the payment, by every domestic corporation and foreign corporation doing business in this state, of an annual registration fee of not less than ten dollars, which fee shall be paid irrespective of any specific license or other tax imposed by law upon such company for the privilege of carrying on its business in this state, or upon its franchise or property; and for the making, by every such corporation, at the time of paying such fee, of such report to the corporation commission of the status, business, or condition of such corporation, as may be prescribed by law. No foreign corporation, except insurers, shall have authority to do business in this state, until it shall have obtained from the corporation commission a license to do business in the state, upon such terms as may be prescribed by law. The legislature may relieve any purely charitable, social, fraternal, benevolent, or religious institution from the payment of such annual registration fee.

Amended, election Nov. 5, 1968, effective Jan. 28, 1969.

§ 18. Contributions to influence elections or official action
Section 18.   It shall be unlawful for any corporation, organized or doing business in this state, to make any contribution of money or anything of value for the purpose of influencing any election or official action.

§ 19. Penalties for violation of article
Section 19.   Suitable penalties shall be prescribed by law for the violation of any of the provisions of this article.

ARTICLE XV
THE CORPORATION COMMISSION

§ 1. Term limits on corporation commission; composition; election; office vacancies; qualifications

Section 1.   A. No member of the corporation commission shall hold that office for more than two consecutive terms. No corporation commissioner may serve again in that office until out of office for one full term. Any person who serves one half or more of a term shall be considered to have served one term for purposes of this section.

B.   A corporation commission is hereby created to be composed of five persons who shall be elected at the general election and whose term of office shall be four years, and who shall maintain their chief office at the state capital. The two additional commission members shall be elected at the 2002 general election for initial two-year terms beginning on the first Monday in January, 2003. Thereafter, all terms shall be four-year terms.

C.   In case of vacancy in the office, the governor shall appoint a commissioner to fill the vacancy. The appointed commissioner shall fill the vacancy until a commissioner shall be elected at a general election as provided by law, and shall qualify. The qualifications of commissioners may be prescribed by law.

Amended, election Nov. 7, 2000, effective Dec. 7, 2000.

§ 2. "Public service corporations" defined

Section 2.   All corporations other than municipal engaged in furnishing gas, oil, or electricity for light, fuel, or power; or in furnishing water for irrigation, fire protection, or other public purposes; or in furnishing, for profit, hot or cold air or steam for heating or cooling purposes; or engaged in collecting, transporting, treating, purifying and disposing of sewage through a system, for profit; or in transmitting messages or furnishing public telegraph or telephone service, and all corporations other than municipal, operating as common carriers, shall be deemed public service corporations.

Amended, election Nov. 5, 1974, effective Dec. 5, 1974; election Nov. 4, 1980, effective Nov. 24, 1980.

§ 3. Power of commission as to classifications, rates and charges, rules, contracts, and accounts; local regulations

Section 3.   The corporation commission shall have full power to, and shall, prescribe just and reasonable classifications to be used and just and reasonable rates and charges to be made and collected, by public service corporations within the state for service rendered therein, and make reasonable rules, regulations, and orders, by which such corporations shall be governed in the transaction of business within the state, and may prescribe the forms of contracts and the systems of keeping accounts to be used by such corporations in transacting such business, and make and enforce reasonable rules, regulations, and orders for the convenience, comfort, and safety, and the preservation of the health, of the employees and patrons of such corporations; provided, that incorporated cities and towns may be authorized by law to exercise supervision over public service corporations doing business therein, including the regulation of rates and charges to be made and collected by such corporations; provided further, that classifications, rates, charges, rules, regulations, orders, and forms or systems prescribed or made by said corporation commission may from time to time be amended or repealed by such commission.

§ 4. Power to inspect and investigate

Section 4.   The corporation commission, and the several members thereof, shall have power to inspect and investigate the property, books, papers, business, methods, and affairs of any corporation whose stock shall be offered for sale to the public and of any public service corporation doing business within the state, and for the purpose of the commission, and of the several members thereof, shall have the power of a court of general jurisdiction to enforce the attendance of witnesses and the production of evidence by subpoena, attachment, and punishment, which said power shall extend throughout the state. Said commission shall have power to take testimony under commission or deposition either within or without the state.

§ 5. Power to issue certificates of incorporation and licenses

Section 5.   The corporation commission shall have the sole power to issue certificates of incorporation to companies organizing under the laws of this state, and to issue licenses to foreign corporations to do business in this state, except as insurers, as may be prescribed by law.

Domestic and foreign insurers shall be subject to licensing, control and supervision by a department of insurance as prescribed by law. A director of the department of insurance shall be appointed by the governor with the consent of the senate in the manner prescribed by law for a term which may be prescribed by law.

Amended, election Nov. 5, 1968, effective Jan. 28, 1969; election Nov. 2, 1976, effective Nov. 22, 1976.

§ 6. Enlargement of powers by legislature; rules and regulations
Section 6.   The law-making power may enlarge the powers and extend the duties of the corporation commission, and may prescribe rules and regulations to govern proceedings instituted by and before it; but, until such rules and regulations are provided by law, the commission may make rules and regulations to govern such proceedings.

§ 7. Connecting and intersecting lines of transportation and communications corporations
Section 7.   Every public service corporation organized or authorized under the laws of the state to do any transportation or transmission business within the state shall have the right to construct and operate lines connecting any points within the state, and to connect at the state boundaries with like lines; and every such corporation shall have the right with any of its lines to cross, intersect, or connect with, any lines of any other public service corporation.

§ 8. Transportation by connecting carriers
Section 8.   Every public service corporation doing a transportation business within the state shall receive and transport, without delay or discrimination, cars loaded or empty, property, or passengers delivered to it by any other public service corporation doing a similar business, and deliver cars, loaded or empty, without delay or discrimination, to other transportation corporations, under such regulations as shall be prescribed by the corporation commission, or by law.

§ 9. Transmission of messages by connecting carriers
Section 9.   Every public service corporation engaged in the business of transmitting messages for profit shall receive and transmit, without delay or discrimination, any messages delivered to it

by any other public service corporation engaged in the business of transmitting messages for profit, and shall, with its lines, make physical connection with the lines of any public service corporation engaged in the business of transmitting messages for profit, under such rules and regulations as shall be prescribed by the corporation commission, or by law; provided, that such public service corporations shall deliver messages to other such corporations, without delay or discrimination, under such rules and regulations as shall be prescribed by the corporation commission, or by law.

§ 10. **Railways as public highways; other corporations as common carriers**
Section 10.   Railways heretofore constructed, or that may hereafter be constructed, in this state, are hereby declared public highways and all railroads are declared to be common carriers and subject to control by law. All electric, transmission, telegraph, telephone, or pipeline corporations, for the transportation of electricity, messages, water, oil, or other property for profit, are declared to be common carriers and subject to control by law.

Amended, election Nov. 4, 1980, effective Nov. 24, 1980.

§ 11. **Movable property as personal property; liability of property to attachment, execution and sale**
Section 11.   The rolling stock and all other movable property belonging to any public service corporation in this state, shall be considered personal property, and its real and personal property, and every part thereof, shall be liable to attachment, execution, and sale in the same manner as the property of individuals; and the lawmaking power shall enact no laws exempting any such property from attachment, execution, or sale.

§ 12. **Charges for service; discrimination; free or reduced rate transportation**
Section 12.   All charges made for service rendered, or to be rendered, by public service corporations within this state shall be just and reasonable, and no discrimination in charges, service, or facilities shall be made between persons or places for rendering a like and contemporaneous service, except that the granting of free or reduced rate transportation may be authorized by law, or by the corporation commission, to the classes of persons described in the act of congress approved February 11, 1887, entitled an act

to regulate commerce, and the amendments thereto, as those to whom free or reduced rate transportation may be granted.

§ 13. Reports to commission
Section 13.   All public service corporations and corporations whose stock shall be offered for sale to the public shall make such reports to the corporation commission, under oath, and provide such information concerning their acts and operations as may be required by law, or by the corporation commission.

§ 14. Value of property of public service corporations
Section 14.   The corporation commission shall, to aid it in the proper discharge of its duties, ascertain the fair value of the property within the state of every public service corporation doing business therein; and every public service corporation doing business within the state shall furnish to the commission all evidence in its possession, and all assistance in its power, requested by the commission in aid of the determination of the value of the property within the state of such public service corporation.

§ 15. Acceptance of constitutional provisions by existing corporations
Section 15.   No public service corporation in existence at the time of the admission of this state into the union shall have the benefit of any future legislation except on condition of complete acceptance of all provisions of this constitution applicable to public service corporations.

§ 16. Forfeitures for violations
Section 16.   If any public service corporation shall violate any of the rules, regulations, orders, or decisions of the corporation commission, such corporation shall forfeit and pay to the state not less than one hundred dollars nor more than five thousand dollars for each such violation, to be recovered before any court of competent jurisdiction.

§ 17. Appeal to courts
Section 17.   Nothing herein shall be construed as denying to public service corporations the right of appeal to the courts of the state from the rules, regulations, orders, or decrees fixed by the corporation commission, but the rules, regulations, orders, or decrees so fixed shall remain in force pending the decision of the courts.

§ 18. Repealed, election Nov. 3, 1970, effective Nov. 27, 1970

§ 19. Power to impose fines

Section 19.   The corporation commission shall have the power and authority to enforce its rules, regulations, and orders by the imposition of such fines as it may deem just, within the limitations prescribed in section 16 of this article.

ARTICLE XVI
MILITIA

§ 1. Composition of militia

Section 1.   The militia of the state of Arizona shall consist of all capable citizens of the state between the ages of eighteen and forty-five years, and of those between said ages who shall have declared their intention to become citizens of the United States, residing therein, subject to such exemptions as now exist, or as may hereafter be created, by the laws of the United States or of this state.

Amended, election Nov. 7, 2000, effective Dec. 7, 2000.

§ 2. Composition and designation of organized militia

Section 2.   The organized militia shall be designated "The National Guard of Arizona," and shall consist of such organized military bodies as now exist under the laws of the territory of Arizona or as may hereafter be authorized by law.

§ 3. Conformity to federal regulations

Section 3.   The organization, equipment, and discipline of the national guard shall conform as nearly as shall be practicable to the regulations for the government of the armies of the United States.

ARTICLE XVII
WATER RIGHTS

§ 1. Riparian water rights

Section 1.   The common law doctrine of riparian water rights shall not obtain or be of any force or effect in the state.

§ 2. Recognition of existing rights

Section 2.   All existing rights to the use of any of the waters in the state for all useful or beneficial purposes are hereby recognized and confirmed.

ARTICLE XVIII
LABOR

§ 1. Eight-hour day
Section 1.   Eight hours and no more, shall constitute a lawful day's work in all employment by, or on behalf of, the state or any political subdivision of the state. The legislature shall enact such laws as may be necessary to put this provision into effect, and shall prescribe proper penalties for any violations of said laws.

§ 2. Child labor
Section 2.   No child under the age of fourteen years shall be employed in any gainful occupation at any time during the hours in which the public schools of the district in which the child resides are in session; nor shall any child under sixteen years of age be employed underground in mines, or in any occupation injurious to health or morals or hazardous to life or limb; nor for more than eight hours in any day.

Amended, election Nov. 7, 1972, effective Dec. 1, 1972.

§ 3. Contractual immunity of employer from liability for negligence
Section 3.   It shall be unlawful for any person, company, association, or corporation to require of its servants or employees as a condition of their employment, or otherwise, any contract or agreement whereby such person, company, association, or corporation shall be released or discharged from liability or responsibility on account of personal injuries which may be received by such servants or employees while in the service or employment of such person, company, association, or corporation, by reason of the negligence of such person, company, association, corporation, or the agents or employees thereof; and any such contract or agreement if made, shall be null and void.

§ 4. Fellow servant doctrine
Section 4.   The common law doctrine of fellow servant, so far as it affects the liability of a master for injuries to his servant resulting from the acts or omissions of any other servant or servants of the common master is forever abrogated.

Constitution of the State of Arizona

§ 5. Contributory negligence and assumption of risk

Section 5. The defense of contributory negligence or of assumption of risk shall, in all cases whatsoever, be a question of fact and shall, at all times, be left to the jury.

§ 6. Recovery of damages for injuries

Section 6. The right of action to recover damages for injuries shall never be abrogated, and the amount recovered shall not be subject to any statutory limitation.

§ 7. Employer's liability law

Section 7. To protect the safety of employees in all hazardous occupations, in mining, smelting, manufacturing, railroad or street railway transportation, or any other industry the legislature shall enact an employer's liability law, by the terms of which any employer, whether individual, association, or corporation shall be liable for the death or injury, caused by any accident due to a condition or conditions of such occupation, of any employee in the service of such employer in such hazardous occupation, in all cases in which such death or injury of such employee shall not have been caused by the negligence of the employee killed or injured.

§ 8. Workmen's compensation law

Section 8. The legislature shall enact a workmen's compensation law applicable to workmen engaged in manual or mechanical labor in all public employment whether of the state, or any political subdivision or municipality thereof as may be defined by law and in such private employments as the legislature may prescribe by which compensation shall be required to be paid to any such workman, in case of his injury and to his dependents, as defined by law, in case of his death, by his employer, if in the course of such employment personal injury to or death of any such workman from any accident arising out of and in the course of, such employment, is caused in whole, or in part, or is contributed to, by a necessary risk or danger of such employment, or a necessary risk or danger inherent in the nature thereof, or by failure of such employer, or any of his or its agents or employee or employees to exercise due care, or to comply with any law affecting such employment; provided that it shall be optional with any employee engaged in any such private employment to settle for such compensation, or to retain the right to sue said employer or any person employed by said employer, acting in the scope of

355

his employment, as provided by this constitution; and, provided further, in order to assure and make certain a just and humane compensation law in the state of Arizona, for the relief and protection of such workmen, their widows, children or dependents, as defined by law, from the burdensome, expensive and litigious remedies for injuries to or death of such workmen, now existing in the state of Arizona, and producing uncertain and unequal compensation therefor, such employee, engaged in such private employment, may exercise the option to settle for compensation by failing to reject the provisions of such workmen's compensation law prior to the injury, except that if the injury is the result of an act done by the employer or a person employed by the employer knowingly and purposely with the direct object of injuring another, and the act indicates a wilful disregard of the life, limb or bodily safety of employees, then such employee may, after the injury, exercise the option to accept compensation or to retain the right to sue the person who injured him.

The percentages and amounts of compensation provided in house bill no. 227 enacted by the seventh legislature of the state of Arizona, shall never be reduced nor any industry included within the provision of said House Bill No. 227[1] eliminated except by initiated or referred measure as provided by this constitution.

1Laws 1925, Ch. 83.
Amended, election Sept. 29, 1925, effective Nov. 2, 1925; election Nov. 4, 1980, effective Nov. 24, 1980.

§ 9. Blacklists
Section 9. The exchange, solicitation, or giving out of any labor "black list," is hereby prohibited, and suitable laws shall be enacted to put this provision into effect.

§ 10. Employment of aliens
Section 10. No person not a citizen or ward of the United States shall be employed upon or in connection with any state, county or municipal works or employment; provided, that nothing herein shall be construed to prevent the working of prisoners by the state or by any county or municipality thereof on street or road work or other public work and that the provisions of this section shall not apply to the employment of any teacher, instructor, or professor authorized to teach in the United States under

the teacher exchange program as provided by federal statutes enacted by the congress of the United States or the employment of university or college faculty members. The legislature shall enact laws for the enforcement and shall provide for the punishment of any violation of this section.

Amended, election Nov. 4, 1930, effective Dec. 1, 1930; election Sept. 11, 1956, effective Oct. 1, 1956; election Nov. 8, 1960, effective Dec. 9, 1960.

ARTICLE XIX
MINES

Note: This Article was amended by two different propositions in the 1992 general election. Both propositions passed. The text of the two propositions was different. Both versions are printed below.

The office of mine inspector is hereby established. The legislature shall enact laws so regulating the operation and equipment of all mines in the state as to provide for the health and safety of workers therein and in connection therewith, and fixing the duties of said office. Upon approval of such laws by the governor, the governor, with the advice and consent of the senate, shall forthwith appoint a mine inspector, who shall serve until his successor shall have been elected at the first general election thereafter and shall qualify. Said successor and all subsequent incumbents of said office shall be elected at general elections, and shall serve for four years. The initial four year term shall be served by the mine inspector elected in the general election held in November, 1994.

Amended by Proposition 102, election Nov. 3, 1992, effective Nov. 23, 1992.

The office of mine inspector is hereby established. The legislature, at its first session, shall enact laws so regulating the operation and equipment of all mines in the state as to provide for the health and safety of workers therein and in connection therewith, and fixing the duties of said office. Upon approval of such laws by the governor, the governor, with the advice and consent of the senate, shall forthwith appoint a mine inspector, who shall serve until his successor shall have been elected at the first general election thereafter and shall qualify. Said successor and all subsequent incumbents of said office shall be elected at general elections, and shall serve for a term of two years. No mine inspector shall serve more than four consecutive terms in that office. No mine inspector, after serving the maximum number of terms, which shall include any part of a term served, may serve in the same office until out of office for no less than one full term. This limitation on the number of terms of consecutive service shall apply to terms of office beginning on or after January 1, 1993.

Amended by Proposition 107, election Nov. 3, 1992, effective Nov. 23, 1992.

ARTICLE XX
ORDINANCE

The following ordinance shall be irrevocable without the consent of the United States and the people of this state:

First.   Toleration of religious sentiment
First.   Perfect toleration of religious sentiment shall be secured to every inhabitant of this state, and no inhabitant of this state shall ever be molested in person or property on account of his or her mode of religious worship, or lack of the same.

Second.   Polygamy
Second.   Polygamous or plural marriages, or polygamous cohabitation, are forever prohibited within this state.

Third.   Introduction of intoxicating liquors into Indian country
Third.   The introduction of intoxicating liquors for resale purposes into Indian country is prohibited within this state until July 1, 1957.

Amended, election Nov. 2, 1954, effective Nov. 23, 1954.

Fourth.   Public lands; Indian lands
Fourth.   The people inhabiting this state do agree and declare that they forever disclaim all right and title to the unappropriated and ungranted public lands lying within the boundaries thereof and to all lands lying within said boundaries owned or held by any Indian or Indian tribes, the right or title to which shall have been acquired through or from the United States or any prior sovereignty, and that, until the title of such Indian or Indian tribes shall have

been extinguished, the same shall be, and remain, subject to the disposition and under the absolute jurisdiction and control of the congress of the United States.

Fifth.   Taxation

Fifth.   The lands and other property belonging to citizens of the United States residing without this state shall never be taxed at a higher rate than the lands and other property situated in this state belonging to residents thereof, and no taxes shall be imposed by this state on any lands or other property within an Indian reservation owned or held by any Indian; but nothing herein shall preclude the state from taxing as other lands and other property are taxed, any lands and other property outside of an Indian reservation owned or held by any Indian, save and except such lands as have been granted or acquired as aforesaid, or as may be granted or confirmed to any Indian or Indians under any act of congress.

Amended, election May 31, 1927, effective June 27, 1927.

Sixth.   Territorial debts and liabilities

Sixth.   The debts and liabilities of the territory of Arizona, and the debts of the counties thereof, valid and subsisting at the time of the passage of the enabling act approved June 20, 1910, are hereby assumed and shall be paid by the state of Arizona, and the state of Arizona shall, as to all such debts and liabilities, be subrogated to all the rights, including rights of indemnity and reimbursement, existing in favor of said territory or of any of the several counties thereof, at the time of the passage of the said enabling act; provided, that nothing in this ordinance shall be construed as validating or in any manner legalizing any territorial, county, municipal, or other bonds, obligations, or evidences of indebtedness of said territory or the counties or municipalities thereof which now are or may be invalid or illegal at the time the said state of Arizona is admitted as a state, and the legislature or the people of the state of Arizona shall never pass any law in any manner validating or legalizing the same.

Seventh.   Public school system; suffrage

Seventh.   Provisions shall be made by law for the establishment and maintenance of a system of public schools which shall be open to all the children of the state and be free from sectarian control, and said schools shall always be conducted in English.

The state shall never enact any law restricting or abridging the right of suffrage on account of race, color, or previous condition of servitude.

Eighth.   English language

Eighth.   The ability to read, write, speak, and understand the English language sufficiently well to conduct the duties of the office without the aid of an interpreter, shall be a necessary qualification for all state officers and members of the state legislature.

Ninth.   Location of state capital

Ninth.   The capital of the state of Arizona, until changed by the electors voting at an election provided for by the legislature for that purpose, shall be at the city of Phoenix, but no such election shall be called or provided for prior to the thirty-first day of December, nineteen hundred and twenty-five.

Tenth.   Repealed, election May 31, 1927, effective June 27, 1927

Eleventh.   Repealed, election Nov. 2, 1954, effective Nov. 23, 1954

Twelfth.   Lands granted to state

Twelfth. The state of Arizona and its people hereby consent to all and singular the provisions of the enabling act approved June 20, 1910, concerning the lands thereby granted or confirmed to the state, the terms and conditions upon which said grants and confirmations are made, and the means and manner of enforcing such terms and conditions, all in every respect and particular as in the aforesaid enabling act provided.

Thirteenth.   Ordinance as part of constitution; amendment

Thirteenth.   This ordinance is hereby made a part of the constitution of the state of Arizona, and no future constitutional amendment shall be made which in any manner changes or abrogates this ordinance in whole or in part without the consent of congress.

ARTICLE XXI
MODE OF AMENDING

§ 1.   Introduction in legislature; initiative petition; election

Section 1.   Any amendment or amendments to this constitution may be proposed in either house of the legislature, or by initiative petition signed by a number of qualified electors equal to fifteen per centum of the total number of votes for all candidates for governor at the last preceding general election. Any proposed amendment or amendments which shall be introduced in either house of the legislature, and which shall be approved by a majority of the members elected to each of the two houses, shall be entered on the journal of each house, together with the ayes and nays thereon. When any proposed amendment or amendments shall be thus passed by a majority of each house of the legislature and entered on the respective journals thereof, or when any elector or electors shall file with the secretary of state any proposed amendment or amendments together with a petition therefor signed by a number of electors equal to fifteen per centum of the total number of votes for all candidates for governor in the last preceding general election, the secretary of state shall submit such proposed amendment or amendments to the vote of the people at the next general election (except when the legislature shall call a special election for the purpose of having said proposed amendment or amendments voted upon, in which case the secretary of state shall submit such proposed amendment or amendments to the qualified electors at said special election,) and if a majority of the qualified electors voting thereon shall approve and ratify such proposed amendment or amendments in said regular or special election, such amendment or amendments shall become a part of this constitution. Until a method of publicity is otherwise provided by law, the secretary of state shall have such proposed amendment or amendments published for a period of at least ninety days previous to the date of said election in at least one newspaper in every county of the state in which a newspaper shall be published, in such manner as may be prescribed by law. If more than one proposed amendment shall be submitted at any election, such proposed amendments shall be submitted in such manner that the electors may vote for or against such proposed amendments separately.

§ 2. Convention
Section 2.   No convention shall be called by the legislature to propose alterations, revisions, or amendments to this constitution, or to propose a new constitution, unless laws providing for such convention shall first be approved by the people on a referendum vote at a regular or special election, and any amendments,

alterations, revisions, or new constitution proposed by such convention shall be submitted to the electors of the state at a general or special election and be approved by the majority of the electors voting thereon before the same shall become effective.

ARTICLE XXII
SCHEDULE AND MISCELLANEOUS

§ 1. Existing rights, actions, suits, proceedings, contracts, claims, or demands; process

Section 1.   No rights, actions, suits, proceedings, contracts, claims, or demands, existing at the time of the admission of this state into the union, shall be affected by a change in the form of government, from territorial to state, but all shall continue as if no change had taken place; and all process which may have been issued under the authority of the territory of Arizona, previous to its admission into the Union, shall be as valid as if issued in the name of the state.

§ 2. Territorial laws

Section 2.   All laws of the territory of Arizona now in force, not repugnant to this constitution, shall remain in force as laws of the state of Arizona until they expire by their own limitations or are altered or repealed by law; provided, that wherever the word territory, meaning the territory of Arizona, appears in said laws, the word state shall be substituted.

§ 3. Debts, fines, penalties, and forfeitures

Section 3.   All debts, fines, penalties, and forfeitures which have accrued, or may hereafter accrue, to the territory of Arizona shall inure to the state of Arizona.

§ 4. Recognizances; bonds; estate; judgments; choses in action

Section 4.   All recognizances heretofore taken, or which may be taken, before the change from a territorial to a state government, shall remain valid, and shall pass to and may be prosecuted in the name of the state, and all bonds executed to the territory of Arizona, or to any county or municipal corporation, or to any officer, or court, in his or its official capacity, shall pass to the state authorities and their successors in office for the uses therein expressed, and may be sued for and recovered accordingly; and all the estate, real, personal, and mixed, and all judgments, decrees, bonds, specialties, choses in action, and claims, demands or debts of whatever description, belonging to the territory of Arizona, shall inure to and vest in the state of Arizona, and may be sued for and recovered by the state of Arizona in the same manner, and to the same extent, as the same might or could have been by the territory of Arizona.

§ 5. Criminal prosecutions and penal actions; offenses; penalties; actions and suits

Section 5.   All criminal prosecutions and penal actions which may have arisen, or which may arise, before the change from a territorial to a state government, and which shall then be pending, shall be prosecuted to judgment and execution in the name of the state. All offenses committed against the laws of the territory of Arizona before the change from a territorial to a state government, and which shall not be prosecuted before such change, may be prosecuted in the name, and by the authority, of the state of Arizona, with like effect as though such change had not taken place, and all penalties incurred and punishments inflicted shall remain the same as if this constitution had not been adopted. All actions at law and suits in equity, which may be pending in any of the courts, of the territory of Arizona at the time of the change from a territorial to a state government, shall be continued and transferred to the court of the state, or of the United States, having jurisdiction thereof.

§ 6. Territorial, district, county, and precinct officers

Section 6.   All territorial, district, county, and precinct officers who may be in office at the time of the admission of the state into the union shall hold their respective offices until their successors shall have qualified, and the official bonds of all such officers shall continue in full force and effect while such officers remain in office.

§ 7. Causes pending in district courts of territory; records, papers, and property

Section 7.   Whenever the judge of the superior court of any county, elected or appointed under the provisions of this constitution, shall have qualified, the several causes then pending in the district court of the territory, and in and for such county, except such causes as would have been within the exclusive jurisdiction of the United States courts, had such courts existed at the time of the commencement of such causes within such county, and the

records, papers, and proceedings of said district court, and other
property pertaining thereto, shall pass into the jurisdiction and possession of the superior court of such county.

It shall be the duty of the clerk of the district court having custody of such papers, records, and property, to transmit to the clerk
of said superior court the original papers in all cases pending in
such district and belonging to the jurisdiction of said superior court,
together with a transcript, or transcripts, of so much of the record
of said district court as shall relate to the same; and until the district courts of the territory shall be superseded in manner aforesaid, and as in this constitution provided, the said district courts,
and the judges thereof, shall continue with the same jurisdiction
and powers, to be exercised in the same judicial district, respectively, as heretofore, and now, constituted.

§ 8.   Probate records and proceedings

Section 8.   When the state is admitted into the union, and
the superior courts, in their respective counties, are organized, the
books, records, papers, and proceedings of the probate court in
each county, and all causes and matters of administration pending
therein, shall pass into the jurisdiction and possession of the superior court of the same county created by this constitution, and the
said court shall proceed to final judgment or decree, order, or other
determination, in the several matters and causes with like effect
as the probate court might have done if this constitution had not
been adopted.

§ 9.   Causes pending in supreme court of territory; records, papers, and property

Section 9.   Whenever a quorum of the judges of the supreme
court of the state shall have been elected, and qualified, and shall
have taken office, under this constitution, the causes then pending
in the supreme court of the territory, except such causes as would
have been within the exclusive jurisdiction of the United States
courts, had such courts existed at the time of the commencement
of such causes, and the papers, records, and proceedings of said
court, and the seal and other property pertaining thereto, shall pass
into the jurisdiction and possession of the supreme court of the
state, and until so superseded, the supreme court of the territory,
and the judges thereof, shall continue, with like powers and jurisdiction as if this constitution had not been adopted, or the state
admitted into the union; and all causes pending in the supreme

court of the territory at said time, and which said causes would have been within the exclusive jurisdiction of the United States courts, had such courts existed, at the time of the commencement of such causes, and the papers, records, and proceedings of said court, relating thereto, shall pass into the jurisdiction of the United States courts, all as in the enabling act approved June 20, 1910, provided.

§ 10. Seals of supreme court, superior courts, municipalities, and county officers

Section 10.   Until otherwise provided by law, the seal now in use in the supreme court of the territory, shall be the seal of the supreme court of the state, except that the word "state", shall be substituted for the word "territory" on said seal. The seal of the superior courts of the several counties of the state, until otherwise provided by law, shall be the vignette of Abraham Lincoln, with the words "Seal of the Superior Court of _____ County, State of Arizona", surrounding the vignette. The seal of municipalities, and of all county officers, in the territory, shall be the seals of such municipalities and county officers, respectively, under the state, until otherwise provided by law, except that the word "territory", or "territory of Arizona", be changed to read "state" or "state of Arizona", where the same may appear on any such seals.

§ 11. Effective date of constitution

Section 11.   The provisions of this constitution shall be in force from the day on which the president of the United States shall issue his proclamation declaring the state of Arizona admitted into the union.

§ 12. Election of representative in congress

Section 12.   One representative in the congress of the United States shall be elected from the state at large, and at the same election at which officers shall be elected under the enabling act, approved June 20, 1910, and, thereafter, at such times and in such manner as may be prescribed by law. (Congressional representation, see 2 U.S.C.A. § § 2a and 2b and A.R.S. § 16-1101.)

§ 13. Continuation in office until qualification of successor

Section 13.   The term of office of every officer to be elected or appointed under this constitution or the laws of Arizona shall extend until his successor shall be elected and shall qualify.

§ 14. Initiative
Section 14.　　Any law which may be enacted by the legislature under this constitution may be enacted by the people under the initiative. Any law which may not be enacted by the legislature under this constitution shall not be enacted by the people.

§ 15. Public institutions
Section 15.　　Correctional and penal institutions, and institutions for the benefit of persons who have mental or physical disabilities, and such other institutions as the public good may require, shall be established and supported by the State in such manner as may be prescribed by law.

Amended, election Nov. 7, 2000, effective Dec. 7, 2000.

§ 16. Confinement of minor offenders
Section 16.　　It shall be unlawful to confine any minor under the age of eighteen years, accused or convicted of crime, in the same section of any jail or prison in which adult prisoners are confined. Suitable quarters shall be prepared for the confinement of such minors.

§ 17. Compensation of public officers
Section 17.　　All state and county officers (except notaries public) and all justices of the peace and constables, whose precinct includes a city or town or part thereof, shall be paid fixed and definite salaries, and they shall receive no fees for their own use.

§ 18. Nomination of incumbent public officers to other offices
Section 18.　　Except during the final year of the term being served, no incumbent of a salaried elective office, whether holding by election or appointment, may offer himself for nomination or election to any salaried local, state or federal office.

Added, election Nov. 4, 1980, effective Nov. 24, 1980.

§ 19. Lobbying
Section 19.　　The legislature shall enact laws and adopt rules prohibiting the practice of lobbying on the floor of either house of the legislature, and further regulating the practice of lobbying.

§ 20. Design of state seal
Section 20.　　The seal of the state shall be of the following design: in the background shall be a range of mountains, with the

sun rising behind the peaks thereof, and at the right side of the range of mountains there shall be a storage reservoir and a dam, below which in the middle distance are irrigated fields and orchards reaching into the foreground, at the right of which are cattle grazing. To the left in the middle distance on a mountain side is a quartz mill in front of which and in the foreground is a miner standing with pick and shovel. Above this device shall be the motto: "Ditat Deus." In a circular band surrounding the whole device shall be inscribed: "Great Seal of The State of Arizona", with the year of admission of the state into the union.

§ 21. Enactment of laws to carry constitution into effect
Section 21.   The legislature shall enact all necessary laws to carry into effect the provisions of this constitution.

§ 22. Judgments of death
Section 22.   The judgment of death shall be inflicted by administering an intravenous injection of a substance or substances in a lethal quantity sufficient to cause death except that defendants sentenced to death for offenses committed prior to the effective date of the amendment to this section shall have the choice of either lethal injection or lethal gas. The lethal injection or lethal gas shall be administered under such procedures and supervision as prescribed by law. The execution shall take place within the limits of the state prison.

Added, election Oct. 3, 1933, effective Oct. 28, 1933; amended, election Nov. 3, 1992, effective Nov. 23, 1992.

ARTICLE XXIII
PROHIBITION

§ § 1 to 3.   **Repealed, election Nov. 8, 1932, effective Nov. 28,**
1932

ARTICLE XXIV
PROHIBITION

§ § 1, 2.   **Repealed, election Nov. 8, 1932, effective Nov. 28,**
1932

ARTICLE XXV
RIGHT TO WORK

Right to work or employment without membership in labor organization
No person shall be denied the opportunity to obtain or retain employment because of non-membership in a labor organization, nor shall the state or any subdivision thereof, or any corporation, individual or association of any kind enter into any agreement, written or oral, which excludes any person from employment or continuation of employment because of non-membership in a labor organization.

Added, election Nov. 5, 1946, effective Nov. 25, 1946.

ARTICLE XXVI
RIGHT OF LICENSED REAL ESTATE BROKERS AND SALESMEN TO PREPARE INSTRUMENTS INCIDENT TO PROPERTY TRANSACTIONS

§ 1. Powers of real estate broker or salesman
Section 1.   Any person holding a valid license as a real estate broker or a real estate salesman regularly issued by the Arizona state real estate department when acting in such capacity as broker or salesman for the parties, or agent for one of the parties to a sale, exchange, or trade, or the renting and leasing of property, shall have the right to draft or fill out and complete, without charge, any and all instruments incident thereto including, but not limited to, preliminary purchase agreements and earnest money receipts, deeds, mortgages, leases, assignments, releases, contracts for sale of realty, and bills of sale.

Added, election Nov. 6, 1962, effective Nov. 26, 1962.

ARTICLE XXVII
REGULATION OF PUBLIC HEALTH, SAFETY AND WELFARE

§ 1. Regulation of ambulances; powers of legislature
Section 1.   The legislature may provide for the regulation of ambulances and ambulance services in this state in all matters

relating to services provided, routes served, response times and charges.

Added, election Nov. 2, 1982, effective Nov. 30, 1982.

ARTICLE XXVIII
ENGLISH AS THE OFFICIAL LANGUAGE

§ 1. English as the official language; applicability
Section 1. (1) The English language is the official language of the state of Arizona.
(2) As the official language of this state, the English language is the language of the ballot, the public schools and all government functions and actions.
(3) (a) This article applies to:
(i) The legislative, executive and judicial branches of government
(ii) All political subdivisions, departments, agencies, organizations, and instrumentalities of this state, including local governments and municipalities,
(iii) All statutes, ordinances, rules, orders, programs and policies.
(iv) All government officials and employees during the performance of government business.
(b) As used in this article, the phrase "this state and all political subdivisions of this state" shall include every entity, person, action or item described in this section, as appropriate to the circumstances.

Added, election Nov. 8, 1988, effective Dec. 5, 1988.

§ 2. Requiring this state to preserve, protect and enhance English
Section 2. This state and all political subdivisions of this state shall take all reasonable steps to preserve, protect and enhance the role of the English language as the official language of the state of Arizona.

Added, election Nov. 8, 1988, effective Dec. 5, 1988.

§ 3. Prohibiting this state from using or requiring the use of languages other than English; exceptions

Section 3.　　(1) Except as provided in subsection (2):
(a)　　This state and all political subdivisions of this state shall act in English and in no other language.
(b)　　No entity to which this article applies shall make or enforce a law, order, decree or policy which requires the use of a language other than English.
(c)　　No governmental document shall be valid, effective or enforceable unless it is in the English language.
(2)　　This state and all political subdivisions of this state may act in a language other than English under any of the following circumstances:
(a)　　To assist students who are not proficient in the English language, to the extent necessary to comply with federal law, by giving educational instruction in a language other than English to provide as rapid as possible a transition to English.
(b)　　To comply with other federal laws.
(c)　　To teach a student a foreign language as a part of a required or voluntary educational curriculum.
(d)　　To protect public health or safety.
(e)　　To protect the rights of criminal defendants or victims of crime.

Added, election Nov. 8, 1988, effective Dec. 5, 1988.

§ 4.　Enforcement; standing
Section 4.　　A person who resides in or does business in this state shall have standing to bring suit to enforce this article in a court of record of the state. The legislature may enact reasonable limitations on the time and manner of bringing suit under this subsection.

Added, election Nov. 8, 1988, effective Dec. 5, 1988.

ARTICLE XXIX. PUBLIC RETIREMENT SYSTEMS

§ 1.　Public retirement systems
Section 1.　　A. Public retirement systems shall be funded with contributions and investment earnings using actuarial methods and assumptions that are consistent with generally accepted actuarial standards.

B.   The assets of public retirement systems, including investment earnings and contributions, are separate and independent trust funds and shall be invested, administered and distributed as determined by law solely in the interests of the members and beneficiaries of the public retirement systems.

C.   Membership in a public retirement system is a contractual relationship that is subject to article II, section 25, and public retirement system benefits shall not be diminished or impaired.

Added, election Nov. 3, 1998, effective December 10, 1998.

TEST BANK

1. What is unique concerning Arizona's native population is that
   a. it represents a broad spectrum on non-indigenous tribes
   b. it is native to Arizona
   c. it is reluctant to remain on reservations
   d. it refuses to promote Indian gaming

2. All but one of the following Spanish explorers set foot in Arizona
   a. Antonio de Espejo.
   b. Marcos de Niza.
   c. Francesco Pizarro.
   d. Juan de Onate.

3. The major activities of the early Spanish in Arizona include
   a. exploration, missions, mines
   b. cattle, mines, agriculture
   c. copper, cotton, cattle
   d. exploration, mines, trade

4. Of significance to state government concerning indigenous populations is
   a. the sizeable percentage of voters they represent
   b. the amount of tax revenue derived from Indian gaming
   c. the amount of non-taxable land controlled by Indian communities
   d. the aging of their members

5. The precipitating event leading to war with Mexico was
   a. the annexation of Texas
   b. American occupation of the Rio Grande valley
   c. a desire to acquire the mines of northern Arizona
   d. the growing number of illegal Mexican immigrants

6. The reason for the Gadsden Purchase was
   a. the mining wealth south of the Gila River
   b. a desire for more slave territory
   c. to make possible a southern transcontinental railroad route
   d. that many Americans had already settled there

7. The effort to combine Arizona and New Mexico was due to all but
   a. limiting the political influence of the West
   b. simplifying the building of a southern transcontinental railroad
   c. the political agenda of Eastern Republicans
   d. diminishing the spread of liberal ideology

8. Arizona's constitution was rejected by President Taft due to its provision related to
   a. the coinage of silver
   b. the recall of judges
   c. female suffrage
   d. its labor provisions

9. During their territorial phase future states
   a. favor diminished federal government services
   b. want no support from the federal government
   c. attempt to prolong their territorial status indefinitely
   d. actively seek the aid of the federal government

10. The general framework for admitting new states into the Union is the
    a. Northwest Ordinance
    b. Tenth Amendment
    c. Ordinance of 1785
    d. United States Constitution

11. In a federal system the national government is
    a. controlled by the various regional governments
    b. supreme within its area of authority
    c. powerless to control state actions
    d. possessed of total authority over the states

12. The population of the Valley of the Sun owes its origins to what territorial era law
    a. Kansas-Nebraska Act
    b. Newlands Act
    c. Foraker Amendment
    d. U"Ren System

13. The federal government uses all of the following to enhance its power except

    a. national defense/security issues
    b. the New Federalism
    c. rights of federal citizenship
    d. the grant-in-aid

14. Ordinary laws passed by the Arizona Legislature go into effect

    a. 30 days after the close of the session in which they were passed
    b. 60 days after the close of the session in which they were passed
    c. immediately upon being signed by the Governor
    d. 90 days after the close of the session in which they were passed

15. Lobbyists are required by state law to

    a. surrender their right to vote for public officials
    b. purchase a license from the Secretary of State
    c. register and file periodic reports with the Secretary of State
    d. get approval from a lobbyist control board

16. The percentage of voter signatures for initiating a protest referendum is

    a. 5%
    b. 10%
    c. 20%
    d. 25%

17. The percentage of voter signatures required for initiating a law and an amendment is
    a. 10% to propose a law and 15% to propose an amendment
    b. 15% to propose either a law or an amendment
    c. 10% to propose either a law or an amendment
    d. 10% to propose a law and 20% to propose an amendment

18. A recall can be initiated against
    a. any elected official
    b. any appointed official
    c. any state employee
    d. any elected official with the exception of judges

19. Excluding legislators the period before a recall may be attempted is
    a. after serving three months in office
    b. 120 days from the date of the initial election
    c. after serving six months but not beyond twelve months
    d. after serving six months in office

20. The initiative allows voters to
    a. propose laws or amendments
    b. pass on all legislation enacted by the legislature
    c. remove elected officials from office before the end of their term
    d. declare which laws shall be emergency laws

21. Not a requirement for voting in Arizona is
    a. United States citizenship
    b. voter registration
    c. payment of taxes
    d. being 18 years of age

22. The impeachment process is accomplished by
    a. a two-thirds vote of the Senate
    b. a majority of the House of Representatives
    c. a joint proclamation of both houses of the legislature
    d. directive of the Arizona Supreme Court

23. The term of office for the Arizona House of Representatives is
    a. four years
    b. six years
    c. two years
    d. one year

24. Special sessions of the state legislature may be called by
    a. a two-thirds vote of both houses
    b. the Secretary of State
    c. the leadership of the House and Senate
    d. the Chief Justice of the Supreme Court

25. The Arizona State Legislature consists of
    a. 30 members
    b. 60 members
    c. 90 members
    d. 120 members

26. Not a power of the legislative body is
    a. investigation
    b. legislation
    c. impeachment
    d. pardon and reprieve

27. The term of office for a state senator is
    a. two years
    b. four years
    c. six years
    d. eight years

28. Certification of election returns for state officials is determined by
    a. county election boards
    b. the Secretary of State
    c. a legislative voting committee
    d. the Credentials Committee of the Supreme Court

29. Effective with the 2002 elections Arizona's congressional delegation consists of
    a. five members
    b. six members
    c. eight members
    d. ten members

30. The residency requirement for voting in a state election is
    a. 30 days
    b. 50 days
    c. 60 days
    d. 90 days

31. The type of election held after a successful initiative drive is called a
    a. special election
    b. referendum
    c. recall
    d. closed

32. Laws invoking the emergency clause go into effect
    a. 30 days after the close of the legislative session in which they were passed
    b. 60 days after the end of the session in which passed
    c. immediately upon being signed by the Governor
    d. as soon as they are printed by the Secretary of State

33. A statute is a
    a. state law
    b. executive proclamation
    c. city charter
    d. local ordinance

34. The majority party in either house of the legislature does all except
    a. select the presiding officer
    b. hold a majority on all committees
    c. possess the exclusive right to introduce legislation
    d. selects all committee chairpersons

35. Compensation for members of the state legislature is established by
    a. action of the legislature subject to executive approval
    b. recommendation of a salary commission subject to executive approval
    c. the voters of the state regardless of source of the proposal
    d. only by a voter initiated proposition

36. Arizona "right to work" means that
    a. labor unions are outlawed
    b. union membership is required as a condition of employment
    c. there exists a constitutional right to have a job
    d. union membership cannot be required as a condition of employment

37. An emergency measure must pass both legislative houses by
    a. a simple majority vote
    b. a two-thirds vote of the membership
    c. a three-fourths vote of the membership
    d. the unanimous vote of those present

38. When the Governor calls a special legislative session the reasons must be
    a. left to the discretion of the legislature
    b. specified by the Governor
    c. determined beforehand by the Governor and legislative leadership
    d. approved by a majority of the elected members of the executive branch

39. Members of either house of the Arizona Legislature are limited to
    a. two consecutive terms
    b. four terms lifetime
    c. an unlimited number of terms
    d. four consecutive terms

40. The Governor must be at least
    a. 35 years of age
    b. 25 years of age
    c. 30 years of age
    d. 21 years of age

41. The elected official immediately in line to succeed to the governorship is
    a. State Treasurer
    b. Lt. Governor
    c. Attorney General
    d. Secretary of State

42. The standard term of office for state elected executive officials is
    a. two years
    b. four years
    c. six years
    d. indefinite subject to periodic voter reassessment

43. The most politically significant power of the Governor is the
    a. veto power
    b. appointment power
    c. pardoning power
    d. foreign affairs power

44. Constitutional requirements for the office of Attorney General include
    a. she must have been a former state judge
    b. he must be a native born American citizen
    c. she must have taught law school for at least five years
    d. he must be licensed to practice before the Arizona Supreme Court

45. The newly revised Corporation Commission consists of
    a. three members
    b. four members
    c. five members
    d. six members

46. Not an elected position within the executive branch is the
    a. Mining Inspector
    b. State Treasurer
    c. State Auditor
    d. Superintendent of Public Instruction

47. The highest salaries of elected officials is found in the
    a. executive branch
    b. county government
    c. judicial branch
    d. legislative branch

48. The Supreme Court exercises original jurisdiction in all cases involving
    a. suits between Arizona counties
    b. violations of state statutes
    c. violations of civil rights
    d. criminal matters involving the death penalty

49. Justices of the Peace obtain office by
    a. selection by a citizen judicial selection committee
    b. appointment by the Supreme Court
    c. appointment by the Governor
    d. election by the voters

50. Two different courts having jurisdiction over the same issue is called
    a. concurrent jurisdiction
    b. appellate jurisdiction
    c. limited jurisdiction
    d. original jurisdiction

51. The Chief Justice of the Arizona Supreme Court is
    a. elected by the voters of the state
    b. chosen by the other justices on the Court
    c. appointed by the Governor from among all sitting justices
    d. chosen by the State Senate from among all sitting justices

52. The term of office for an Arizona Supreme Court Justice is
    a. lifetime
    b. four years
    c. five years
    d. six years

53. Administrative supervision over all Arizona courts is exercised by the
    a. Commission on Judicial Conduct
    b. Governors Committee on the Judiciary
    c. Supreme Court
    d. Commission on Judicial Proceedings

54. The term "general courts" applies to
    a. municipal courts
    b. Justice of the Peace Courts
    c. Superior Court
    d. Court of Appeals

55. Arizona Supreme Court Justices are chosen by
   a. gubernatorial appointment based on committee recommendation
   b. appointment by a legislative joint committee on the judiciary
   c. general election partisan vote
   d. general election with no party affiliation allowed

56. The term of office of a Superior Court judge is
   a. two years
   b. four years
   c. six years
   d. lifetime

57. No formal academic preparation is required for judges at this level
   a. Court of Appeals
   b. Superior Court
   c. Justice of the Peace Courts
   d. Supreme Court

58. The Commission on Judicial Performance was designed to
   a. propose a quality control system for Arizona judges
   b. provide information to voters to aid in their evaluation of judicial fitness
   c. identify and remove poorly performing judges
   d. investigate and make recommendations to the Supreme Court

59. Which of the following is entitled to exemption from some property tax
    a. all Arizona veterans who have had overseas duty
    b. all widows and widowers
    c. senior citizens with at least fifty years Arizona residency
    d. disabled veterans

60. The Chair of the State Board of Investment is the
    a. Secretary of State
    b. Governor
    c. State Treasurer
    d. State Auditor

61. This state function accounts for the greatest expenditure of funds
    a. highway construction
    b. irrigation and flood control projects
    c. public education
    d. health and safety

62. The aggregate amount of state operating debt may not exceed
    a. an amount determined by each session of the legislature
    b. one million dollars indexed to 1960
    c. $350,000
    d. $550,000

63. The major source of state revenue is derived from the
    a. income tax
    b. property tax
    c. sales tax
    d. corporate tax

64. The Budget Stabilization Fund was established to
    a. level out income and outgo over a five year period
    b. provide reserve funds for times of economic need
    c. investigate the feasibility of abolishing the state income tax
    d. accrue funds for future major capital expenditures

65. An Arizona county is
    a. a sovereign political body
    b. an independent political subdivision of state government
    c. a political subdivision of state government
    d. more independent than charter city government

66. Not a constitutionally mandated county official is the
    a. Recorder
    b. Clerk of Superior Court
    c. Sheriff
    d. Assessor

67. Services and functions of county government include all except
    a. libraries
    b. penitentiaries
    c. sewerage treatment
    d. health facilities

68. Motor vehicle registration is the responsibility of the
    a. county treasurer
    b. county assessor
    c. board of supervisors
    d. county recorder

69. County ordinances are created by the
    a. sheriff
    b. county attorney
    c. state legislature
    d. board of supervisors

70. Not a function of the county sheriff is to
    a. maintain the county jail
    b. perform search and rescue operations
    c. maintain records and enforce decisions of the Superior Court
    d. function as custodian of recovered lost and stolen property

71. The county Board of Supervisors is
    a. the same for all fifteen Arizona counties
    b. appointed by the state legislature
    c. elected to oversee county government
    d. reports to the county manager

72. The compensation of elected county officials is
    a. determined by the voters of each county
    b. established by the state legislature
    c. mandated in the state constitution
    d. set by the county board of supervisors

73. The charter of incorporated cities and towns is granted by the

    a. Superior Court
    b. Board of Supervisors
    c. State Legislature
    d. Secretary of State

74. The term "charter" is practically synonymous with

    a. compact
    b. ordinance
    c. constitution
    d. statute

75. Not a form of Arizona school district is

    a. union high school district
    b. common school district
    c. consolidated school district
    d. unified school district

76. Neighborhood improvement associations have the power to do all except

    a. place property liens and enforce by foreclosure
    b. enforce covenants through civil action
    c. set architectural and landscaping standards
    d. assess fees according to the dictates of their boards of directors

77. Which of the following is not true concerning city charters

    a. they may be initiated by voter petition
    b. the city council is responsible for writing proposed city charters
    c. they may be initiated by an existing city council
    d. voter approved charters are subject to approval by the Governor

78. Councils of Governments (COGs) were established to

    a. provide government in those regions where none existed
    b. provide for regional coordination of planning
    c. consolidate the activities of various tribal councils
    d. minimize the growing influence of county governments

79. The most unique and controversial feature of tribal government concerns

    a. legislative organization
    b. separation of tribal functions
    c. sovereignty
    d. the tribal judicial system

80. The grant of authority governing tribal lands emanates from

    a. state government
    b. federal government
    c. county government
    d. the tribal itself

81. Tribal judges are generally appointed by
    a. a tribal judicial screening committee
    b. the tribal chairperson
    c. the tribal council
    d. federal district court

82. Tribal jurisdiction extends to
    a. all Indians on the reservation regardless of tribal affiliation
    b. all Indians and non-Indians while physically on the reservation
    c. only registered members of the tribe
    d. any issue in which a registered tribal member is involved

83. Congress passed the Indian Gaming Act primarily
    a. to encourage gambling on the reservation
    b. as a means of increasing federal revenues
    c. to provide for economic development on the reservations
    d. to provide leisure time activities for senior citizens

84. The percentage of Arizona children living in poverty per the 2000 Census is
    a. 15%
    b. 22%
    c. 12%
    d. 28%

85. The fastest growing minority population in the state is
   a. African-American
   b. Asian-Pacific Islander
   c. Hispanic
   d. Native American

86. In what sector is the greatest number of Arizonians employed
   a. agriculture and cattle
   b. service industry
   c. mining and logging
   d. high tech industry

87. The fact that 76% of the population resides in two counties
   a. focuses attention on the rural urban disparities in the state
   b. makes it quite easy to determine boundaries for political districts
   c. indicates that a majority of Arizonians are urban sophisticates
   d. lessens the cost of maintaining infrastructure

88. Characteristics of Arizona's senior population include all except
   a. longer and healthier life span
   b. tend to be economically solvent
   c. tend to be active in a variety of community issues
   d. fiscally and politically liberal at the polls

89. Arizona has ranked poorly in its funding of social programs because
    a. the state possesses a very limited economic base
    b. a sizeable minority population is opposed to social programs
    c. little demand for such programs existed until quite recently
    d. people moving into the state have little interest in their development

90. Environmental issues in Arizona are compounded by all except
    a. inability of the land and vegetation to tolerate heavy use
    b. presence of naturally occurring contaminants in desert air
    c. scarcity of water in an arid climate
    d. the lack of a body of law to regulate such issues